Health Extension

TRANSFORMATIONS IN HIGHER EDUCATION: THE SCHOLARSHIP OF ENGAGEMENT

Health Extension

COMMUNITY-BASED HEALTHCARE AND THE FUTURE OF COOPERATIVE EXTENSION

Edited by Cheryl L. Eschbach,
Elizabeth H. Weybright, and Jeffrey W. Dwyer

Michigan State University Press | East Lansing

Michigan State University Press
East Lansing, Michigan 48823-5245

Library of Congress Cataloging-in-Publication Data
Names: Eschbach, Cheryl L., editor. | Weybright, Elizabeth H.
(Elizabeth Hall), editor. | Dwyer, Jeffrey W., editor.
Title: Health extension : community-based healthcare and the future of
cooperative extension / edited by C. L. Eschbach, E. Weybright, and J. W. Dwyer.
Description: East Lansing : Michigan State University Press, 2024. |
Series: Transformations in higher education : the scholarship
of engagement | Includes bibliographical references.
Identifiers: LCCN 2024015210 | ISBN 9781611865158 (paperback) |
ISBN 9781609177737 | ISBN 9781628955330
Subjects: LCSH: Rural health services—United States. | Community health services—United
States. | Cooperative Extension System (U.S.) | Health services accessibility—United States.
Classification: LCC RA771.5 .H434 2024 | DDC 362.10973—dc23/eng/20240509
LC record available at https://lccn.loc.gov/2024015210

Cover design by Becca Dwyer, beccadwyer.com, @beccadwyerdesign

---

Visit Michigan State University Press at *www.msupress.org*

Transformations in Higher Education: Scholarship of Engagement

The Transformations in Higher Education: The Scholarship of Engagement book series is designed to provide a forum where scholars can address the diverse issues provoked by community–campus partnerships that are directed toward creating innovative solutions to societal problems. Numerous social critics and key national commissions have drawn attention to the pervasive and burgeoning problems of individuals, families, communities, economies, health services, and education in American society. Such issues as child and youth development, economic competitiveness, environmental quality, and health and health care require creative research and the design, deployment, and evaluation of innovative public policies and intervention programs. Similar problems and initiatives have been articulated in many other countries, apart from the devastating consequences of poverty that burdens economic and social change. As a consequence, there has been increasing societal pressure on universities to partner with communities to design and deliver knowledge applications that address these issues, and to co-create novel approaches to effect system changes that can lead to sustainable and evidence-based solutions. Knowledge generation and knowledge application are critical parts of the engagement process, but so too are knowledge dissemination and preservation. The Transformations in Higher Education: The Scholarship of Engagement series was designed to meet one aspect of the dissemination/preservation dyad.

This series is sponsored by the National Collaborative for the Study of University Engagement (NCSUE) and is published in partnership with the Michigan State University Press. An external board of editors supports the NCSUE editorial staff in order to ensure that all volumes in the series are peer reviewed throughout the publication process. Manuscripts embracing campus–community partnerships are invited from authors regardless of discipline, geographic place, or type of transformational change accomplished. Similarly, the series embraces all methodological approaches from rigorous randomized trials to narrative and ethnographic studies. Analyses may span the qualitative to quantitative continuum, with particular emphasis on mixed-model approaches. However, all manuscripts must attend to detailing critical aspects of partnership development, community involvement, and evidence of program changes or impacts. Monographs and books provide ample space for authors to address all facets of engaged scholarship, thereby building a compendium of praxis that will facilitate replication and generalization, two of the cornerstones of evidence-based programs, practices, and policies. We invite you to submit your work for publication review and to fully participate in our effort to assist higher education to renew its covenant with society through engaged scholarship.

HIRAM E. FITZGERALD
BURTON BARGERSTOCK
LAURIE VAN EGEREN

Contents

Preface

In this volume we share curated content with the intent to spur engaging conversations about the future of the Cooperative Extension System (CES) and its impact on human health. We are inspired to share this collection of ideas and opinions on the state of the CES and the possibilities of the future because we are passionate advocates of the land-grant mission and have devoted much of our professional lives to working for or partnering with Cooperative Extension in various roles and states. This edited volume addresses the future of Extension by focusing on health and community-based healthcare and giving voice to creative, thoughtful, and diverse scholars who have much to say but have not always had a platform from which to be heard.

Three goals have guided this collective effort. The first is to promote Health Extension within CES and land-grant universities (LGUs) as an authentic partnership between healthcare and community organizations by sharing models and proven strategies that can transform lives, families, and communities in the twenty-first century. The second is to frame the history of the United States, the CES, and the emergence of health as a growing emphasis in CES, in ways that show linkages and underscore the extent to which normative gatekeeping and oppression of scholars, ideas, and communities threaten the central role that CES can and should play in community-based healthcare. In this context, contributors provide history, facts, personal experiences, and timelines not often discussed in journal articles, but that are essential to consider in building the future of Cooperative Extension's role in community-based healthcare. Third, we gift readers with literature reviews, recommended readings, and critical reviews of popular health frameworks while exploring connecting constructs (i.e., equity, oppression, justice, abolition, liberation) that are vitally important in charting a path for the future of Health Extension. These resources may serve to build capacity both generally, and specifically for Health Extension. We hope that the ideas conveyed are insightful and provocative and generate new and expanded efforts to incorporate an emphasis on all aspects of health in CES and among LGUs.

This volume is needed today because higher education, LGUs, and the CES are at a crossroads. If CES aspires to incorporate health authentically into its twenty-first-century mission, then health equity must be a core principle guiding organizational and programming priorities. Many CES administrative and programmatic leaders are interested in the concept of health equity but are not yet well versed in its meaning and utility. This volume offers perspectives, strategies, and a comprehensive review of the literature establishing a foundation for identifying research questions, partnerships, and interventions to explore health equity in the future. As a system, we must reckon with history, call out past failures, and share current behaviors that replicate the past more than they enhance the future. Health equity is defined in different ways by different organizations and scholars, but nearly all definitions affirm that the opportunity to be healthy should be freely available to everyone, regardless of their circumstance, social conditions, economic conditions, or any other unfair preventable difference. We believe that optimal health and access to appropriate healthcare is a fundamental right and that the CES can play a central role in prioritizing health equity by effectively leveraging its history, community presence, and sustainable infrastructure.

This publication arrives at time when diversity, equity, and inclusion (DEI) initiatives at U.S. colleges and universities are being challenged in many ways. We believe that conversation addressing discrimination and oppression is critical in the context of Health Extension and offer this edited volume as a constructive opportunity to identify and understand gatekeeping in CES, and the protection of whiteness, sexism, and other forms of power imbalances that serve to obfuscate the promotion of health justice. We agree with Fields and Shaffer (2022) that Extension "must have a reckoning ourselves if we see the next century of our work being as meaningful and as impactful as possible" (165).

Contributors to this volume are a talented group of intellectual and administrative leaders, researchers, and Extension professionals in varying roles and disciplines who have been contributing to the national Health Extension conversation in one way or another for the last decade. This is a like-minded group of disruptors and innovators, some of whom have not had a platform for advocating change. This volume reviews the origins of the Health Extension concept, cites evidence for how the movement can keep advancing, and offers urgent calls for action and system change. This collection of chapters is an opportunity for a creative and intellectually insightful group of mostly early and mid-career scholars to shape the foundation for what we now call Health Extension in a way that will improve the lives of all people, generate new knowledge, shape public policy and programming, and advance CES and community-based healthcare for decades to come. We believe that this can only be done by enhancing collaboration among 1862, 1890, and 1994 LGUs, better serving underrepresented and historically marginalized populations, and incorporating CES-led Health Extension into the existing community-based healthcare infrastructure.

The volume editors bring to this project a broad range of professional experiences that allow bringing both significant academic expertise and personal and insider knowledge to the Health Extension debates. Dr. Dwyer is a sociologist who has held tenured full professor positions in three disciplines throughout a thirty-five-year career (medicine, sociology, agriculture). After beginning his career in a college of nursing, he held leadership roles in both medicine (senior associate dean for research & community engagement) and agriculture (director of Michigan State University Extension) and was the first to include Extension professionals to facilitate research and program implementation in the federally funded Geriatric Education Centers (2008–2015). Dr. Eschbach is a gerontologist with a background in human development and family sciences; is a prolific Extension scholar and grant writer/recipient who has been a part of Michigan State University Extension for sixteen years, currently serving as Director of the Health and Nutrition Institute; and was a collaborator and contributor to Cooperative Extension's most recent National Framework for Health Equity and Well-Being (2021). Dr. Weybright has a background in prevention science and more than fifteen years of experience at LGUs; has written extensively on healthy behaviors and health risks across the life span; and is a tenured faculty member and Extension professional with significant competitive funding on topics ranging from substance use to youth development and rural firearm culture.

Three specific audiences may be interested in this volume: (1) Cooperative Extension professionals in the vast CES network in the United States, and those in similar systems around the world, who recognize the potential for CES to play a significant role in addressing community-based healthcare; (2) health care providers, researchers, and policymakers who have little or no experience or knowledge of the potential for CES to play a significant role in providing community-based healthcare interventions and programming in the coming decades; and (3) academic-based medical schools and health sciences such as pharmacy, nursing, and allied health fields, especially those with a community focus and part of LGUs. We hope readers enjoy the journey and are inspired to join us in shaping the future of Health Extension in the CES.

REFERENCE

Fields, N. I., & Shaffer, T. J. (2022). *Grassroots engagement and social justice through Cooperative Extension.* Transformations in Higher Education Series. East Lansing: Michigan State University Press.

Cooperative Extension and Healthcare: Origins of Health Extension

Jeffrey W. Dwyer and Cheryl L. Eschbach

The Cooperative Extension System (CES) is affiliated with the land-grant university (LGU) system in the United States and was formalized in 1914 by the Smith–Lever Act (Rasmussen, 1989; U.S. Congress, 1914). The CES has been engaged in health education and community-based health interventions (primarily in food science and nutrition) since the beginning of the land-grant system. During the last decade, CES has utilized its presence across the United States, with substantial human resource and leadership infrastructure, more than a hundred years of organizational history, relationships in agriculture, rural communities, and underserved populations, and the ability to quickly adapt to emergent needs, to explore a more comprehensive focus on human health in diverse populations with education and interventions implemented comprehensively and sustainably.

The CES was established as a partnership among LGUs, the federal government (specifically the U.S. Department of Agriculture), state and local governments, and academic professionals at colleges and universities to empower farmers, policymakers, youth, and citizens in leadership roles to improve their lives by explicitly linking university research to communities (Seevers et al., 1997). By 1935, "virtually all of the 3,150 counties in the nation had at least one extension agent" (Rogers, 1988, 497). CES has been referred to as "the largest education system of its kind in the world" (U.S. General Accounting Office, 1981, i) and has historically emphasized agriculture, community development, youth enrichment (4-H), and family and consumer sciences. More recently, due to changing population, cultural, and technological dynamics, many scholars have argued that "Extension's survival depends on addressing new societal problems and reaching new audiences" (Morse et al., 2009, 9). Moreover, specialization and regionalization have been a common response to funding pressures and societal changes and there is significant variability in how state extension programs are organized, funded, and staff and faculty are appointed or resourced (Morse, 2011; Powers et al., 2017). Nevertheless, it remains important that programming be present in every county and that Extension professionals are valued as friends and neighbors, as well as for their technical expertise, to maintain local support (Rasmussen, 1989; Warner & Christenson, 1984).

At its inception, CES served a large segment of the United States because of the emphasis on agriculture and rural communities, populations that have noticeably declined over the past century. To retain the same relevance for the next one hundred years, human health and health equity must become central to the core mission of CES across the entire organization. The focus on health equity is consistent with the original mission of CES and central to becoming part of the broader community-based healthcare system. However, to effectively focus on health in a way that changes lives and builds meaningful partnerships, there are historical, systemic, and contemporary issues that CES must factor into current conversations. Health Extension represents a movement within CES and an expanding conceptual approach with an evolving compilation of strategies that can address important and emergent healthcare issues while taking full advantage of CES's ubiquitous presence in the nation. Hence, it is a critical element for providing new resources to traditional audiences and reaching new populations, thus ensuring the future of CES.

We define the term "Health Extension" as health-focused education, programming, intervention, and research in which the assets of CES are leveraged as an authentic partner to enhance community-based healthcare, academic health systems including medical schools, public health, and prevention outcomes. This reorientation of traditional programming, target audiences, and resources has led to the development of significant community-based healthcare and public health interventions in mental health, substance use prevention, disaster management, and health promotion that have measurable impacts on human health and integrate with the already well-established healthcare infrastructure. Throughout this volume, we advocate for Health Extension as an integral part of the LGU system and as a significant partner in providing community-based healthcare (i.e., person-centered care provided in the home or community) in the United States and countries around the world.

The assertion that Health Extension should be an integral part of the CES and contributor to the community-based healthcare system is predicated in no small part on the ability to comprehensively address the social determinants of health for diverse and dispersed populations. Health Extension strategies such as building wide-ranging partnerships, preparing Extension professionals for participation in community-based participatory research, increasing primary care patient referrals and enrollment into CES health programs from healthcare for prevention and disease self-management, and exploring innovative funding opportunities have proven effective and are addressed in detail in this volume. These strategies hold the potential to benefit all communities in our nation, especially those that have experienced historical discrimination and marginalization and that represent the perpetually underserved.

Health is "a state of physical, mental, and social well-being and not merely the absence of disease and infirmity" (World Health Organization, 1946, 1); healthy built environments are "places where people are born, live, learn, work, play, worship, and age" with infrastructure designed to promote good health (Office of Disease Prevention and Health Promotion, n.d.); and "Public health is the science and the art of preventing disease, prolonging life, and promoting health and efficiency through organized community efforts . . . which will ensure to every individual in the community a standard of living adequate for the maintenance of health" (Winslow, 1920, 30).

Healthy People 2030 (Office of Disease Prevention and Health Promotion, n.d.) defines the social determinants of health as "the conditions in the environments where people are born, live, learn, work, play, worship, and age that affect a wide range of health, functioning, and quality-of-life outcomes and risks." In general, social determinants of health (SDOH) are the nonmedical factors that influence health outcomes and are an underlying cause of most of today's major societal health issues such as obesity, heart disease, diabetes, and depression (Magnan, 2017). Examples of SDOH include safe housing, experiences of systematic racism and discrimination, violence, food access, pollution, and language and literacy skills that contribute to health inequities and disparities. Social determinants also influence health outcomes associated with emergent issues such as COVID-19 (Abrams & Szefler, 2020). Impacting the social determinants of health is one of the core themes of CES's recent iteration of the National Framework for Health Equity and Well-Being (Burton et al., 2021) and a fundamental premise of Health Extension.

In this volume, we extend earlier work as a foundation for the future of Health Extension in CES and recommend strategies for establishing CES as an important partner in providing community-based healthcare through the extraordinary scholarship and insight of colleagues from around the country, several of whom participated in the development of the 2021 Cooperative Extension National Framework for Health Equity and Well-Being (Burton et al., 2021). This chapter explores the history of health-related education and Health Extension in LGUs and CES, critiques alternative frameworks for implementing Health Extension, and reviews Health Extension strategies to date that underscore the value of incorporating Health Extension fully into the CES system and including CES as an important partner in the provision of community-based healthcare. Efforts at Michigan State University (MSU) to begin and sustain a Model of Health Extension are described in detail and linkages to health equity, community-based health systems, dissemination science, disaster management planning, and mental health are explored to underscore the potential benefits of Health Extension in multiple domains.

The Land-Grant University and Cooperative Extension Systems

Although Extension has been a well-known and integral part of agriculture and rural communities since 1914, too few people in other parts of the population know of its presence, impact, and potential. CES is often referred to as the "best kept secret" and an organization with an antiquated image that does not effectively market the range of services it offers to wide-ranging populations (Harder et al., 2009). Warner and Christenson (1984) observed four decades ago that the relative absence of an Extension literature was remarkable, and while the volume of Extension content has increased in the ensuing years, the failure to publish findings regularly in the peer-reviewed literature and in disciplinary areas outside of the historically normative outlets for CES persists. A survey of family and internal medicine physicians in Michigan, for example, revealed that many were completely unaware of community-based health programs provided by CES and available in their communities (Khan et al., 2020). This limited constituency and lack of public awareness often constrain opportunities to explore and implement new programming despite the long-standing aim to help people improve their lives by bringing the vast knowledge and resources of LGUs directly to individuals, families, communities, and businesses.

LGUs include institutions of higher education that receive the benefits of the Morrill Acts of 1862 or 1890. The purpose of the Morrill Act of 1862 was to emphasize teaching, research, and service in agriculture, science, military training, engineering, and industrial arts while making higher education more accessible to the working classes. The second Morrill Act of 1890, in addition to providing additional resources to all land-grant institutions, established in each of the then-segregated Southern states land-grant institutions for Blacks that are generally known as the 1890 land-grants or historically Black colleges and universities (HBCUs). In 1994, land-grant status was conferred to Native American tribal colleges that are typically referred to as 1994 land-grants or tribal colleges and universities (TCUs).

Currently, there are 112 designated land-grant institutions: fifty-eight are 1862 versions; nineteen are 1890 versions; and thirty-five are 1994 versions (see the figure). The exact number of LGUs has varied over time, and those interested are encouraged to check the U.S. Department of Agriculture (USDA) website for updated maps regarding the locations of the nation's LGUs. Although land-grant institutions have many and varied sources of funding, federal funding of research (Agricultural Experiment Stations) through the Hatch Act of 1887 and funding of the CES through the Smith–Lever Act of 1914, together with the one-to-one state matching funds these incentivize, are the foundation for funding research and outreach/engagement in the land-grant system. Academic health centers, which generally have an allopathic or osteopathic medical school, at least one other health professions school at the university, and at least one teaching hospital, can be an important partner for CES in the context of Health Extension and community-based health education, research, and outreach. Therefore, the map also shows which states have an academic health center on the main campus of an LGU in that state.

Cooperative Extension was established based on the realization that as of the early 1900s, the knowledge, research, and outcomes of land-grant institutions were not yet reaching all state residents who might benefit from them. In 1914, the CES was funded and formally charged with taking the resources and knowledge of land-grant universities to the public at large, regardless of where they might be located, to "improve lives through

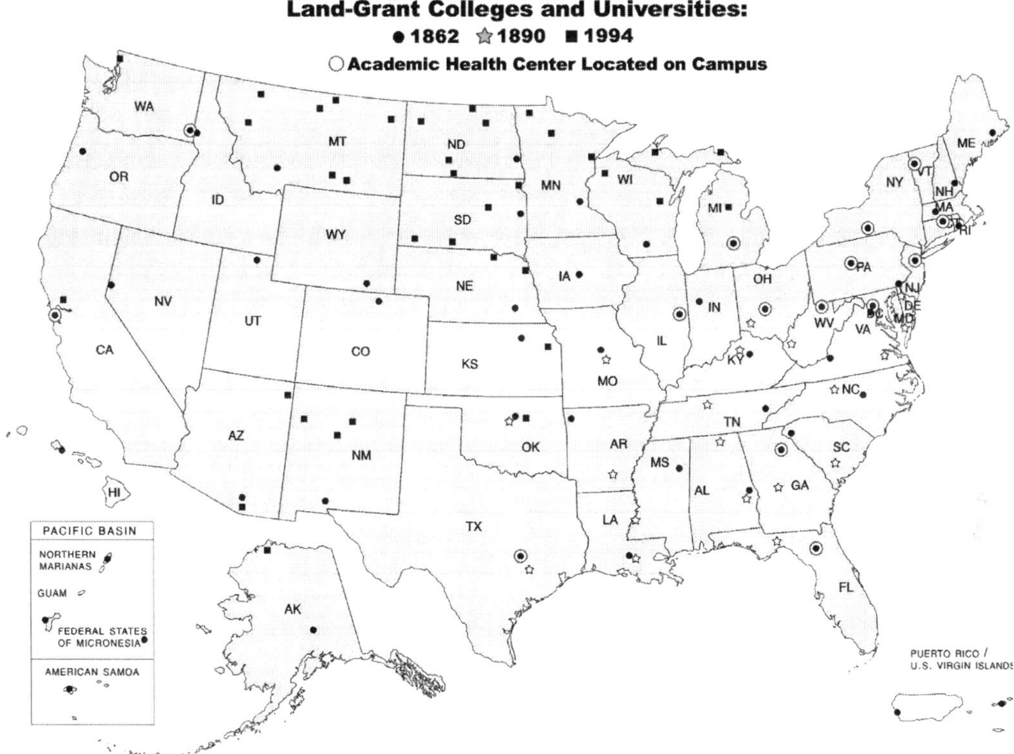

Map of U.S. land-grant colleges and universities (LGUs) system. Adapted from the U.S. Department of Agriculture, National Institute for Food and Agriculture. (https://www.nifa.usda.gov/land-grant-colleges-universities-map).

an educational process that uses scientific knowledge focused on issues and needs" (Rasmussen, 1989, 4). Rogers (1988) has remarked that the "extension model is undoubtedly the most widely recognized system in the world for the diffusion of technological innovations" (493). Today, CES is a vast network of thirty-five thousand professionals working in the nation's 3,150 counties along with more than two million volunteers (Extension Foundation, 2023). Moreover, the sustainable impact of CES over time has led to similar systems in other countries (Michigan State University Extension, 2021). Cooperative Extension across states and within different LGUs is variable in structural and functional aspects such as funding sources, geography, staffing, and faculty/staff promotion processes. Despite this variability, the national system has strength in what state systems have in common (i.e., history, mission).

In this volume, we refer to CES as the entire national system and historical organization of Cooperative Extension built under the USDA through congressional acts. We use the term "Extension" when examples are state-level and not necessarily true across the whole system. Similarly, we reference "Extension professionals" as a collective group that can consist of CES educators, agents, specialists, faculty, administrators, and others employed under the CES funding allocations and who are embedded in the LGU systems with varying titles and program areas which reflect the collective work.

Unfortunately, 1890 and 1994 land-grant institutions are historically and systemically under-resourced relative to 1862 LGUs as a function of both their differing sources and amounts of federal funding and disparities in the extent to which these institutions receive the full expected funding match from their state (Lee & Keys, 2013). Funding disparities in federal and state capacity-building allocations to 1862, 1890, and 1994 LGUs create a context for disparities to be exacerbated, as reflected in success in obtaining other sources of competitive funding that are essential for sustaining vital education and intervention programs. A 2022 National Academies of Sciences, Engineering, and Medicine (NASEM) report titled "Enhancing Coordination and Collaboration Across the Land-Grant System" identified 247 current multistate research projects among LGUs and found that "participants from the 1890 or 1994 (HBCU and TCU) institutions are seldom involved" (NASEM, 2022, 1). Understanding the limited coordination and collaboration among LGUs is especially important because "once these projects are established, they are open to other institutions, including other land-grant and non-land-grant colleges and universities, federal agencies, and the private sector, which bring their own sources of funding to participate" (NASEM, 2022, 1). Hence, variability in federal and state capacity funding and the exclusion of HBCU and TCU partners in federally funded multistate projects in the land-grant system limits 1890 and 1994 LGU access to additional collaboration and funding opportunities. These funding disparities have important implications for the utilization of the CES as a framework for Health Extension and community-based healthcare, especially in reaching underserved populations.

Health Programming in the CES

For the first one hundred years of the CES, the inclusion of health in programming and research was almost exclusively focused on nutrition and related topics (e.g., obesity prevention). The Association of Public and Land-Grant Universities' (APLU) Extension Committee on Organization and Policy published the first "National Framework for Health and Wellness" (Braun et al., 2014) that captured a shift in health priorities for CES. This emphasis was reinforced in 2016 when the APLU commissioned a report titled "Healthy Food Systems, Healthy People" that, while advocating for a public health approach and greater collaboration among related entities, was primarily focused on physical health and nutrition. The CES has also implemented SNAP-Ed (Supplemental Nutrition Assistance Program—Education) for nearly four decades and the Expanded Food and Nutrition Education (EFNEP) since 1968 (Rasmussen, 1989). EFNEP was a direct outgrowth of the "War on Poverty" of the 1960s (Rogers, 1988) and the Food Stamp Act of 1977. These opportunities laid the foundation for cooperative and matching SNAP-Ed-funded programming that expanded the reach of nutrition education to low-income communities and that by 2004 was being provided throughout the country by CES (USDA, 2023c).

Historically, there was resistance to adding nutrition education in CES because of concern that these efforts would detract from resources typically available to production agriculture. Rogers (1988) has argued that the inclusion of EFNEP in CES programming was "undoubtedly the most radical single change in extension services in the past 50 years" (504) because EFNEP had nothing to do with production agriculture, the use of community-based aides (rather than degreed professionals) was a first for CES, and the target audience included both low-income rural *and* urban families. EFNEP funding at LGUs and CES changed hiring practices (Entenmann, 1989), and as a result, the CES workforce became more racially and ethnically diverse. The initial EFNEP priorities were for aides or paraprofessionals to teach nutrition, demonstrate food preparation, and inform consumers about food buying for low-income and minority audiences (Entenmann, 1989). Over time, however, the benefits of adding community nutrition programming into CES as enhancements to food systems, food safety, and food product entrepreneurship education have been widely accepted. While SNAP-Ed, EFNEP, and other nutrition- and physical health-related education continue to be an important part of CES, impacting hundreds of thousands of people each day, it was only in the mid 1990s that behavioral health was discussed as a possible emphasis for CES and well into the 2010s before the potential for CES to impact behavioral health and other important health behaviors and outcomes (e.g., prevention) became a more prominent emphasis (Dwyer et al., 2017a; Hill & Parker, 2005; Molgaard, 1997). Part of the timing for the most recent emphasis was influenced by debates around the human right of healthcare coverage for all that was associated with the Affordable Care Act (ACA) of 2010.

National Movements Intersecting with Health Extension

Over the last two decades, references to Health Extension have underscored two very important but differing perspectives. Our definition of Health Extension (Dwyer et al., 2017b) contrasts with other uses of the term that emphasize creating new infrastructure "like" Extension and/or using Extension as a resource but not an authentic partner. Efforts to operationalize Health Extension outside of CES required new funding and infrastructure "modeled on" or "adapted from" (Kaufman et al., 2010; Kaufman et al., 2017) the CES when referring to Health Extension. These efforts have proven costly, politically confusing, and unsustainable (Dwyer et al., 2017b), despite funding from prominent sources such as the Agency for Healthcare Research and Quality (AHRQ), the Commonwealth Fund, and, more recently, the Health Resources and Services Administration (HRSA) Area Health Education Centers.

The ACA of 2010 charged AHRQ to create the Primary Care Extension Program "modeled on" the agricultural extension service but did not fund this effort. Leong and Roberts (2013) argue that the ACA focused attention on the social determinants of health and the fact that they impact marginalized communities in different ways. Solomon and Kanter (2018) state that "the question is no longer whether there is an appropriate role for the U.S. health care system in addressing the social determinants of health, but what that role is, how to create the right policy context for innovation and how health care can partner more effectively with providers of social services to meet patients' most pressing needs" (18). Since the implementation of the ACA, conversations among health professionals have increasingly focused on social determinants of health and methods for reaching marginalized and historically underrepresented communities. This identified need to address root causes of health represents a major opportunity for CES to have a role in community-based healthcare.

A cursory look at maps published by HRSA that show medically underserved areas/populations reveals two important facts. First, despite decades of effort to address this complex dilemma by focusing on the recruitment of physicians and other health professionals, large portions of the United States remain underserved, especially communities that are characterized as rural or are disproportionately comprised of minority populations. Second, CES does not have to "go to" these communities to provide services . . . CES is already there! In addition to the vast rural areas served by 1862 institutions, 1890 and 1994 institutions are geographically located in many of the regions identified as medically underserved. Enhancing the primary care workforce to address underserved communities and health equity is essential (Cohen et al., 2023; NASEM, 2022); nevertheless, conflating the expansion of primary care with the potential role of CES serves to undermine the unique characteristics that make CES an important leader and partner in providing community-based healthcare in the twenty-first century. The future of Health Extension will require the inclusion of CES as an authentic partner providing a broad range of community-based health education and intervention in close collaboration with medical and health professions colleagues, especially those in primary care specialties.

Several national movements and policy discussions have influenced the development of Health Extension concepts. Leading up to the ACA, debates and policies focused on healthcare utilization and costs, Medicare and Medicaid and implications for payment reform, and the patient-centered medical home each gained traction as elements of transformation. Early definitions of Health Extension mirrored this healthcare context. Health Extension was initially viewed as a method of helping communities, and the primary care practices that serve them, to overcome barriers to practice transformation by sharing common resources including local expertise coupled with technical resources of universities, health departments, and social service agencies available during and after the clinical practice transformation process.

In an early attempt to operationalize Health Extension, Grumbach and Mold (2009) proposed a Primary Care Cooperative Extension Service with a focus on patient education and linking practices to community resources. Advocacy continues for this approach that is modeled on the CES and that requires substantial new funding and infrastructure (Cohen et al., 2023), even though implementation efforts have been largely unsuccessful and adoption not widespread. Subsequent efforts to establish effective frameworks for healthcare or primary care extension without including CES as an authentic partner have been largely unsustainable. Preliminary frameworks of health extension or primary care extension in the United States were supported by grants from AHRQ and the Commonwealth Fund between 2011 and 2013. Seventeen states participated as health extension project sites and learning communities, including four lead states (North Carolina, Oklahoma, New Mexico, Pennsylvania). North Carolina and Oklahoma built infrastructure for primary care quality improvement and then shared resources for practice transformations with partners. Pennsylvania supported primary care practices to become patient-centered medical homes. Perhaps the best known of these is the Health Extension Rural Offices (HEROs) introduced by Kaufman et al. (2010, 2017, 2019) in New Mexico and based at the University of New Mexico School of Medicine (not the LGU). Financial support from AHRQ and The Commonwealth Fund produced a Health Extension Toolkit website as a response to states that wanted to learn new models of practice transformation (Health Extension Toolkit, n.d.). The toolkit is aimed at states, academic health centers, and Tribal Nations to adopt aspects of a health extension movement. The online toolkit contains helpful resources and tools, but the website has not been maintained or updated over time.

During this same time, Cooperative Extension produced a National Framework for Health and Wellness (Braun et al., 2014). The framework identified the need for CES to create partnerships and secure resources to respond to America's health conditions and disparities. This national framework was a tool to help CES methodically address health and wellness at the individual, community, environmental, and policy levels. The hope at the time, and still today, is that a national framework for CES can transform and innovate the health field in the twenty-first century as it did for agriculture in the twentieth century.

As an authentic partner in Health Extension, CES has many attributes that have been characteristic of successful implementation efforts thus far. First, Extension is present in every state and has maintained essential programming and acted as sentinels in communities for more than a hundred years. Second, CES has sustainable, core funding from federal, state, county, and other sources that, although always subject to alteration, have been largely unchanged for many years. Third, in every state, CES has a well-established human infrastructure with expert staff and distributed leadership that is buttressed by the resources of a land-grant university. Fourth, because CES professionals typically live in the communities they serve, often for many years, the relationships they develop are meaningful and often transferable to their colleagues. For example, when MSU Extension first implemented mental health education in farming communities, the effort was successful from the outset largely because unknown mental health experts were able to walk in the door with their agriculture colleagues who knew nothing about mental health but had lived and worked in those communities for decades. Finally, more authentic inclusion of 1890 and 1994 institutions in Health Extension offers the opportunity to provide outreach and education with underserved populations that may need it the most and that have been systematically blocked from investments because of oppressive systems of power and control. These are the building blocks of Health Extension predicated on CES as an authentic partner.

Development and History of the MSU Model of Health Extension

The MSU Model of Health Extension (Dwyer et al., 2017a) was the first to demonstrate effectiveness in several domains of human health education, research, and outreach by utilizing and leveraging CES at an LGU where there is also a community-based medical school. This innovative report documented several initial strategies for enhancing Health Extension, including marketing Extension relationships and capabilities to university research faculty, training Extension staff in the basics of research (including human subjects protocol), detailing to primary care offices (i.e., visiting primary care offices to provide information to physicians, nurses, and other health care staff) to create awareness and facilitate patient referrals to community-based Extension programs, and creating an "Rx for Health" prescription pad with Extension's health programs listed for promotion in physician offices as program referrals. Collectively, these initial strategies were pursued to broaden the scope of health and public health topics addressed by Extension and to enhance opportunities for external funding. In roughly the same time frame, two public health crises in the state of Michigan (the Flint water crisis, and agricultural producers dying by suicide), described later in this chapter, helped to formalize the adoption of the MSU Model of Health Extension in ways that highlight the unique ability of CES to be a critical partner in responding to emerging and complex health issues.

Early Days and Foundational Steps

Earlier projects and foundational steps of collaboration assisted the development of a model of Health Extension. Beginning in 2008, MSU's College of Human Medicine (CHM) involved and funded Extension professionals to be a part of the Geriatric Education Center of Michigan (GECM), a HRSA-funded effort where Jeffrey W. Dwyer served as principal investigator from 2008 to 2015. Extension worked with medical faculty to provide impactful geriatrics training to health care providers to prepare them to work with older adults. With CES involved in the funded effort, multidisciplinary teams of family/internal medicine faculty and community-based Extension staff provided workshops for nurses, social workers, physicians, and allied health clinic staff. In the northern part of Michigan's lower peninsula (where Cheryl L. Eschbach was involved as an educator from 2008 to 2011), there was success in reaching Tribal health clinics (Proctor, 2013a), partly because MSU Extension had connections to tribal communities from past outreach related to natural resources management and well-received good governance education known as Building Strong Sovereign Nations (Proctor, 2013b). The GECM trainings were impactful in part because the clinics would shut down for a few hours and the entire staff (MDs to front-door receptionists and appointment schedulers) attended; emphasis was placed on expected caregiving trajectories due to normal aging and common diseases; and GECM faculty and staff attended professional development together (conferences) to build relationships within the interdisciplinary training team and to learn about current research and strategies to use in the twenty-six MSU GECM training modules.

Building on the success of engaging MSU Extension in the GECM project effort, in February 2014, Dwyer convened a group of Extension professionals while still in an administrative leadership role with the MSU CHM. The original group included four Extension educators and one specialist who were titled "health liaisons" to facilitate community-campus and clinic connections across the university. These positions were supported by MSU's CHM, MSU Extension, and the MSU Vice President Office for Research to fund 0.5 full-time equivalent staff salary per person as a pilot. Dwyer then added team support by inviting individuals from university advancement, grants and research administration, and communications to assist the emerging Extension Health Research team. An early objective of the new model was that health liaisons would support research activities in, with, and for communities.

In 2015, in addition to presenting at the Beyond Flexner conference (Miller et al., 2010; Social Mission Alliance, 2023), the Health Extension team at MSU hosted a national webinar through eXtension, "Extension Health Research in Michigan," which included testimonials of medical faculty working with Extension professionals to disseminate research findings to target populations in Michigan. This national webinar focused on how MSU's community-based medical school and its affiliated research activity provide a form of community engagement in the state. Dwyer and colleagues highlighted the fact that medical school faculty often lack the time investments in communities to excel in the beginning and ending cycles of translational research—that is, the needs assessment and research dissemination phases. This gap in health research shaped the focus for the original core four strategies proposed in the MSU Model of Health Extension, which emphasized CES's role in advancing health research (Dwyer et al., 2017a).

One advantage of the MSU Model of Health Extension is the range of possibilities for collaboration with professionals who share the same mission. MSU established one of the nation's first community-based medical schools with multiple campuses in 1969 (Mavis et al., 2012), "as a state-funded medical school with specific legislative directives to educate primary care physicians who would serve the needs of the state, particularly those of underserved areas" (1705). A recent review of the physician workforce in Michigan revealed that 20 percent of MSU CHM graduates practiced within fifty miles of their medical school campus (Phillips et al., 2018). These findings show the value of dispersing clinical campuses across the state as a strategy to recruit and retain a healthcare workforce and underscore the potential for Extension professionals and medical faculty to develop long-term relationships and community collaborations. Internally at MSU, we spend time conducting "in-reach" (equivalent to outreach to external partners), staying connected to the two medical schools, the College of Nursing, the College of Veterinary Medicine, and MSU Health Care (the academic health center of Michigan's 1862 LGU). As of February 2024, MSU Health Care includes 650 clinical faculty and more than 9,300 community-based medical faculty across fourteen clinical and twenty-one academic departments (Michigan State University, 2023). Combined, the two human health colleges at MSU have nearly twenty thousand alumni, a disproportionate number of whom live and practice in Michigan.

Warner and Christensen (1984) noted that, historically, "flexibility has been one of Extension's strengths" (9), an observation also noted in the evolution of the MSU Model of Health Extension over the past decade. This organizational flexibility, with the growing literature supporting Health Extension in the context of CES, is also reflected in real-time community impacts. The initial focus of the MSU Model of Health Extension (Dwyer et al., 2017a) included activities related to four strategies. These strategies are now proven and continue to evolve.

1. Increasing familiarity of Extension's health programs among family medicine physicians (Khan et al., 2020), which involved surveying physicians to determine scalable state-level models for increasing awareness of chronic disease prevention and other community-based educational programs in efforts to improve the health of the nation. Health care providers need awareness, familiarity, and incentives for program referrals.
2. Creating and trying different program participant referral pathways from primary care, which were piloted in the form of patient referrals to community-based education (Tiret et al., 2019). Michigan's Rx for Health Referral Toolkit marketed Extension programs to primary care clinics for healthcare settings (mostly physicians and receptionists) to promote quality healthcare experiences for patients by connecting to community resources like free, online health education programs. Current efforts at MSU Extension include promoting a QR code and accepting online referrals for self, other, or patient.
3. Training Extension professionals in research design, partnership formation, and grant writing with the creation and implementation of "Are You Research Ready?" and "Are You Partnership Ready?" professional development workshops (Eschbach et al., 2019). This set of professional development experiences increased capacity of Extension staff and encouraged collaborative efforts for innovative programming, engaging in research, and building community partnerships for Health Extension. Additional trainings are needed systemwide for using secondary data in program planning, and to learn participatory and engaged research methods, including trauma-informed approaches.
4. Speed meetings with MSU's medical college faculty to connect with MSU Extension professionals and programs, a simple in-reach activity, which yielded benefits in grant proposals both submitted and awarded for new projects (Eschbach et al., 2018). Other Health Extension activities could include multistate, regional, and national gatherings of Extension professionals with health care providers, academic health center faculty, and agricultural experiment station researchers.

The table offers an updated listing of strategies for the MSU Model of Health Extension based on achievements and lessons learned between 2017 and 2023.

Expanded Four Strategies of the MSU Model of Health Extension

BUILDING PARTNERSHIPS	PREPARING PROFESSIONALS FOR HEALTH EXTENSION	INCREASING REFERRALS FROM HEALTHCARE	EXPLORING INNOVATIVE FUNDING
Government (federal, state, local)	Training workshops for Extension professionals—human subject protocol, research designs, sampling, funding partnerships	Health care providers refer patients to CES health programs (interventions)	Multisource funding on specific, strategic issues
Healthcare entities	Grant writing skills—objectives, budgets, timelines, biosketch, conflict of interest, current and pending	Familiarity and awareness of CES programs at LGU—all program areas	Multiyear initiatives with grants as primary, subaward, key personnel
Health care providers and allied health professionals	Professional development on participatory and engaged research methods, trauma-informed approaches	Participant and partner incentives for referrals and completing research- or evidence-based educational program series	Establishing interdisciplinary teams with university faculty to pursue atypical funding
Academic health centers			Train-the-trainer contracts and income
Multistate CES collaborations, Extension regions			
Agricultural Experiment Stations			

MSU Model of Health Extension Resulted in Innovative Grant Funding

Making connections and supporting frequent communications between medical faculty and Extension professionals has proven successful. In 2019, as the opioid crisis raged in the state (and nation) with overdose deaths on the rise, the MSU Family Medicine Department chair reached out to Dwyer (then director of MSU Extension) about a funding announcement from the Substance Abuse and Mental Health Services Administration (SAMHSA). Eschbach (as director of the Health and Nutrition Institute, MSU Extension) took lead as project director and included as grant co-principal investigators (co-PIs) the Family Medicine Department chair, associate chair of research, and the director of the Rural Medicine Curriculum. This SAMHSA funding was part of the Rural Opioid Technical Assistance program (2019–2022), and the MSU project was awarded $1 million to provide evidence-based trainings to increase awareness of opioid use disorder and treatment options and to support recovery in Michigan's rural communities (Eschbach et al., 2023). The funded project and team became known as Michigan Substance Use

Prevention, Education and Recovery (MISUPER) and collaborated with the Health Department of Northwest Michigan. The project built upon MSU Extension's past rural opioid misuse prevention initiatives, most notably state funding from the Department of Health and Human Services for a state opioid response project (Eschbach et al., 2022).

Having multiple funded initiatives, concurrently, to address Michigan's opioid crisis allowed Extension to hire new health staff, expand the focus beyond prevention to include treatment options and recovery supports, and go much further into the work of creating healthcare referral pathways (Eschbach et al., 2022). MSU Extension provides community-based educational programs as interventions to help people reduce the interference of their symptoms caused by chronic conditions and pain, and to promote self-management strategies (Eschbach et al., 2022). MSU Extension delivers health education in series, with evidence- and research-based curricula and trained facilitators that collect pre- and postsurvey data so that health outcomes are captured and reported for funders and published in peer-reviewed outlets. Between 2019 and 2020, MSU Extension received four grants totaling $2.1 million in funding to work on addressing rural opioid misuse in Michigan through evidence-based health education programs (direct program delivery), telehealth, distance learning (virtual programs), and digital media campaigns. Collaboration between Extension and the College of Human Medicine faculty was a key contributor to project success, because there is a need for technical expertise and community-based connections for implementation.

During this same period, between 2019 and 2023, MSU Extension received steady funding with six grants from national and state funding sources ($2.4 million) for farm stress outreach. MSU addresses farm stress through Extension mental health literacy programs and effective behavioral health outreach training programs with agricultural audiences (Cuthbertson et al., 2021; Eschbach et al., 2022). Eschbach and colleagues at MSU created a statewide network for farm and ranch stress assistance in a project called Legacy of the Land. The farm stress (suicide prevention) funding supported new growth in hiring CES staff with mental health backgrounds and clinical-community-setting experience. Hiring graduates from master of public health degree programs has been a good match for these funded CES projects in Michigan. Recently, MSU Extension become lead on the state's AgrAbility program (2022–2026), once again (AgrAbility is the USDA's Assistive Technology Program for Farmers with Disabilities), flipping leadership roles with the MSU CHM, who served as PI on the previous grant awards with Extension as a partner. Having multiple funding sources in core content areas and long-standing academic partners has been a successful way to bring in new CES program areas and project teams with funded plans of work.

The last example of innovative grant funding from the MSU Model of Health Extension strategies occurred when COVID-19 funding ($25,000) became available on short notice from the Extension Foundation via the Centers for Disease Control and Prevention (CDC) to facilitate a national vaccination education effort called EXCITE—Extension Collaboration on Immunization Teaching and Engagement. MSU Extension worked with two 1994 LGUs in the state (Bay Mills Community College and Keweenaw Bay Ojibwa Community

College) that also received EXCITE funding to provide outreach to tribal communities about the safety and availability of the COVID-19 vaccine. A Tribal Extension educator with a health background was the project manager. Subsequently, the state of Michigan Department of Health and Human Services (MDHHS) approached MSU Extension with different CDC funding, available through the Coronavirus Response and Consolidated Appropriations Act of 2021 and the American Rescue Plan Act of 2021 designed to address health equity and prioritize populations disproportionately affected by COVID-19, as the ideal partner to reach rural adults and youth.

MDHHS knew of MSU Extension health work through SNAP-Ed community nutrition education and the state opioid response project. Given this recent, proven record and established connections with state agency officials, the state health department awarded MSU Extension $7 million to spend between July 2021 and September 2024. Funding for vaccine education has resulted in hiring seventeen new staff members since the start of the Michigan Vaccine Project, thus infusing the organization with new talent and capacity. Vaccine education is not new to MSU Extension. MDHHS has funded a collaboration between MSU Extension, health care professionals, and local health departments since 1995. Using a cohort of practicing physicians, MSU Extension's Physician Peer Education Project on Immunizations (PPEPI) works in conjunction with MDHHS's Immunization Division to provide education sessions to health care providers (i.e., practicing physicians, physician assistants, nurse practitioners). The PPEPI project reaches approximately two thousand health care providers each year. The history of the PPEPI collaborative project is interesting because it surfaced from the need for a response to the state's rapidly declining immunization rates in the mid 1990s. The PPEPI partnership began in 1994 when Michigan's childhood immunization rate was the lowest in the nation. Over the years, Michigan's rate neared the national average at about 75 percent. However, since the start of the pandemic in early 2020, immunization rates for Michigan's children once again fell below the national average, prompting the need for additional educational efforts.

As long as CES continues to respond to emergent public health issues, the community-based information delivery and dissemination network possible through CES will remain viable and active. There is no shortage of health crises to address, especially with the acceleration of climate change and the prevalence of natural and human-made disasters impacting our health environments and opportunities to thrive and reach our full health potential. If CES listens to state residents, helps U.S. government agencies get information and services to people, and aligns plans of work strategically with the best intervention designs and innovative methods possible, then CES can continually evolve and build upon Health Extension efforts using LGUs' strengths, stability, and trust as a foundation. It is also important to note that one reason for past funding success from nontraditional sources (for CES) is that Extension professionals have been full partners and intellectual leaders in these funded projects. Extension offers traditional mechanisms for information exchange, such as the peer review process, while also achieving impactful community-focused outcomes. This combination of a strong connection to state needs, foundation in the literature, and Extension professionals holding skill sets in current methodology was validated by collaborations with academic colleagues, and ultimately seen in the outcomes of funded projects and community engagement.

Emergent Public Health Issues

Sometimes CES is already addressing public health issues and new partners join efforts; at other times, partners are overwhelmed and seek Extension to help them address complex social issues. Regardless, a focus on Health Extension is important because it broadens the opportunity to improve lives by bringing science to issues and problems and utilizes the unique capabilities of CES. Two examples of statewide needs and opportunities are presented here to showcase MSU Extension responses to contemporary public health issues.

In 2016, the (then) director of the Michigan Department of Agriculture and Rural Development reached out to Dwyer (then the director of MSU Extension), indicating that he and his team sensed an increase in farmers attempting and dying by suicide and asked whether MSU Extension could help. As sentinels in the community, MSU Extension agriculture staff had recently noted the same concern, and we immediately tasked one of our existing educators, with expertise in mental health, to begin developing education in this area. Within weeks Extension was providing direct education in the community and, by all accounts, saving lives. MSU Extension subsequently hired full-time professionals in mental health, and there are several now employed in the Health and Nutrition Institute directed by Eschbach. It is important to note, however, that this reorientation of resources did not occur without significant pushback. Our CES colleagues nationally, our agriculture constituents locally, and even our staff were quite adamant in voicing some version of "that is not what MSU Extension does or should do." Before long, however, it became clear that CES was an ideal organization for promulgating this type of information, and by 2023, virtually every state Extension program had one or more mental health professionals on staff. At MSU, Extension culture was further transformed by the director mandating and financially supporting all employees to become trained in Mental Health First Aid, a comprehensive day-long training focused on signs, symptoms, and actions associated with depression and other mental health issues in daily life. This mandate helped to immediately grow the capacity of MSU Extension professionals to continue to be sentinels in their communities and the ability of all employees to recognize and respond to mental health issues presented in their personal and professional lives. This intentional staff capacity investment continues to benefit the organization's cultural climate and ability to support the public.

In very early 2016 the magnitude and long-term implications of the Flint water crisis were becoming known, based on the careful research of Dr. Mona Hanna-Attisha and colleagues (Hanna-Attisha et al., 2016). Dr. Mona (a term of endearment by which she is known in Michigan) concluded that the "percentage of children with elevated blood lead levels increased after water source change, particularly in socioeconomically disadvantaged neighborhoods. Water is a growing source of childhood lead exposure because of aging infrastructure" (283). In his second week as MSU Extension director, Dwyer and MSU Extension were asked by the provost to take the lead for MSU in Flint. In those early months, Extension was able to utilize the resources of twenty staff members already working in Flint and supplement their expertise and relationships by drawing on the expertise of more than seven hundred MSU Extension colleagues statewide and more than three thousand faculty at MSU. This redirection of resources was also not without significant pushback. Commonly heard statements included "What does Extension know about lead in the water?" and "Extension does not work in urban areas!" Soon, however, the ability of MSU Extension to respond to an emerging health crisis while incorporating long-standing partnerships became clear.

A get-acquainted meeting with the CEO of the Michigan Milk Producers Association (MMPA) was on the calendar for Dwyer on the same Monday when the provost asked that CES in Michigan take the lead for MSU's response in Flint. During the discussion, it came up that Dwyer was heading next to Flint. The CEO asked why, which provided an opportunity to explain what was happening related to the lead/water situation in Flint and the short- and long-term impacts for children. He asked whether there was anything that MMPA could do, opening the door to reviewing research that suggested that food rich in vitamin D had the potential to ameliorate some of the initial consequences of lead exposure for children. By the next morning a call from the CEO informed Dwyer that MMPA members had agreed to send twelve thousand gallons of whole milk to Flint by Friday and hoped to do much more. We like to say that essential nutrition went from cows to kids in less than seventy-two hours. Perhaps more importantly, MMPA has since donated tens of thousands of gallons of milk to Flint and other communities, and in 2021, the USDA established a Dairy Donation Program modeled in part on these Michigan-based efforts. Leveraging diverse partnerships and long-standing relationships to impact a critical and emerging health issue is a unique characteristic of Health Extension with CES as an authentic partner.

These Michigan examples characterize the potential for a Health Extension that utilizes the vast network, partners, and expertise of the CES and LGUs to provide resources, make connections between otherwise unconnected parties, and benefit underserved and affected communities in a timely and coordinated fashion. Leveraging these connections is possible because of a well-established physical infrastructure, a vast network of human expertise and relationships, and a leadership framework effective in a dispersed statewide organization. It is also effective because CES staff members are sentinels in their communities. In the public health context, a sentinel event is a preventable health-related issue that serves as an early warning sign to public health officials and health care providers that patients and populations may be at risk (Rutstein et al., 1983). Human sentinels are people able to be aware of warning signs or changes in communities who also have a mechanism for reporting those. For example, CES sentinels were the initial impetus for MSU Extension's investment in opioids misuse and overdose prevention education in 2017–2018. Several simultaneous reports from Extension professionals from different parts of the state reporting personal and community losses due to opioid-related deaths created awareness and interventions followed. The adoption of the role of sentinel in a health/public health context by MSU Extension staff was an adaptation of the long-standing role of Extension professionals as sentinels in detecting new or emerging diseases, pests, and invasive species in agriculture.

Conclusion

It bears reminding that the mission of CES is to "improve lives through an educational process that uses scientific knowledge focused on issues and needs" (Rasmussen, 1989, 4). As the needs of the U.S. population evolved over the course of the twentieth century it became necessary to redirect attention and resources to priority areas not anticipated at its inception. As we conceptualize the concept and begin sharing associated outcomes, Health Extension is a range of strategies for utilizing the many resources of CES to support community-based healthcare that has proven successful in both addressing emerging health issues (e.g., COVID-19, opioid use disorder, suicide) and providing ongoing training and education in communities for prevention and recovery. As new health-related issues alter the needs of the U.S. population, CES and LGUs can be there to provide education, interventions, innovations, and dissemination of science-based information, but only if historical and structural barriers are addressed and new strategies are adopted to integrate Health Extension fully into CES and establish CES as an effective partner in providing community-based healthcare.

REFERENCES

Abrams, E. M., & Szefler, S. J. (2020). COVID-19 and the impact of social determinants of health. *The Lancet: Respiratory Medicine, 8*(7), 659–661.

Braun, B., Bruns, K., Cronk, L., Kirk Fox, L., Koukel, S., LeMenestrel, S., Lord, L., Reeves, C., Rennekamp, R., Rice, C., Rodgers, M., Samuel, J., Vail, A., & Warren, T. (2014). *Cooperative Extension's national framework for health and wellness.* Washington, DC: Extension Committee on Organization and Policy.

Burton, D., Canton, A., Coon, T., Eschbach, C., Gunn, J., Gutter, M., Jones, M., Kennedy, L., Martin, K., Mitchell, A., O'Neal, L., Rennekamp, R., Rodgers, M., Stluka, S., Trautman, K., Yelland, E., & York, D. (2021). *Cooperative Extension's national framework for health equity and well-being.* Washington, DC: Extension Committee on Organization and Policy.

Cohen, D. J., Grumbach, K., & Phillips, R. L. (2023). The value of funding a primary care extension program in the United States. *JAMA Health Forum, 4*(2), e225410.

Cuthbertson, C., Eschbach, C., & Shelle, G. (2021). Addressing farm stress through Extension mental health literacy programs. *Journal of Agromedicine, 27*(2), 124–131.

Dairy Donation Program. (August 2023). Rules and regulations: United States Department of Agriculture. *Federal Register, 88*(160).

Dwyer, J., Contreras, D., Eschbach, C., Tiret, H, Newkirk, C, Carter, E., & Cronk, L. (2017a). Cooperative Extension as a framework for health extension: The Michigan State University

Model. *Academic Medicine, 92*, 1416–1420.

Dwyer, J., Contreras, D., Eschbach, C., Tiret, H., Newkirk, C., Carter, E., & Cronk, L. (2017b, September/October). Cooperative Extension as a framework for health extension. *Annals of Family Medicine*. Letter to editor.

Entenmann, F. (1989). *The next 25 years, 1960–85: An update of the history of Cooperative Extension, Washington State University*. Pullman: Cooperative Extension, College of Agriculture and Home Economics, Washington State University.

Eschbach, C., Arnetz, B., & Arnetz, J. (2023). Designing and evaluating opioid misuse prevention training for rural communities and health care providers. *Health Promotion Practice*. https://doi.org/10.1177/15248399231174920

Eschbach, C., Carter, E., Newkirk, C., Tiret, H., Millet, M., Cronk, L., & Dwyer, J. (2018). Using speed meetings to connect Extension experts with university health researchers. *Journal of Extension, 56*(4), article 20.

Eschbach, C. L., Contreras, D. A. & Kennedy, L. E. (2022). Three Cooperative Extension initiatives funded to address Michigan's opioid crisis. *Frontiers in Public Health, 10*, 921919.

Eschbach, C. L., Cuthbertson, C., Shelle, G., & Bates, R. O. (2022). Expanding effective behavioral health literacy programs to address farm stress. *Journal of Extension, 60*(2), article 19.

Eschbach, C., Tiret, H., Carter, E., & Newkirk, C. (2019). Preparing Extension educators for community-based research and grant partnerships. *Journal of Extension, 57*(6), article 12.

Extension Foundation. (2023, August). *Find Cooperative Extension in your state*. https://extension.org/find-cooperative-extension-in-your-state

Grumbach, K., & Mold, J. W. (2009). A health care cooperative extension service: Transforming primary care and community health. *Journal of the American Medical Association, 301*(24), 2589–2591.

Hanna-Attisha, M., LaChance, J., Sadler, R. C., & Champney Schnepp, A. (2016). Elevated blood lead levels in children associated with the Flint drinking water crisis: A spatial analysis of risk and public health response. *American Journal of Public Health, 106*(2), 283–290.

Harder, A., Lamm, A., & Strong, R. (2009). An analysis of the priority needs of Cooperative Extension at the county level. *Journal of Agricultural Education, 50*(1), 11–21.

Hill, L. G., & Parker, L. A. (2005). Extension as a delivery system for prevention programming. Capacity, barriers, and opportunities. *Journal of Extension, 43*(1), article 4.

Health Extension Toolkit. (n.d.). *The United States Department of Health and Human Services Agency for Healthcare Quality & Research (AHQR) and The Commonwealth Fund*. http://healthextensiontoolkit.org

Kaufman, A., Boren, J., Koukel, S., Ronquillo, F., Davis, C., & Nkouaga, C. (2017). Agriculture and health sectors collaborate in addressing population health. *Annals of Family Medicine, 15*(5), 475–480.

Kaufman, A., Dickinson, P. W., Fagnan, L., Duffy, F., Parchman, M. & Rhyne, R. (2019). The role of health extension in practice transformation and community health improvement: Lessons from 5 case studies. *Annals of Family Medicine, 17*(Suppl. 1), S67–S72.

Kaufman, A., Powell, W., Alfero, C., Pacheco, M., Silverblatt, H., Anastasoff, J., Ronquillo, F.,

Lucero, K., Corriveau, E., Vanleit, B., Alvesson, D., & Scott, A. (2010). Health extension in New Mexico: An academic health center and the social determinants of disease. *Annals of Family Medicine, 8*(1), 73–81.

Khan, T., Eschbach, C., Cuthbertson, C. Newkirk, C., Contreras, D., & Kirley, K. (2020). Connecting primary care to community-based education: Michigan physicians' familiarity with Extension programs. *Health Promotion Practice, 21*(2), 175–180.

Lee, J. M., & Keys, S. W. (2013). *Land-grant but unequal. State one-to-one match funding for 1890 land-grant universities.* APLU Office of Access and Success publication no. 3000-PB1. Washington, DC: Association of Public and Land-grant Universities.

Leong, D., & Roberts, E. (2013). Social determinants of health and the Affordable Care Act. *Rhode Island Medical Journal, 96*(7), 20–22.

Magnan, S. (2017). *Social determinants of health 101 for health care: Five plus five. NAM perspectives.* Discussion paper. Washington, DC: National Academy of Medicine.

Mavis, B., Sousa, A., Osuch, J., Arvidson, C., Lipscomb, W., Brady, J., Green, W., & Rappley, M. D. (2012). The College of Human Medicine at Michigan State University: Expansion and reinvention. *Academic Medicine, 87*(12), 1705–1709.

Miller, B. M., Moore, D. E., Stead, W., & Balser, J. R. (2010). Beyond Flexner: A new model for continuous learning in the health professions. *Academic Medicine, 85*(2), 266–272.

Molgaard, V. K. (1997). The Extension Service as key mechanism for research and services delivery for prevention of mental health disorders in rural areas. *American Journal of Community Psychology, 25*, 515–544.

Morse, G. W. (2011). Regionalization with or without specialization: A call for a national research agenda. *Journal of Extension, 49*(2), Article 10.

Morse, G. W., Markell, J., O'Brien, P., Ahmed, A., Klein, T., Coyle, L., & Martin, M. V. (2009). *The Minnesota response: Cooperative Extension's money and mission crisis.* iUniverse. University of Minnesota Digital Conservancy.

Michigan State University. (2023, August). *About MSU health care.* https://healthcare.msu.edu.

Michigan State University Extension. (2021). *Innovations in agricultural education.* https://www.canr.msu.edu/resources/innovations-in-agricultural-extension

National Academies of Sciences, Engineering, and Medicine (NASEM). (2022). *Enhancing coordination and collaboration across the land-grant system.* Washington, DC: National Academies Press.

Office of Disease Prevention and Health Promotion. (n.d.). *Healthy people 2030.* U.S. Department of Health and Human Services. https://health.gov/healthypeople

Phillips, J. P., Wendling, A. L., Fahey, C. A., & Mavis, B. E. (2018). The effect of a community-based medical school on the state and local physician workforce. *Academic Medicine, 93*(2), 306–313.

Powers, W., Cockett, N., & Lardy, G. (2017). Getting the most out of your Extension appointment and still having a life. *Journal of Animal Science, 95*(4), 1827–1835. https://doi.org/10.2527/jas.2016.1266

Proctor, E. (2013a). *The Geriatric Center of Michigan.* https://www.canr.msu.edu/news/

the_geriatric_education_center_of_michigan
Proctor, E. (2013b). *Building Strong Sovereign Nations.* https://www.canr.msu.edu/news/building_strong_sovereign_nations
Rasmussen, W. D. (1989). *Taking the university to the people: Seventy-five years of Cooperative Extension.* Ames: Iowa State University Press.
Rogers, E. M. (1988). The intellectual foundation and history of the agricultural extension model. *Knowledge: Creation, Diffusion, Utilization*, 9(4), 492–510.
Rutstein, D. D., Mullan, R. J., Frazier, T. M., Halperin, W. E., Melius, J. M., & Sestito, J. P. (1983). Sentinel health events (occupational): A basis for physician recognition and public health surveillance. *American Journal of Public Health*, 73(9), 1054–1062.
Seevers, B., Graham, D., Gamon, J., & Conklin, N. (1997). *Education through Cooperative Extension.* Boston: Delmar.
Social Mission Alliance (2023, August). *Beyond Flexner Alliance: History of the movement.* https://socialmission.org/history
Solomon, L. S., & Kanter, M. H. (2018). Health care steps up to social determinants of health: Current context. *Permanente Journal*, 22, 18–139.
Tiret, H., Eschbach, C. L., & Newkirk, C. (2019). Rx for Health Referral Tool Kit techniques to promote Extension programs. *Journal of Human Sciences and Extension*, 7(3), 173–185.
U.S. Congress. (1914). Smith-Lever Act, Agricultural Extension Work Act. 63 P.L. 95, 63 Cong. Ch. 79, 38 Stat. 372.
U.S. Department of Agriculture. (2023a, August). *Cooperative Extension System.* National Institute of Food and Agriculture. https://www.nifa.usda.gov/about-nifa/how-we-work/extension/cooperative-extension-system
U.S. Department of Agriculture. (2023b, August). *A short history of SNAP.* Food and Nutrition Service. https://www.fns.usda.gov/snap/short-history-snap
U.S. Department of Agriculture. (2023c, August). *The Supplemental Nutrition Assistance Program—Education (SNAP-Ed).* https://www.nifa.usda.gov/grants/programs/capacity-grants/efnep/snap/supplemental-nutrition-education-program-education-snap-ed
U.S. General Accounting Office (1981, August 21). *Cooperative Extension Service's mission and federal role need congressional clarification.* Report to the Congress by the Comptroller General. https://www.gao.gov/assets/ced-81-119.pdf
Warner, P., & Christenson, J. A. (1984). *The Cooperative Extension Service: A national assessment.* Boulder, CO: Westview Press.
Winslow, C. E. (1920). The untilled fields of public health. *Science*, *51*(1306), 23–33.
World Health Organization (1946). Constitution of the World Health Organization. https://apps.who.int/gb/bd/PDF/bd47/EN/constitution-en.pdf?ua=1

Health Equity in Extension: Accounting for Our History and Forging an Authentic Path Forward

Lauren E. Kennedy, Cheryl L. Eschbach, and Erin L. Martinez

If the Cooperative Extension System (CES) is to maximize its potential by engaging in Health Extension to improve population health and well-being for all, health equity must be a systemwide value. Many Extension professionals are seeking ways for equity to serve as a grounding concept across CES, necessitating a review of the concept's history and the connecting movements related to health equity, as well as strengths and shortcomings of recent frameworks. We are at a time in history when we can see the possibilities of health equity sparking systems change that ultimately assists CES goals to achieve health justice for all. In this chapter, we explore the politics of health equity, visit familiar topics such as the social determinants of health (SDOH), and engage the curious reader in less familiar, connecting constructs or movements (i.e., oppression, liberation) important to advance equity. We also describe recent efforts by the Association of Public and Land-Grant Universities (APLU) to publish two Cooperative Extension National Frameworks for Health (Braun et al., 2014; Burton et al., 2021) in less than a decade. Our critical review is based, in part, on our experience as co-authors of the more recent national framework. These reflections help inform the chapter's concluding calls to action for modernizing Extension's research, education, and interventions to address health equity. Health Extension is proposed as a mechanism or collection of strategies for transforming traditional CES program areas and reorientating resources to center Extension work on the pursuit of health equity and justice.

The Politics of Health Equity

In some states, health equity in the context of CES research, education, and interventions is avoided in conversations or met with ambivalence. When we have presented on health equity topics among colleagues in recent years, individuals have responded that the topic is "too political" to address in their state or community. Yet these reticent Extension professionals also acknowledged that working for higher education is already political because CES receives public funding and has connections to government policy and congressional mandates. In other states, staff and administrative leadership are beyond assessing readiness and are actively trying strategies and initiatives that advance equity as an organizational priority. Politics of health equity are relevant because forces stand in favor of or against certain movements that intend progress or change.

The attainment and maintenance of health itself, or being healthy, is also complex and inherently political. Decades of health disparities research have revealed numerous differences in health outcomes across population groups. According to the National Institutes of Health, "Health disparities are differences that exist among specific population groups in the United States in the attainment of full health potential that can be measured by differences in incidence, prevalence, mortality, burden of disease, and other adverse health conditions" (n.d., 1). Disparities often refer to racial or ethnic differences; however, disparities also exist across age, gender, disability status, educational background, income, and residence (National Academies of Sciences, Engineering, and Medicine, 2017). Disparities mean some individuals disproportionately face higher burdens of disease, experience poorer quality of care and health outcomes, and have greater challenges to access healthcare. These health disparities are documented in higher rates of disease and death. The Centers for Medicare & Medicaid Services (2022) calls attention to "disparities in chronic and infectious diseases such as diabetes, chronic kidney disease, cancer, dementia, cardiovascular disease, maternal and infant health, behavioral health, as well as HIV/AIDS, and COVID-19, which disproportionately impact members of underserved communities due to prevalence, complexity, and social risk factors" (6).

Health disparities research is important because it documents differences in outcomes for different groups, but to impact the future, we must address root causes. Looking through a health equity lens, one can see that most of the differences observed between groups are not randomly occurring. Instead, they are often the result of unjust, preventable conditions that inequitably structure the opportunity to access or achieve health, making it easier for some groups to be healthy or maintain health, while for others health may be unattainable, leading to chronic health conditions and accelerating premature death.

The attainment and maintenance of health are partly influenced by social, environmental, economic, and political contexts and histories that impact health outcomes. These determinants of health are defined as the nonmedical factors or conditions that people are born into and live, grow, and age in. Healthy People 2030, published by the Office of Disease Prevention and Health Promotion at the U.S. Department of Health and Human Services (n.d.), cites education access and quality, healthcare access and quality, neighborhood and built environment, social and community context, and economic stability as key SDOH (see the social determinants of health figure).

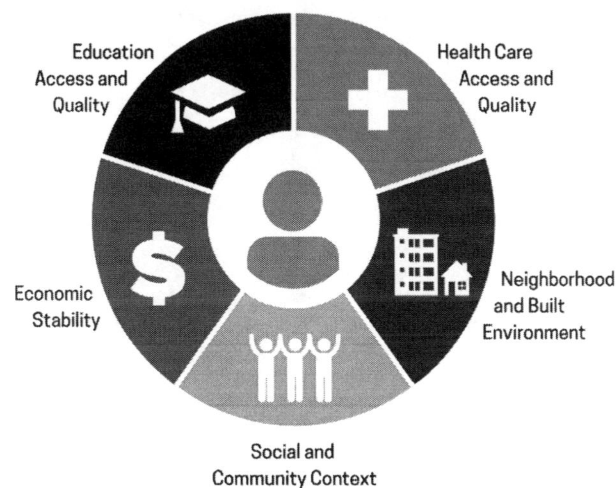

Social determinants of health, from Healthy People 2030. U.S. Department of Health and Human Services, Office of Disease Prevention and Health Promotion.

Healthy People 2030 is a 10-year plan to measure important public health outcomes including overall health and well-being measures. Leading health indicators (LHIs) help define trackable measures for health disparities, priority populations, health equity, and health literacy. One way that Healthy People 2030 changed the dialogue among researchers in 2020 was by changing health literacy definitions. Literacy programs and associated evaluation studies had been focused on personal understanding; revised definitions highlight organizational literacy (Santana et al., 2021) to reduce health information complexity and simplify health systems. This is an example of how health equity principles are shifting the research and education topic of literacy to a policy, systems, and environmental (PSE) change perspective where our healthcare systems have responsibility to translate terms and procedures for prevention and medical treatment services, as well as to purposely reduce barriers to healthcare. Individuals need health information that is easy to understand to make informed decisions, and this practice is necessary to avoid systemic racism that is reproduced when information unjustly disadvantages American Indian and Alaska Native, Black, and Hispanic patients (Coleman et al.2023). One goal of the updated definition of organizational literacy in

Healthy People 2030 was to support efforts to integrate health literacy principles into policy. Energy spent on systems becoming a "health literate organization" (Santana et al., 2021, S262) through PSE changes, in combination with individuals gaining health literacy skills to navigate these systems, demonstrates commitment in applying health equity principles to change the nature of interventions and policies.

Although SDOH are helpful to frame initiatives and plan programs, even these social determinants do not cover all possible connections to health. In November 2022, the U.S. Department of Health and Human Service's Office of Disease Prevention and Health Promotion released a Federal Plan for Equitable Long-Term Recovery and Resilience (ELTRR) that elaborated seven vital conditions that can be used with SDOH and has seventy-eight recommendations to bring federal resources together to address health for all (Federal Plan for ELTRR, 2022). An opportunity to expand upon the SDOH exists through these vital conditions for health and well-being. The vital conditions provide actionable, asset-based recommendations that are needed to address inequities and enhance health and well-being for thriving communities. The Vital Conditions and Health and Well-Being Framework advances an entire government perspective (twenty-eight agencies) and complements other frameworks, including SDOH, the Federal Emergency Management Agency Recovery Core Capabilities, the National Disaster Recovery Framework, and Healthy People 2030. The conditions expand upon SDOH to include roles of civic sectors in creating, maintaining, and advancing resilient and thriving communities. Aspects like belonging and civic muscle, a thriving natural world, basic needs for health and safety, humane housing, meaningful work and wealth, lifelong learning, and reliable transportation are considered.

Root Causes of Inequitable Structures: Connecting Constructs to Health Equity

This section defines key concepts and connects larger civic movements to CES and Health Extension to assist in preparing a conceptual foundation for the adoption of health equity as a systemwide value. These constructs may be less familiar to the CES audience, but they are important in dismantling oppressive and inequitable structures and ensuring the fair participation and decision making of those who are historically and systemically oppressed. Root causes of inequitable structures in the United States derive from various forms of oppression and, consequently, power imbalances. David and Derthick (2014) offer the following definition of oppression:

> Oppression occurs when one group has more access to power and privilege than another group and when that power and privilege is used to maintain the status quo (i.e., domination of one group over another). Thus, oppression is both a state and a process, with the state of oppression being unequal group access to power and privilege, and the process of oppression being the ways in which inequality between groups is maintained. (3)

Oppressions, such as racism, sexism, ableism, classism, and others, are structures that impact health at different levels by influencing policies, systems, the environment, and our cultural norms. This makes the experience of being oppressed virtually inescapable for members of oppressed groups. Each of us inhabits a range of identities and memberships to various groups, and the intersection and overlap of these identities lead to additional variance in power imbalances and lived experiences of oppression.

Health equity is both a process and an outcome of trying to ensure that the opportunity to be healthy is maximally available to everyone. "Health justice" builds on the concept of health equity by addressing the jurisprudential and regulatory constraints to individual health. Health justice is concerned with guaranteeing not only that inequities are prevented from (re)occurring, but also that foundational liberties are protected, and individuals are unrestrained to pursue their fullest potential (Benfer, 2015). Therefore, the pursuit of health justice necessitates critical examination of laws, the ways they are enforced and upheld, how they benefit dominant groups, and how they result in state-sanctioned exploitation and vulnerability to premature death for minoritized groups (Gilmore, 2007). This positions CES, and anyone else in community health, as integral to the critical analysis of systems that are deleterious to people's health, are producing and reproducing trauma, and inhibit being authentically engaged in community and meeting basic needs. Community development experts, planners, and others already in CES working in systems are well suited to join forces with their health and nutrition colleagues doing this work.

Health equity and health justice are intertwined. If we pursue health equity, we must also pursue health justice. The eventual outcome of health justice is liberation. "Liberation" is the freedom to self-direct your life and chosen purpose and to reevaluate that purpose and change direction through socially acquired values, and the freedom from being prevented from doing those things (Campbell, 1995; McDowell et al., 2014).

The World Health Organization (WHO, 2023) defines another layer of SDOH, called commercial determinants of health, as private sectors such as supply chains of goods or services that impact health. The prison-industrial complex has been an example (Klein & Lima, 2021) of a commercial determinant of health with a multitude of systems and institutions causing significant health-related harm. Documented harms to people's health can be attributed to direct or vicarious encounters with law enforcement, healthcare, public education, and criminal-legal pipelines, to name a few (Alang et al., 2017; Duarte et al., 2020; Nichols et al., 2018; Riley et al., 2022; Wahbi & Beletsky, 2022). By looking at systems deeply and identifying the harms or supports that structure human health inequities, one can see larger concepts connected to individual health outcomes (e.g., power, oppression).

To engage in the work of health justice, we find ourselves grappling with history and laws to dismantle harm-producing systems, leading us into conversations about abolition. The core of abolition is not just dismantling oppressive systems and institutions, but it is also what Ruth Wilson Gilmore (2007) calls a "constant becoming." This means

Summary of Key Terms and Recommended Readings for Concepts Connected to Centering Health Equity as a Systemwide Value Within Health Extension

KEY TERM	SUMMARY	RECOMMENDED ADDITIONAL READINGS
OPPRESSION	A state and a process of systematically disadvantaging some groups while benefiting others, as a result of one group having prejudice and more access to power and privileges than the other. Examples: racism, sexism, ableism.	David (2014). Freire (1970).
ABOLITION	The elimination of law enforcement violence, ending of prison expansions, divesting from punishment and incarceration, and the restructuring of society to meet everyone's needs.	American Public Health Association (2018, 2021). Gilmore (2007). Iwai et al. (2020).
HEALTH JUSTICE	The expansion of health equity to include protection of foundational liberties that constrain an individual's health and life.	Rodriguez et al. (2022). Braveman et al. (2011).
LIBERATION	The freedom to self-direct your life and chosen purpose, the freedom to reevaluate that purpose and change direction through socially acquired values, and the freedom from being prevented from doing those things.	McDowell et al. (2014).

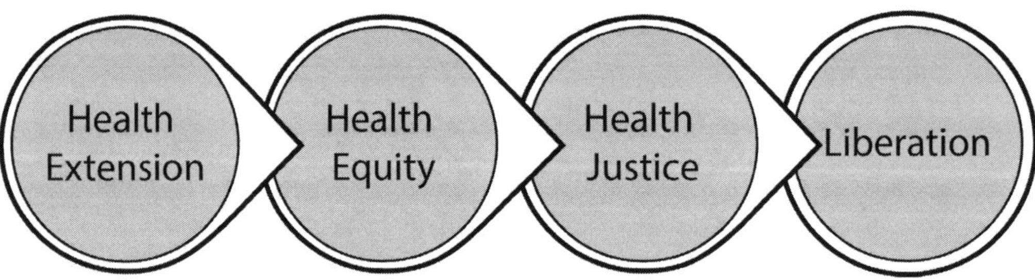

Continuum for addressing health disparities and oppression through Health Extension strategies that advance health equity and promote health justice to ultimately achieve liberation for all.

that abolition affords us the opportunity to reimagine and reconstruct our society in ways that meet everyone's needs and do not rely on punishment and violence to give the illusion of safety. There are inevitably questions about what that reconstruction will look like. However, we do not need to have all the answers to those questions to begin the process of making a world with less harm. That is the beauty of the "constant becoming." We recognize that it is beyond the scope of this chapter to fully explore the connections among power, oppression, abolition, and liberation as they relate to health equity and health justice. We offer recommended readings for concepts related to CES efforts around centering equity as a systemwide value in health initiatives (see the table). Key terms are only briefly defined.

A thoughtful review of abolition and liberation in the context of health will be needed in future CES research, education, and interventions to fully embed and embrace equity. In this chapter, we aim to offer a vision ahead for CES and a foundation for exploring this continuum for addressing oppression in Health Extension (see the figure illustrating the continuum).

The Cooperative Extension System's History with Oppression

CES's history is inextricably tied to the land-grant university (LGU) system. In their essay "Early Chapters of Extension: Land Grants, Segregation, and the Development of Cooperative Programming," Shaffer et al. (2022) describe the legislative foundation for LGU and CES. The Morrill Act of 1862 appropriated land in each state for the founding of a public university or college, with a particular focus on agricultural and mechanical studies. At the time of the Morrill Act of 1862, neither the federal nor state governments possessed the land being granted for the LGUs (Phillips, 2003; Williams et al., 2021). Instead, nearly eleven million acres of land were stolen from Indigenous people and redistributed to states. As the "Land-Grab Universities" investigation points out (Lee & Ahtone, 2020; Lee et al., 2020; Lomawaima et al., 2021), dispossession was necessary to grant land to states through the Morrill Act. The land granted through the Morrill Act also included land beyond college campuses, which could be sold or developed, contributing to ongoing LGU wealth that continues to accumulate even today.

It is argued that fifty-two land-grant institutions and 245 Tribal Nations are tied to this shared history of the Morrill Act of 1862 (Lee & Ahtone, 2020). The increase in universities exhibiting institutional consciousness (Martin & Hipp, 2018) has generated important conversations about the value of that land and modern access, use, and caretaking of that land for and by Indigenous peoples. Tribal land acknowledgments by LGUs have been a positive, albeit performative, step forward in the ongoing dialogue about this history and today's "land back" movement led by Indigenous people (Red Shirt-Shaw, 2020) is starting to impact the conversation about LGUs. Still, people identifying as Alaskan or Native American (Indigenous people) are underrepresented today in student populations and in staff and faculty positions within the 1862 institutions. Phillips (2003) reminds us that education was once used as an assimilation tool for Indigenous populations and that there were low participation rates of American Indian students in higher education that persisted even before the 1994 investment in tribal land-grant institutions. Of note, twenty-nine tribal colleges and university were working as the American Indian Higher Education Consortium before the Equity in Educational Land-Grant Status Act of 1994 (Phillips, 2003).

There is a growing interest in actions that can be prioritized to take responsibility for this history (William et al., 2021). Forms of restorative action are needed; recommendations include hiring Indigenous faculty at all LGUs and inviting descendants of disposed lands be included and compensated to serve on university councils, boards, and other forms of university governance (McCoy et al., 2021). Crazy Bull and White Hat (2019) share examples of how the sovereignty of Tribal Nations drives quality education in the land-grant structure, and they highlight the growth of tribal land grants since 1994.

Inequities in the establishment of LGUs are extensive, as neither the eighteen 1890 historically Black colleges and universities (HBCUs) nor the thirty-four 1994 tribal colleges and universities (TCUs) received any land as permanent endowments (Martin & Hipp, 2018). This history and the decades of underfunding to support 1890 and 1994 LGUs leaves repair and retribution to be made by modern-day administrators and university boards of trustees. At the very least, 1862 LGUs and the APLU could send messages to Congress that the unequal LGU funding investments perpetuates systematic racism in the CES and could advocate for equitable funding. Leaders and lawmakers can recognize that 1890 LGUs and 1994 TCUs receiving increased funding does not reduce the capacity of 1862 LGUs; rather, increased funding investments to all higher education institutions in each state supports those residents to engage in sustainable agriculture, manage land and natural resources, and promote healthy and thriving communities.

The Morrill Act of 1862 has additional history with oppression because at the time the law was passed, LGUs only admitted white students (men or women). During Reconstruction, Southern U.S. states were opposed to admitting students of color, refusing to integrate. However, the second Morrill Act of 1890 required those Southern states to do so, mandating them to admit Black students to their state's LGU or provide a separate but equal institution for them (National Archives, n.d.). Unsurprisingly, the Southern states decided they would rather create a separate institution than allow Black students to enroll at their existing LGUs. This was the advent of HBCUs as LGUs.

Southern state leaders also devised ways to make sure that these separate institutions were not equal. Principal among these strategies was limiting the amount of matching funds that came from the state government, by including a provision in the legislation that allowed state legislatures to decide how to distribute Smith-Lever funds in states with more than one LGU (Harris, 2008). The result of this provision is that racist state legislatures have been disproportionately appropriating federal funds since the inception of 1890 land grants, in favor of the 1862 LGUs. For example, Lee and Keys (2013) found that in the years 2010–2012, 1890 LGUs had more than $31 million in CES funds withheld from them by state legislatures that refused to adhere to the matching requirement in federal law. This strategy continues today, with most 1890 LGUs receiving significantly less state funds than their 1862 counterparts, resulting in tremendous disparities in the capacity of each university to educate students, conduct research, and do CES outreach. Further, the Smith-Lever Act of 1914, which established the CES, pushed out African Americans' demonstration work in the South to ensure that control of Extension work, land, and funding was held by white workers (Crosby, 1986; Ramírez Solís & Montgomery, 2021).

Overt racism against people of color was pervasive, even encouraged, and some firmly felt as though those without citizenship, perceived or actual, should not be served by the CES (Harris, 2008). Therefore, resources were directed at white farmers, who were believed to be more capable of learning and implementing best practices that would enhance the nation's agricultural productivity (Schor, 1986).

In 1994, the Equity in Educational Land-Grant Status Act (EELGSA) offered land-grant status to TCUs, funding research, education, and teaching and increased CES capacity for tribal communities. The EELGSA authorized a $4.6 million endowment rather than an actual land grant (Phillips, 2003). Keep in mind that the nation provided $5 million in 1917 to the 1862 and 1890 LGUs to operate their new Smith-Lever Act-funded Extension Service. As a comparison, in the late 1990s, TCUs were each given $50,000 per year in operating funds (Phillips, 2003). Congress has not yet passed capacity funding for 1994 land grants. In 2021, the endowment for TCUs was $5 million shared with 35 institutions, and by comparison, between 2019 and 2020, the 1862 land grants received $574 million and 1890 land grants received $124 million in capacity funds (Congressional Research Service, 2022). The endowment has since built up much-needed capacity for 1994 LGUs to conduct research, teaching, and extension, but these inequitable beginnings have long-lasting consequences.

Despite the status designation and the limited funds that come with it, little to nothing has been done to repair the past harms caused, return stolen lands, or provide financial reparations to tribal communities for the profits earned from their land for more than a century. Based on quantitative calculations of modern land values, the federal government could offer $5.4 million per year to each 1890 and 1994 LGU as a small step to correct this history of injustice (Martin & Hipp, 2018). This national investment would be small in scale compared to current federal government spending, but a symbolic step in the right direction.

The result of this history is that today we have three separate and unequal land-grant Extension systems. The disparities in funding for each system often mean CES staff located at 1890 or 1994 LGUs are paid significantly less, have fewer institutional resources such as supplementary funding (e.g., grants or endowments), and are often expected to take on additional responsibilities that support the department or institution, limiting actual CES capacity.

The Need to Modernize Family and Consumer Science

Family and consumer sciences (FCS) is a traditional programming area first launched to support rural homemakers using home demonstrations on topics such as gardening, food preservation, laundry, sewing, and cooking (Scholl, 2013). However, Atiles and Eubanks (2014) explain that in the South, FCS agents and programs were segregated by race. African American home agents were employed from 1912 (Oklahoma) until the late 1960s, when the Civil Rights Act of 1964 changed hiring practices. After this time, rather than build out an Extension workforce that was representative of communities, CES FCS agents became more homogeneous because CES tended to hire white, college-educated women with degrees from accredited home economics college programs at the 1862 LGUs (Atiles & Eubanks, 2014). Regardless of the time in history or the health behavior, the emphasis of recent FCS programming has predominantly been on providing educational programs in group settings from an expert-teaching model. CES FCS program efforts have long operated on executing plans of work that include naming learning objectives for participants and then delivering direct education. Some educators are moving away from this expert-teaching model by including participatory learning methods, but many traditional FCS programs still instruct programs only from an expert-teacher model. This dynamic, called the banking concept of education by Freire (1970), serves an insidious goal when examined through the lens of structural oppression. Freire describes how when oppressors are threatened, they deliberately lead the oppressed to change instead. This serves only the oppressor's purpose—to maintain power and inequity. The adoption of the banking model for FCS education, particularly for reaching marginalized and oppressed audiences, is therefore incompatible with the pursuit of equity.

Freire (1970) offers us a ready solution: transform the structures so that the oppressed are liberated. Liberation is obviously new for Health Extension and CES. We have not overtly focused on health equity, let alone liberation, before, but this chapter serves as a call to action for systems change. This requires intentional practice and action from systems (like LGUs and CES) and their personnel. The modernization of FCS and the expansion of Health Extension as a movement are ripe for this type of actionable disruption.

Health Extension as a Way to Transform FCS and Advance Health Equity

Health Extension presents an opportunity for CES program areas to advance health equity and lay the foundation for health justice and liberation. It is no longer enough to only build knowledge; the CES must act to change society's conditions. We must also confront the systemic and institutional racism and oppression perpetuated by our own system(s) and the systems we wish to collaborate with in this endeavor (e.g., legal, medical, and healthcare). One way to do so is to build power in Black, Indigenous, and people of color (BIPOC) communities (Brock-Petroshius et al., 2022). However, communities need to be approached authentically for mutual benefit and meaningful involvement. This is particularly critical within CES and FCS, as nationwide efforts and models are attempting to guide Extension work toward contributing to the achievement of improved population health and health equity and justice for all.

LGUs and CES cannot simply pivot to just folding health equity into existing efforts. There is a caution that even with good intent, such a sudden departure from previous work (i.e., traditional FCS) to that of health equity pursuits can be flagrantly insensitive toward systemically oppressed populations and in public health fields where researchers and practitioners have worked in equity space for decades. Health equity cannot be just a buzz word within CES and there should not be a haphazard reactionary approach. Doing so will make these institutions, their leaders, scholars, and CES educators "health equity tourists" (Lett et al., 2022)—those who simply jump into this work without any prior experience, knowledge, or commitment because of sudden societal or academic interest, mandates to chase funding streams, and the need to meet "check the box" standards of diversity, equity, and inclusion. White scholars must be respectful and inclusive of existing efforts of Black researchers and stay sensitive to not taking over funding or publishing opportunities as health equity tourists. One example of tourist behavior is when researchers of color are asked to provide feedback on manuscripts or grant applications without compensation and are blocked from authorship (McFarling, 2021).

Extension's Two National Frameworks for Health in Less Than a Decade

LGUs elect individuals to represent their institution on a collective body referred to as the APLU Extension Committee on Organization and Policy (ECOP). It was late 2012 when the ECOP chair at the time added health to the ECOP national priorities and requested programming ideas, outcome indicators, and potential partners to be presented at the March 2013 National Extension Director's meeting. ECOP assembled a task force with members who ultimately published the 2014 National Framework for Health and Wellness (Braun et al., 2014). The document writers were a group of CES employees, not necessarily with health expertise backgrounds, primarily from high-ranking administrative positions. One of the authors was, at the time, an employee of an 1890 LGU. This framework was meant to usher in an approach to programming that went beyond nutrition, to include broader health and wellness topics. Since many states already offered health programs at this point, parallel goals of the framework were to solidify Extension's presence as a collaborator in community health and to mobilize new resources. The published framework was a tremendous step forward for CES, and it was assumed at the time that health programming might fall under FCS.

The framework potentially represented a shift in Extension and FCS program identities, and it successfully brought in new national funding through partnerships with the Robert Wood Johnson Foundation (RWJF) and Centers for Disease Control and Prevention (CDC). Since 2014, Extension has made incredible strides in most state systems, if not all, with implementation of this framework and the recommendations made. Examples include hiring personnel, particularly those with public health backgrounds, rebranding the Priester Conference as the National Health Outreach Conference, exploring partnerships with clinical translational science institutions, and initiating a stronger presence in areas of health that were new to FCS, like substance use and behavioral or mental health. Notably, Health Extension as a movement (Dwyer et al., 2017) was able to flourish because of this 2014 national framework.

Key themes of the 2014 framework reflect where CES was at that time. Strengthening CES organizationally to build upon existing health programming and capacity seemed the easiest first step, followed by building capacity within states and for CES nationally by enhancing the leadership and professional development at all levels of the organization. Strategic marketing and communications related to Extension's health work were identified as needed. Finally, CES recognized the need to build partnerships to acquire new resources.

The 2014 framework attempted to leverage CES's traditional models and infrastructure to influence health, but it fell short in several ways. Chief among its shortcomings was how little attention was offered to root causes of health, the social or structural determinants of health, or how PSE changes could be adopted as a strategy to increase impact. The 2014 framework outlined a section on "health disparities" as a national trend, but there was no mention of disparities in the resulting priorities. Most of the priorities recommended in the 2014 framework dealt with arranging buy-in and further legitimizing CES as a visible presence in public health settings. Nevertheless, five of the six stated priorities were clearly targeting individual-level behaviors, putting the onus of health on the individual and ignoring systemic and structural contributors to health altogether. This was a missed opportunity, but it is painfully unsurprising if we consider the history of LGUs, CES, and FCS.

Following both the 2016 ECOP report "Innovation in Extension" and the 2019 ECOP report "Innovation Scoping Report," APLU's ECOP established a new Health Innovation Task Force as a two-year committee in September 2019. ECOP charged the group with providing recommendations for system-level changes that would further advance CES's health-related work. The new ECOP Task Force had sixteen members in total who split efforts. One group focused on a big idea forum exploring workforce development and aligning local, state, and national resources to advance health, economic vitality, youth opportunities, and educational attainment in underserved communities. The other group was charged with updating the 2014 framework as an output (i.e., product deliverable). The sixteen individuals in the writing group included ten from 1862s, two from 1890s, none from 1994s, three national administrators, and one government agency partner.

This new National Framework for Health Equity and Well-Being (Burton et al., 2021) represents tremendous progress in CES. Health equity is acknowledged as an important part of community health, and the framework declares racism as a public health issue and key driver of inequity. The framework incorporated contemporary definitions of health equity from the RWJF, CDC, and World Health Organization. Trends were highlighted again, but this time, an example of the inequities observed within each trend was also noted.

The current framework (Burton et al., 2021) positions five systemwide recommendations as future goals: (1) advance health equity as a core system value to ensure that all people have a fair and just opportunity to be as healthy as they can be; (2) utilize community assessment processes that integrate data science and resident voices to identify and address health inequities with greater precision; (3) invest in the success and visibility of extension's health-related professionals, programs, and initiatives; (4) establish partnerships with academic units, universities, government agencies, corporations, nonprofit organizations, and foundations that share a commitment to reducing or eliminating health inequities; and (5) utilize a community development approach to advance the work of coalitions focused on influencing the SDOH.

Despite the progress of the new framework, there are major limitations and failures that necessitate exploration and accountability. The authors of this chapter have first-hand experience with the writing process and a thorough understanding of the final framework's content and early drafts. Even though this framework attempted a focus on health equity (going so far as changing the framework title), the final product is mostly performative and presents only a narrow view of health inequities, oppression, health justice, and liberation.

Critiques of the 2021 National Framework for Health Equity and Well-Being

This section is a reflection on the development and distribution of ECOP's 2021 National Framework for Health Equity and Well-Being by three authors of the framework who made significant contributions to the content. The purpose of sharing these reflections is to provide context for the historical developments and to present an alternative view of the timeline, processes, outputs, and outcomes from Extension professionals personally involved.

Authorship, Writing, and Editing Processes

Authorship for a national guiding document like the health framework should reflect CES, including different personnel roles, different identities and backgrounds, different LGUs and TCUs, and more. Instead, ECOP selected Task Force members based on rank and seniority, and from there, those members self-selected into the writing group. This resulted in a group primarily composed of 1862 deans, directors, and administrators, which means this was a predominantly white group. Attempts were made several times by the authors of this chapter in the early stages of writing to advocate for including 1890 and 1994 co-authors, by appealing to Extension's national leadership and the chairs of the Health Innovation Task Force, but those appeals were heard and even acknowledged but not acted upon immediately nor with an open process. Not until early 2021 were two 1890 professionals added to the writing group for framework review. Notably, no 1994 employees were included in the framework review, writing, or editing. In addition to the exclusion of critical voices, there was no effort to follow professional standards to determine authorship. Hence, Task Force members were included as authors regardless of their contribution, despite an over-reliance on a few early and mid-career Extension professionals in idea generation and writing. These authors were not recognized commensurate to their contributions, were left vulnerable to a mysterious editing process, and were removed from decision making on the final product ahead of the framework's approval by ECOP in July 2021.

The new framework is not just an update of the 2014 document; it is a complete overhaul, a brand-new document (Burton et al., 2021). Undertaking a writing project like a national framework typically entails a stated process for writing, assignment of sections, collaborating with co-authors, and the full participation of anyone intending to be listed as a co-author on the final product. However, the development of the new framework lacked any semblance of a process. Some co-authors attempted to write collaboratively, but others preferred to keep their contributions limited to providing feedback. This disjointed approach led to rogue writing and editing, with limited opportunity for meaningful input and synergetic discussion. The timeline for completing the new framework was vague, with only an endpoint in mind. This meant the new framework had less than a full year to be completely updated, rushing a process that should have been more thoughtful and inclusive.

Framework Content, Editorial Process, and Publication Standards

Attempting to create a foundation for the framework's update, the contributing co-authors conducted a review of relevant literature and summarized that research to be included in the document. The final product had much of this cited research removed during discussions among the noncontributing co-authors, with the caveat that it could be included as appendices to the framework document. However, that content was scrubbed from the final versions posted online without discussion. An executive summary was created from the original twenty-two-page framework document and published online with references removed (i.e., the cited research) and reworded recommendations, as well as retitled this shorter, eight-page document the "popular report." Additionally, a flipping book publication was produced by Extension Foundation after the task force and writing group disbanded. The flipping book is an online publication that requires a download (with collection of name/e-mail) to view and has the framework text used with new content, photos, and resource links added that were not vetted during the review process and, in some instances, were not consistent with the core content. Taken together, this means that there are three different versions of the 2021 National Framework for Health Equity and Well-Being (Burton et al., 2021). This matters because readers will likely draw differing conclusions about CES's commitment to health equity and other issues depending on which version they read.

Throughout the editing process, the deeper analysis of CES's history and the influence of structural racism became more superficial and palatable for the status quo leadership and stakeholders. For example, the framework states, "More recently, racism is increasingly being elevated as a dimension of social identity that deserves increased attention at this current point in time." This nonsensical statement incorrectly labels racism as a dimension of social identity. The wording of the sentence also insinuates that racism only recently rose to the level of deserving our attention, which is false and offensive. The co-authors responsible for most of the writing made numerous suggestions to remove or rewrite this text and to align the framework with established health equity theories and metrics, but those suggestions were mostly ignored.

Drafts of the framework were vetted in early 2021 through seventeen presentations that reached 478 individuals, including leaders of 1862 and 1890 land-grant institutions. In addition, a Qualtrics survey to gather input from institutional health contacts and members of the health and well-being subgroup of Connect Extension was created and managed by the University of Wisconsin. However, only twenty-nine respondents provided feedback on that national survey, with respondents self-reporting as 90 percent women, 100 percent white, and 96 percent representing 1862 LGUs. These white, 1862 LGU stakeholders who responded to the feedback survey reported that the framework recommendations were supported. Although this was seen as validation for the framework by task force leaders, academic scholars who publish in scientific fields would not count this data set as rigorous or representative.

Finally, the way the current framework is published online, rather than in the peer-reviewed literature, limits its visibility, circulation, and potential longevity. APLU offers a PDF download of the twenty-two-page full framework document on a website. However, the Extension Foundation only offers the flipping book version and, until very recently, the ECOP website hosted by APLU (containing documents and information for CES leaders) only included the popular report version of the framework. Moreover, the link to access the published framework has already changed twice since 2021, and the lack of professional publishing standards puts the document at risk. Another central document that the 2014 framework was built upon was the 2010 U.S. Department of HHS Strategic Plan that included performance measures. As of 2023, this HHS website was written over with the strategic plan for Fiscal Year 2022–2026. Hence, not only are there three different versions of the framework document that were subjected to a less than ideal review process, but these versions are variously accessible to those who might be interested in the content. To avoid these shortcomings, CES needs to publish important national frameworks in the peer-reviewed literature following generally accepted professional standards to ensure that the full framework content can remain accessed over time.

Framework Adoption by ECOP and Dissemination

The dissemination of the updated framework continues to be critical to expanding its reach and encouraging its uptake. However, a dissemination plan was never collaboratively designed nor were efforts discussed. Although purposeful and appropriate webinars, publications, and document distribution have taken place within ECOP and 1862 LGUs, a strategic dissemination approach with input from a variety of stakeholders would have promoted a more inclusive reach. Many webinars have been provided to traditional CES leadership, partners, and stakeholders, with arguably limited reach to non-1862 Extension institutions and professionals. Members of the ECOP 2020 Health Innovation Task Force—some of whom were not involved in the writing or editing of the framework—have led presentations to CES and LGU leadership audiences, which only reinforced the hierarchical power of particular task force members, while revoking any opportunity for mid-career writers to dialogue with high-level LGU/CES leaders. The content within dissemination efforts has also varied and has been subject to editorialized vernacular and commentary that showed blatant disregard for actual framework content and displayed inexcusable ignorance of systemic and oppressive structures that drive health inequity.

Multilevel System Capacities with Cooperative Extension

Something omitted from the framework was an exploration of the multilevel system capacities within Extension—that is, the capabilities and resources at various levels of the institution that address and mitigate health disparities. Rather, reflection on the system's recent capacity building highlighted the increased use of the word "health" in Extension's lexicon, the intent to hire more individuals with health-related backgrounds, the National Health Outreach Conference, and, later in the narrative, the development of an APLU-funded Extension Health director position. The framework utterly failed to address past and present systemic racism and oppression within CES's institutional structure (as outlined in this chapter and mentioned as removed from early 2021 framework drafts) that have directly diminished the system's capacity for success and opted instead to provide accolades for a few surface-level accomplishments and future priorities. In fact, early drafts of the 2021 framework contained numerous instances of revising the LGU and CES history. For example, one author wrote that the Smith-Lever Act was a "measure of equity" at its core, which is something we have undoubtedly proven false in this chapter, but a myth that apparently others in CES continue to believe in and propagate. The only loose connection to building a semblance of institutional capacity was the high-level recommendation to "promote health equity as a core system wide value."

Time for Urgent Action

Like other U.S. systems and the institutions that accompany them, CES and the LGUs must change. The 1862 LGU network and associated Extension systems must be the main initiators and drivers of this change since they enjoy the privilege and power of inequitable and long-standing funding investments. Considering the history of CES and LGU described in this chapter, trust is likely low with individuals and communities where health justice is most needed and with 1890 and 1994 LGU partners. To be clear, it is not that those individuals and communities lack trust, but that we, as a system, an institution, and actors within the system, have demonstrated ourselves to be untrustworthy. Therefore, the onus of reversing that falls to us. In CES, change needs to take place locally, in counties and communities where overt interpersonal racism and discrimination is still the norm. It needs to take place at the state level, where LGU campus staff, legislators, and partners work together to determine funding priorities, program priorities, staffing decisions, and overall organizational culture. It also needs to happen at the national level, where CES leadership, partners, and policymakers are coordinating to determine

CES's future. Without these system overhauls, CES and Health Extension as a movement working on equity have no credibility with which to operate. The calls to action in the following reflect areas of emphasis for the future that would help CES progress to demonstrate trustworthiness and avoid health equity tourism (Lett et al., 2022).

Stop Revising History and End Gatekeeping

Progress includes being upfront about the nation's history, as well as the difficult past of CES and LGUs. During the writing of the 2021 framework there was a desire from the group to embed health equity as a new topic. There was internal questioning on whether our programs and funding are truly open to all and reach all, but that questioning turned into a reluctance to list the core issue of racism directly within health equity. There was a deliberate effort to not place racism central in the model, but instead to broaden out the list to include several root causes of structural inequity in addition to racism.

Sometimes revising history is accomplished through false statements in publications about the nation's history of land acquisition for LGUs, as was done by Gavazzi and Gee (2018) in their recent book that has received wide attention. Gavazzi and Gee (2018) noted that the Morrill Acts granted "federally owned" land to states—a convenient, yet predictable, inaccuracy that seems unlikely to have been made from ignorance. They also describe the 1890 Morrill Act as a kind of neutral policy designed to "support the land-grant institutions."

"Gatekeeping" is a strategy used by a dominant group to maintain power and the status quo (Coleman et al., 2021). Gatekeeping information permits those in power to keep dominance by selecting when, where, how, and with whom to share power. Traditionally, and from our experiences, gatekeepers of power at LGUs and within CES are white men, or occasionally white women (particularly in FCS and nutrition), trend toward an older age, and almost exclusively represent 1862 LGUs as (past or current) employees or alumni. Gatekeepers recently complicated the framework development process and evaded accountability for their inaction, but this is not the only recent example.

In the North Central Region, FCS program leaders brought health specialists (from within CES) to Chicago in April 2023 to explore the potential for multistate collaborations and overlapping priorities. Attendees overwhelmingly expressed they wanted to adopt a community-based participatory approach that would center equity and community voices, yet meeting facilitators and some state leaders pressured specialists to pick high-need topic areas anyway (e.g., workforce development, food access, social connectedness) and form regional groups that could begin suggesting relevant tools and programs to act on when the meeting ended. When the specialists declined to do that, explaining that this was not compatible with their preferred approach to center community voice, the meeting facilitators and state leaders insisted they do it anyway. When asked how health equity processes would be integrated into each regional group, the leaders decided that it was at the discretion of each group to include equity considerations, refusing to integrate it into the directives. Unfortunately, Cooperative Extension's National Framework for Health Equity and Well-Being (2021) was not mentioned at this 2023 meeting. Not using the framework limited possible discussions about systemic changes needed and showed a disconnect with the recently developed national recommendations.

Gatekeeping in CES and FCS can end only when new leaders are allowed to step up. CES needs leaders who are bold and brave, who have a health equity and health justice commitment and expertise, and who support the facilitation of necessary systems change with greater urgency.

Let Others Lead

The 1890 and 1994 land-grant institutions' distinct missions to serve people racialized as Black, Indigenous, and people who are marginalized for any reason means that they already have the blueprints, expertise, and trust of those individuals and communities. The role of the 1862 LGUs and CES in working toward health equity and justice, and ultimately liberation, should be more supportive than assertive. If 1862 LGUs and CES used their power to advocate for more equitable, sustainable base funding for the 1890 and 1994 systems, it would also increase their capacity to continue being the leaders in advancing health justice. Further, this type of change aligns with the field of social work, which is trying to shift from social justice with antiracist practices to building power in BIPOC communities targeting sources of racism and developing interventions that prevent and mitigate racism at the macro level (Brock-Petroshius et al., 2022). CES should be thoughtful, careful, and intentional with marginalized and exploited populations because government distrust is high for good reasons and immigration status threats remain (Owens et al., 2022). It is advised that CES professionals spend time in the communities that they serve. By being involved and embedded into the community, Extension professionals can recognize and involve champions to provide leadership and support health equity education and research. This includes finding key community voices to empower and involve in CES work and measuring the outcome of this work.

Measure Progress

Measuring health equity can be challenging, but it is a critical part of being accountable to this commitment and the communities we serve (Hoyer et al., 2022). CES leaders must ask, "How do we know if we are successful at addressing health equity?" There is no need for CES to develop its own set of metrics for health equity. In fact, CES will be stronger if it can align its measurements with the evolving SDOH research, the seven vital conditions for health, or by adopting the National Academies of Sciences, Engineering, and Medicine (2016, 2017) recommendations. What is important is for CES to review the peer-reviewed literature and connect to other research-based or national efforts to measure health equity. Using a data-driven approach is one strategy, but there may be limitations of different types of data used that need to be considered (e.g., undercounting of children and families of color in U.S. Census data; allowing Extension professionals to assign participant's race/ethnicity/gender in state reporting systems based on their visual perception of the person). Another way to align recommendations with established health equity metrics and frameworks is to consider intersectional inquiry. López and Gadsden (2016) recommend:

> When developing or applying an intersectionality health equity lens, the researcher engages in deep self-reflection that contextualizes and recognizes the ways in which race, gender, class, sexual orientation, disability, and other axes of inequality constitute intersecting systems of oppression. (4)

Extension Workforce Diversification

CES needs to diversify its workforce to stay relevant in public health spaces. LGUs must hire BIPOC, LGBTQIA+ individuals, and other historically excluded individuals into the CES workforce and promote them to leaders and administrators. Specific attention is needed to diversify the FCS program area and adjust staffing demographics and program names to be reflective of social work, public health, and health equity principles. Beyond civil rights efforts for parity of program participants at Extension events, this work is intentional and strategic and requires long-term efforts. Real change is needed in the hiring, onboarding, retention, and promotions of CES's future workforce. Increasing capacity of the system and employees will require leadership, authenticity, institutional commitment, trust, and truth. Having conversations with partners and communities to explain CES commitment to equity, addressing reluctance, resistance, and distrust is needed. Professional development on health equity as an outcome and as a process will remain important to advance the concept as a systemwide value (e.g., program planning, development, implementation, evaluation). Some states are integrating health equity processes and competencies into job descriptions (including support staff), onboarding, and ongoing professional development as action steps. Ultimately, advancing health equity will look like applying equity-focused PSE work across all program areas and in all CES job descriptions.

Adopt the Community Development Model

Health equity involves doing the work of community development and not just saying that CES should engage community. Doing this community development work may require implementation guides and ongoing technical assistance for state and local use. Cooperative Extension's National Framework for Health Equity and Well-Being (2021) has high-level recommendations and some more specific recommendations, but they are not adequately detailed to inform next steps for a system like CES. Community-based staff will require guidance on implementation, including selecting community implementation strategies, participatory program planning and evaluation models, and assistance with balancing program fidelity and adaptations. Without this implementation guidance, state systems that are in the process of increasing their capacity for advancing health equity will be trying to initiate new programs and initiatives with little practical support. The likely result will be more of the same, up to and including inflicting additional harm on communities we are purporting to serve.

Adopt New Ways to Measure Health and Health Equity Beyond Rurality and ZIP Code

CES was founded to serve rural communities with awareness of differences in the culture, daily life, and accessibility to resources, services, and knowledge compared to urban counterparts. However, the landscape (pun intended) has changed. Through partnerships with RWJF, the national leadership of CES (e.g., APLU, Extension Foundation) has enthusiastically adopted descriptors for place-based inequities—the ZIP Code. In the past, RWJF led very successful public information campaigns and offered funding to researchers and communities to propagate the idea that our ZIP Codes could determine our health outcomes (even our life expectancy). Significant differences could be revealed, even if those ZIP Codes were adjacent, by matching ZIP code to health outcome data. But what determines someone's ZIP Code? Are we randomly assigned a ZIP Code at birth? No. The history of residential housing segregation in this country reflects decades of racist policies (Julian & Daniel, 1989; Kenn, 2001; Lamb, 2005; Nodjimbadem, 2017) that permeate ZIP Codes to this day, both because of the residual effects and because policies and practices that discriminate against people racialized as Black persist. Furthermore, data show that many places in the United States with the deepest inequities are both rural and racially and ethnically diverse. Counties with the most persistent poverty rates often have the highest percentage of Black and Indigenous residents (Benzow et al., 2023). These places also tend to map directly on to locations that have long histories of racial and ethnic exploitation (Cook et al., 2018). ZIP Code is, therefore, a proxy for race. Furthermore, if equity is of interest to CES, the system must critically examine its focus on rural communities if that means continuing to serve mostly white people. Because rurality is mutable and confounded by ZIP Codes, there is a call to adopt new ways to measure health and health equity that do not rely on rurality or ZIP Code.

Change Traditional Funding and Programming Models

Policies that structure the availability of and access to resources often result in the disenfranchisement of minoritized groups. For CES, federal and state policies on funding allocation, program content, audiences, and evaluation contribute to inequities in both program outcomes (e.g., reach) and the disenfranchisement of certain communities. These actions are often traceable to government policies designed to disenfranchise. For example, the U.S. Department of Agriculture's (USDA) adoption and "forced compliance," as Zabawa and Lunsford (2022) note, of adherence to MyPlate and other Western diet ideals is discriminatory toward Black Americans and the myriad ethnic and cultural foodways present in the United States. However, MyPlate guidance is the foundation of the majority of CES nutrition education programs, particularly for low-income audiences. Similarly, Black farmers have been structurally excluded from the agriculture industry through USDA lending discrimination and government-supported land loss policies (e.g., heir's property). Funding for farm stress programming and initiatives, like USDA's Farm and Ranch Stress Assistance Network program, do not require participating states to develop plans that address structural root causes of stress; therefore, most do not.

Our collective actions to promote justice are long overdue. Fixing the myriad of problems will not happen overnight and we should not expect a system as old and rooted as CES to be immediately receptive and responsive to our calls and recommendations for change. However, accountability for taking urgent action and making the right actions are of utmost importance to this process. It is okay to move methodically, intentionally, and carefully, so that we do not repeat past mistakes. At the same time, we cannot let precision prevent us from making change. The actions that we must take to repair harms, reimagine new systems, and reconstruct them should have been completed long ago—or better yet, never needed in the first place. But this is where we are, and we must hold ourselves and the system accountable to forge an authentic path forward.

REFERENCES

Alang, S., McAlpine, D., McCreedy, E., & Hardeman, R. (2017). Police brutality and black health: Setting the agenda for public health scholars. *American Journal of Public Health, 107*(5), 662–665.

American Public Health Association. (2018, November 13). *Addressing law enforcement violence as a public health issue.* Policy number 201811. https://www.apha.org/policies-and-advocacy/public-health-policy-statements/policy-database/2019/01/29/law-enforcement-violence#:~:text=APHA%20recommends%20the%20following%20actions,accountability%20measures%2C%20(3)%20increase

American Public Health Association. (2021, October 26). *Advancing public health interventions to address the harms of the carceral system.* Policy number 202117. https://www.apha.org/Policies-and-Advocacy/Public-Health-Policy-Statements/Policy-Database/2022/01/07/Advancing-Public-Health-Interventions-to-Address-the-Harms-of-the-Carceral-System

Atiles, J. H., & Eubanks, G. E. (2014). Family & consumer sciences and Cooperative Extension in a diverse world. *Journal of Extension, 52*(3), article 28.

Benfer, E. A. (2015). Health justice: A framework (and call to action) for the elimination of health inequity and social justice. *American University Law Review, 65*(2), article 1.

Benzow, A., Fikri, K., Kim, J., & Newman, D. (2023, September). *Advancing economic development in persistent-poverty communities.* Economic Innovation Group. https://policycommons.net/artifacts/4553119/advancing-economic-development-in-persistent-poverty-communities-c-a-s-e/5376678/

Braun, B., Bruns, K., Cronk, L., Kirk Fox, L., Koukel, S., LeMenestrel, S., Lord, L., Reeves, C., Rennekamp, R., Rice, C., Rodgers, M., Samuel, J., Vail, A., & Warren, T. (2014). *Cooperative

Extension's National Framework for Health and Wellness. Washington, DC: Extension Committee on Organization and Policy.

Braveman, P. A., Kumanyika, S., Fielding, J., LaVeist, T., Borrell, L. N., Manderscheid, R., & Troutman, A. (2011). Health disparities and health equity: The issue is justice. *American Journal of Public Health, 101*(Suppl. 1), S149–S155.

Brock-Petroshius, K., Mikell, D., Washington, D. M., & James, K. (2022). From social justice to abolition: Living up to social work's grand challenge of eliminating racism. *Journal of Ethnic & Cultural Diversity in Social Work, 31*(3–5), 225–239.

Burton, D., Canton, A., Coon, T., Eschbach, C., Gunn, J., Gutter, M., Jones, M., Kennedy, L., Martin, K., Mitchell, A., O'Neal, L., Rennekamp, R., Rodgers, M., Stluka, S., Trautman, K., Yelland, E., & York, D. (2021). *Cooperative Extension's National Framework for Health Equity and Well-Being.* Washington, DC: Extension Committee on Organization and Policy.

Campbell, A. V. (2005). *Health as liberation: Medicine, theology, and the quest for justice.* Cleveland, OH: Pilgrim Press.

Centers for Medicare & Medicaid Services. (2022). *The CMS framework for health equity (2022–2032).* U.S. Department of Health and Human Services. https://www.cms.gov/files/document/cms-framework-health-equity.pdf

Coleman, C., Birk, S., & DeVoe, J. (2023). Health literacy and systemic racism-using clear communication to reduce health care inequities. *Journal American Medical Association: Internal Medicine, 183*(8), 753–754.

Coleman, B. R., Collins, C. R., & Bonam, C. M. (2021). Interrogating whiteness in community research and action. *American Journal of Community Psychology, 67*(3–4), 486–504.

Congressional Research Service. (2022, January 4). 1994 *Land-grant universities: Background and selected issues. In focus.* CRS report IF12009/2. https://crsreports.congress.gov/product/pdf/IF/IF12009/2

Cook, L. D., Logan, T. D., & Parman, J. M. (2018). Racial segregation and southern lynching. *Social Science History, 42*(4), 635–675.

Crazy Bull, C., & White Hat, E. (2019). Cangleska Wakan: The ecology of the Sacred Circle and the role of tribal colleges and universities. *International Review of Education, 65*(1), 117–141.

Crosby, E. W. (1986). The struggle for existence: The institutionalization of the black county agent system. *Agricultural History, 60*(2), 123–136.

David, E. J. R. (Ed.). (2014). *Internalized oppression: The psychology of marginalized groups.* New York: Springer Publishing.

David, E. J. R., & Derthick, A. O. (2014). What is internalized oppression, and so what? In E. J. R. David (Ed.), *Internalized oppression: The psychology of marginalized groups* (p. 3). New York: Springer Publishing.

Duarte, C. D. P., Salas-Hernández, L., & Griffin, J. S. (2020). Policy determinants of inequitable exposure to the criminal legal system and their health consequences among young people. *American Journal of Public Health, 110*(S1), S43–S49.

Dwyer, J., Contreras, D., Eschbach, C., Tiret, H, Newkirk, C, Carter, E., & Cronk, L. (2017). Cooperative Extension as a framework for health extension: The Michigan State University model. *Academic Medicine, 92*, 1416–1420.

Federal Plan for ELTRR. (2022, January 20). *Federal plan for equitable plan for long-term recovery and resilience for social, behavioral and community health.* Office of the Assistant Secretary for Health (OASH). https://health.gov/our-work/national-health-initiatives/equitable-long-term-recovery-and-resilience

Freire, P. (1970). *Pedagogy of the oppressed.* New York: Seabury Press.

Gavazzi, S. M., & Gee, E. G. (2018). *Land-grant universities for the future: Higher education for the public good.* Baltimore, MD: Johns Hopkins University Press.

Gilmore, R. W. (2007). *Golden gulag: Prisons, surplus, crisis, and opposition in globalizing California.* Oakland: University of California Press.

Harris, C. V. (2008). "The Extension Service is not an integration agency": The idea of race in the Cooperative Extension Service. *Agricultural History, 82*(2), 193–219.

Hoyer, D., Dee, E., O'Leary, M. S., Heffernan, M., Gelfand, K., Kappel, R., & Fromknecht, C. Q. (2022). How do we define and measure health equity? The state of current practice and tools to advance health equity. *Journal of Public Health Management and Practice, 28*(5), 570–577.

Iwai, Y., Khan, Z. H., & DasGupta, S. (2020). Abolition medicine. *Lancet,* 396(10245), 158–159.

Julian, E. K., & Daniel, M. M. (1989). Separate and unequal—The root and branch of public housing segregation. *Clearinghouse Review,* 23, 666.

Kenn, D. (2001). Institutionalized, legal racism: Housing segregation and beyond. *Boston University Publications International Law Journal, 11,* 35.

Klein, D. E., & Lima, J. M. (2021). The prison industrial complex as a commercial determinant of health. *American Journal of Public Health, 111*(10), 1750–1752.

Lamb, C. M. (2005). *Housing segregation in suburban America since 1960: Presidential and judicial politics.* New York: Cambridge University Press.

Lee, J. M., & Keys, S. W. (2013). *Land-grant but unequal. State one-to-one match funding for 1890 land-grant universities.* APLU Office of Access and Success publication 3000-PB1. Washington, DC: Association of Public and Land-Grant Universities.

Lee, R., & Ahtone, T. (2020, March 30). Land grab universities: Expropriated Indigenous land is the foundation of the land-grant university system. *High Country News.* https://www.hcn.org/issues/52-4/indigenous-affairs-education-land-grab-universities/

Lee, R., Ahtone, T., Pearce, M., Goodluck, K., McGhee, G., Leff, C., Lanpher, K., & Salinas, T. (2020). *Land-grab universities.* https://www.landgrabu.org

Lett, E., Adekunle, D., McMurray, P., Asabor, E. N., Irie, W., Simon, M. A., Hardeman, R., & McLemore, M. R. (2022). Health equity tourism: Ravaging the justice landscape. *Journal of Medical Systems, 46*(3), article 17. https://doi.org/10.1007/s10916-022-01803-5

Lomawaima, K. T., McDonough, K., O'Brien, J. M., & Warrior, R. (2021). Editors' introduction: Reflections on the Land-Grab Universities project. *Native American and Indigenous Studies, 8*(1), 89–91.

López, N., & Gadsden, V. L. (2016). *Health inequities, social determinants, and intersectionality. Discussion paper.* Washington, DC: National Academy of Medicine.

Martin, M. V., & Hipp, J. S. (2018). A time for substance: Confronting funding inequities at land grant institutions. *Tribal College Journal of American Indian Higher Education,* 29(3).

McCoy, M., Risam, R., & Guiliano, J. (2021). The future of land-grab universities. *Native American and Indigenous Studies, 8*(1), 169–175.

McDowell, T. L., Moore, N., & Holland, J. N. (2014). Working through bound liberation: A community engagement framework for health partnerships. *Progress in Community Health Partnerships: Research, Education, and Action, 8*(4), 465–470.

McFarling, U. L. (2021, September 23). "Health equity tourists": How white scholars are colonizing research on health disparities. *STAT News*. Boston Globe Media.

National Academies of Sciences, Engineering, and Medicine. (2016). *Metrics that matter for population health action*. Washington, DC: National Academies Press.

National Academies of Sciences, Engineering, and Medicine. (2017). *Communities in action: Pathways to health equity*. Washington, DC: National Academies Press.

National Archives. (n.d.). *Morrill Act (1862). Milestone documents*. https://www.archives.gov/milestone-documents/morrill-act

National Institutes of Health. (n.d.). *Health disparities*. National Heart, Lung, and Blood Institute. https://www.nhlbi.nih.gov/health/educational/healthdisp

Nichols, V. C., LeBrón, A. M., & Pedraza, F. I. (2018). Policing us sick: The health of Latinos in an era of heightened deportations and racialized policing. *Political Science & Politics, 51*(2), 293–297.

Nodjimbadem, K. (2017, May 30). The racial segregation of American cities was anything but accidental. *Smithsonian Magazine* (pp. 1–5).

Office of Disease Prevention and Health Promotion. (n.d.). *Healthy people 2023*. U.S. Department of Health and Human Services. https://health.gov/healthypeople

Owens, M. H., Krehbiel, M., & McCoy, T. (2022). Cultural competence in evaluation: One size does not fit all. In N. I. Fields & T. Shaffer (Eds.), *Grassroots engagement and social justice through cooperative extension* (pp. 63–75). Transformations in Higher Education Series. East Lansing: Michigan State University Press.

Phillips, J. L. (2003). A tribal college land grant perspective: Changing the conversation. *Journal of American Indian Education, 42*, 22–35.

Ramírez Solís, J. L., & Montgomery, B. (2021). Agricultural service disparities between white and non-white farmers provided by the Federal Extension Service during the Jim Crow Era. *University of South Carolina Upstate Student Research Journal, 14*, article 6.

Red Shirt-Shaw, M. (2020, August). *Beyond the land acknowledgement: College "land back" or free tuition for native students*. Hack the Gates: Policy and Practice Brief. https://sustainability.stanford.edu/sites/sustainability/files/media/file/redshirt-shaw_landback_htgreport.pdf

Riley, T., Zia, Y., Samari, G., & Sharif, M. Z. (2022). Abortion criminalization: A public health crisis rooted in white supremacy. *American Journal of Public Health, 112*(11), 1662–1667.

Rodriguez, S. M., Rakes, H., Healy, K., & Ben-Moshe, L. (2022). Depathologization as healing justice. *QED: A Journal in GLBTQ Worldmaking, 9*(3), 11–34.

Santana, S., Brach, C., Harris, L., Ochiai, E., Blakey, C., Bevington, F., Kleinman, D., & Pronk, N. (2021). Updating health literacy for Healthy People 2030: Defining its importance for a new decade in public health. *Journal of Public Health Management and Practice, 27*(Suppl. 6),

S258–S264.

Scholl, J. (2013). Extension family and consumer sciences: Why it was included in the Smith-Lever Act of 1914. *Journal of Family & Consumer Sciences, 105*(8), 8–16.

Schor, J. (1986). The Black presence in the U.S. Cooperative Extension Service to 1983: An American quest for service and equity. *Agricultural History, 60*(2), 137–153.

Shaffer, T. J., Peters, S. J., & Smith, M. D. (2022). Early chapters of Extension: Land grants, segregation, and the development of cooperative programming. In N. I. Fields & T. J. Shaffer (Eds.), *Grassroots engagement and social justice through cooperative extension* (pp. 3–29). Transformations in Higher Education Series. East Lansing: Michigan State University Press.

Wahbi, R., & Beletsky, L. (2022). Involuntary commitment as "carceral-health service": From healthcare-to-prison pipeline to a public health abolition praxis. *Journal of Law, Medicine & Ethics, 50*(1), 23–30.

Williams, R. B., Gavazzi, S. M., Roberts, M. E., Chaatsmith, M. L., Hoy, C., Low, J., & Snyder, B. (2021). Paying old debts. *Journal of American Indian Higher Education, 33*(2).

World Health Organization. (2023, March 21). *Commercial determinants of health.* WHO. https://www.who.int/news-room/fact-sheets/detail/commercial-determinants-of-health

Zabawa, R., & Lunsford, L. (2022). The USDA and land-grant Extension: A legacy of continuing inequities. In N. I. Fields & T. Shaffer (Eds.), *Grassroots engagement and social justice through cooperative extension* (pp. 79–96). Transformations in Higher Education Series. East Lansing: Michigan State University Press.

Engagement with Health Systems, Providers, and Payors

Allison Myers and Leslie Lytle

A set of both long-standing and emerging trends in healthcare offers opportunities for and actual movement toward a health system that promotes health, and supports the broader mission of public health, which is to create conditions for health and well-being for all people across the United States (Institute of Medicine, 1988). The purposes of this chapter are to describe promising trends in healthcare that move the system toward becoming one that is health promoting; articulate why and how Health Extension (i.e., utilizing the existing infrastructure of Cooperative Extension) could and should become a health promotion and disease prevention partner of choice for health care providers and payors; offer examples of current health system and Health Extension partnerships that can be replicated and evaluated across the United States; and recommend a set of actions that must be taken to optimize the future of Health Extension and health system collaboration.

U.S. Health System and Community-Based Healthcare

The U.S. healthcare system is unmatched in the world from the perspective of investing in research and clinical innovations. Conversely, from the perspective of serving as a truly health-promoting system, we are at minimum suboptimal and, more realistically, woefully behind peer countries. The U.S. system is built for sick care rather than health care (Marvasti & Stafford, 2012). The United States has the highest per-person spending on healthcare in the world—and some of the worst health outcomes (Schneider et al., 2021). In 2020, for example, the United States reported the highest infant mortality rate and the highest rate of people with chronic conditions across 12 high-income countries (Gunja et al., 2023). In addition, the United States spends $2 for health care for every $1 for social needs, which is exactly the opposite of other countries that support population health through a focus on supporting social needs (Bradley & Taylor, 2013). We are also perhaps the most inequitable health system in the world. Disparities in care and outcomes exist by race and ethnicity, income, and access to care. In the United States, in 2019, life expectancy at birth was four years lower for non-Hispanic Black Americans (74. 8 years) and seven years lower for non-Hispanic American Indians or Alaskan Natives (71.8 years) than for non-Hispanic whites (78.8 years) (Gunja et al., 2023). Life expectancy at birth for all Americans declined by 2.2 years in 2021 due to COVID-19 deaths and Black and Latino populations experienced declines about two times those of Whites (Adrasfay & Goldman, 2022). Similar disparities by race, ethnicity, and income exist for risk of smoking (Centers for Disease Control and Prevention, 2018), morbidity and mortality from cardiovascular disease (Diez-Roux et al., 1997), cancer (Alcaraz et al., 2020), diabetes (Tucker et al., 2000), infant mortality (Matoba & Collins, 2017), and infectious diseases (Lopez et al., 2021).

Inequities in health outcomes are attributed to myriad factors, including population, social conditions, and the policies that influence those conditions such as access to health care and the quality of available care (Institute of Medicine, 2003). Other factors that contribute to inequities are the social and physical contexts that are experienced in neighborhoods. These factors include access to healthy and economical foods, safe places to walk and play, and quality air and water (Escarce, 2019; Warnecke et al., 2008). Promoting health and well-being—particularly for those diverse individuals and population groups who are most at risk for poor health outcomes across the United States—will require well-designed educational approaches, as well as changes in policies, systems, and environments.

Quintuple Aim for Health Systems

For nearly two decades, leaders in the U.S. health care system have been working toward quality improvement initiatives that address health disparities. What began as the "Triple Aim" and is now the "Quintuple Aim" (Itchhaporia, 2021) is an important trend in health care that has the power to catalyze partnerships between Health Extension and health systems. The Triple Aim was introduced in 2007 as a new paradigm in the health care system. It was led by the Institute for Healthcare Improvement, under the leadership of pediatrician Don Berwick, who later led the Center for Medicare & Medicaid Services (CMS) under the Obama Administration (McCarthy & Klein, 2010). The Triple Aim was meant to guide optimization of health system performance, and centered improvement in three goals: improving the health of the patients themselves (also called populations), improving the patient experience and quality of care, and reducing the costs of care for each patient (Berwick et al., 2008). Later, recognizing that symptoms of burnout (e.g., loss of enthusiasm for work) and associated poor health behaviors (e.g., alcohol use and suicidal ideation) were widespread among physicians, it was suggested that preventing clinician and staff burnout be added to create a Quadruple Aim (Bodenheimer & Sinsky, 2014). Also noting a need to increase collaboration with varying provider types, proponents of the Quadruple Aim recommended expanding roles for other staff such as medical assistants as a way to increase the capacity for preventive health or chronic disease management (Bodenheimer & Sinsky, 2014). In more recent years, as our health system has continued to reckon with the long-standing truth of unequal treatment (Institute of Medicine, 2003) and health disparities based on race and ethnicity, the concept of health equity has been added, resulting now in the Quintuple Aim related to health system performance (Nwando Olayiwola & Rastetter, 2020). This commitment to undoing health disparities is aligned with national public health goals, the National Cooperative Extension Framework for Health Equity and Well-being (Burton et al., 2021), and the foundation of Health Extension.

Value-Based Payments

Another health system trend that offers a tailwind for health promotion and disease prevention is attention to what are called alternative payment models, such as value-based payments or global budgets, which involves movement away from traditional fee-for-service models. Traditional fee-for-service involves a payor offering a provider a fixed amount for a service, without regard to whether a patient's health status improves, whereas value-based payment involves a payor offering a provider a variable, higher or incentive amount if and when a patient's health status improves. A helpful example of this has to do with 2023 incentive measures for coordinated care organizations (CCOs) that coordinate and provide care for Oregon Health Plan (Medicaid) beneficiaries. A CCO is a geographically based network of physical, dental, and behavioral health care providers who work together in defined communities to serve Medicaid beneficiaries. CCOs are provided a global per-member, per-month budget, and are eligible for shared savings according to a set of incentive metrics (Mendez & Myers, 2022). Given this payment model, CCOs are incentivized to focus on disease prevention and the management of chronic conditions. CCOs are an innovation beyond accountable care organizations, which have been studied with Medicare populations as part of the U.S. Center for Medicare & Medicaid Services Innovation Center research programs (e.g., 1115 waivers). As an example, comprehensive diabetes care is an incentive measure offered via CCOs and is defined by the percentage of patients eighteen to seventy-five years of age with diabetes under care of the CCO who had hemoglobin A1c greater than 9 percent (showing "poor control") during a measurement period (Oregon Health Authority, 2022). The fewer patients there are with "poor control" based on claims and clinical data, the greater is the incentive payment to the CCO. This CCO incentive measure is akin to the accountable care organization measure number 27 in the shared savings program (CMS, 2011).

In short, incentive metrics (Oregon Health Authority, 2021) that are set at the federal level by CMS and by state Medicaid programs are a mechanism that pushes upstream investments in health interventions that promote health, rather than simply treating disease. These payment changes in public and private insurance have created financial incentives for health systems to reshape the ways they provide care, and where they invest in health promotion and disease prevention activities. For example, these financial incentives generate demand for more community-based self-management and health promotion education delivered to patients outside the clinic setting. As value-based care initiatives proliferate, increasing attention is paid to population health, with the goals of promoting healthy behaviors and preventing the onset or progression of disease.

When we bring together the trends of outsized U.S. spending on clinical care and limited investment in health promotion, disease prevention, and social needs; the health systems' stated commitment to the Quintuple Aim of improving quality, lowering costs, improving outcomes, improving well-being of care providers, and undoing health disparities; and changes in health care payment models that encourage health-promoting behaviors and improved outcomes instead of simply paying for services, an opportunity exists for Health Extension to rise to prominence as an integral partner to the health system for the purpose of preventing and managing disease. Perhaps most importantly, the Cooperative Extension System (CES) shares a stated goal related to health equity at the population level (Burton et al., 2021).

Health Extension as a Health Promotion and Disease Prevention Partner of Choice

The CES, also known as the Extension Service, is guided by the Extension Committee on Organization and Policy, which is one of several commissions housed at the Association of Public and Land-Grant Universities. Today, there are three kinds of land-grant universities (LGUs): the 1862s, the 1890s, and the 1994s. The 1862s were original land-grant universities (and remain predominately white institutions), created when the Morrill Act gave land to states, so that they could create a university "for the people," rather than for the wealthy male elites who were generally able to attend university at the time. The 1890s were designated as land-grant universities when Congress granted cash to what are historically Black colleges and universities; an endowment that provided a smaller cash grant was used to establish the 1994s, which are institutions serving predominately Native Americans. Across all land-grant universities, CES is a long-standing mechanism to serve the people of a state with science-based education and information; to disseminate and implement university-generated knowledge to local communities; and, to bring community expertise in to the university system. Extension professionals live and work in all of the more than three thousand counties across the United States and are positioned to build on community strengths to improve the health behaviors and outcomes of diverse populations, according to locally identified needs.

In the beginning of the land-grant history, community needs were related to agriculture, science, engineering, and military science, and to Agricultural Extension, including the 4-H youth development program. About one hundred years ago, home science or home economics (today called family and consumer sciences) was included as part of the Extension repertoire. The current Health Extension programs are both an expansion and a pivot from family and consumer sciences (FCS). While FCS programming traditionally focused on nutrition education, food safety, and food preparation, the current health extension has expanded to also focus on physical activity promotion, gerontology and healthy aging, mental health promotion including suicide prevention and substance use disorder prevention, and disaster/emergency preparedness. CES has moved out of the kitchen and into the community and has expanded its health focus beyond nutritional issues.

It is notable that the vision we articulate for the future of Health Extension may be different from past perspectives. In the past, others have suggested a "health extension" model that can serve the purpose of optimizing primary care or other medical practices through the discipline of practice management (or practice transformation, practice facilitation, or practice support). It is likely that the Primary Care Extension Programs that were described in the Patient Protection and Affordable Care Act (Section 5405) and funded by the Agency for Healthcare Research and Quality for practice transformation and addressing social determinants of health (Kaufman et al., 2010, 2017, 2019) had impacts on population-level health behaviors and outcomes. However, health improvements were not the highest priority for providers; instead, data from a survey of 556 primary care providers in Pennsylvania indicated that coordinating mental health services, improving the efficiency of the office, increasing revenue, and improving the use of evidence-based clinical guidelines were among the most desired outcomes (Parisi & Gabbay, 2015).

Health Extension leverages the assets of CES as an authentic partner to enhance community-based healthcare, public health, and prevention outcomes, and is aligned with national agenda-setting guidelines like Healthy People (Office of Disease Prevention and Health Promotion). The challenge is to utilize this foundation and alignment to expand the ways in which CES can use its infrastructure, relationships, history, and ubiquitous presence to improve health outcomes and address current inequities. The Healthy People national objectives, issued by the U.S. Centers for Disease Control and Prevention, have guided health promotion work in public health since the first set of goals were issued in 1990. Among all ages, there is a set of Healthy People 2030 leading health indicators (LHIS) (a subset of twenty-three high-priority core objectives) that are already matched to work that is common within CES nationally. For example, a reduction in the consumption of calories from added sugars by persons aged two years and older, a reduction in household food insecurity and hunger, a reduction in the prevalence of children and adolescents with obesity, and an increase in the proportion of adults who meet current minimum guidelines for aerobic physical activity and muscle strengthening activity are indicators that match well to the federally funded Supplemental Nutrition Assistance Program—Education (SNAP-Ed) and Expanded Food and Nutrition Education Program (EFNEP) led by many family and community health or family and consumer sciences units nationally. SNAP-Ed and EFNEP are two programs funded by the U.S. Department of Agriculture (USDA) with the specific purposes of improving the nutritional health of Americans. SNAP-Ed is an evidence-based program that includes nutrition education classes, social marketing campaigns, and efforts to improve policies, systems, and the nutritional environments of communities (USDA, 2023). EFNEP provides nutrition education specifically targeting low-income families with the goal of reducing food insecurity (USDA, 2022) and involves a workforce comprised of members of the population to whom programming is offered. Both of these programs are charged to specifically meet the needs of low-income populations, and often this results in reaching racially and ethnically diverse populations. The LHIs of increasing the proportion of adults with hypertension whose blood pressure is under control and reducing the incidence of new cases of diagnosed diabetes in the population may also be affected at the population level by Extension efforts to promote healthy nutrition and physical activity with evidence-based interventions (EBIs) from the SNAP-Ed Toolkit, such as BE Physically Active 2Day (BEPA 2.0), Cooking Matters, and Walk with Ease.

Other Healthy People LHIs are matched to emerging areas of effort for Health Extension. For example, recent grant funding from the USDA National Institute for Food and Agriculture and the U.S. Substance Abuse and Mental Health Services Administration has focused CES efforts on mental health and substance use (also known as behavioral health). With federal grant funding, Extension partners are contributing to reducing drug overdose deaths and suicides in communities. The LHI of reducing exposure to unhealthy air has been a focus of the Extension Disaster Education Network and other grant-funded initiatives led by Extension faculty (e.g., Oregon State University's ASPIRE Center for advancing children's environmental research health translation). Finally, in the future, given that Health Extension professionals bring expertise as community builders, educators, and conveners for policy and environmental change, Health Extension could play a role in addressing the LHIs of reducing current use of any tobacco products among adolescents; cigarette smoking in adults; and adults engaging in binge drinking of alcoholic beverages during the last thirty days.

CES has physical infrastructure across the country and can be considered "the front door" to states' land-grant universities (LGUs) (Gutter et al., 2020). The presence of a local office, staffed with university-connected local expertise, also creates conditions where Extension is a trusted resource in communities, particularly among populations who are burdened by limited opportunities for health, and associated poor health outcomes, or who are distrusting of governmental public health or the health system. Extension professionals understand the LGU of which they are a part and can bridge research and practice; they are also aware of local economic conditions, health interests and concerns, and culture (Molgaard, 1997). In addition to CES's physical infrastructure, there also exists a business and operational infrastructure for human resources, marketing and communication, and grant accounting or other fiscal management. Extension professionals engage in regular professional development internal to their universities and also externally as part of Extension and non-Extension professional organizations. They are also expected to track and report on their activities, including process and outcome evaluations that are used over time for granting promotion and/or tenure.

Health Extension efforts involve university campuses and county offices to provide experiences, education, and training to state residents. Health Extension professionals' backgrounds also vary, from those who have completed high school, earned a community health worker certificate, and serve in Extension as an education program assistant, to those who have completed a master of public health degree and work at the county level as an outreach program coordinator or professor of practice, to those who have completed a doctoral degree and/or postdoctoral fellowship and serve as campus-based professors or statewide "specialists." It is notable that the training professional backgrounds of Health Extension professionals, in recent years, may differ from Extension professionals who focused on more traditional family and consumer sciences. For example, CES had no formal positions related to mental or behavioral health before about 2017, although there were sometimes Extension professionals with some expertise in new areas working in more traditional programs. An emphasis has been placed on broadening the CES/FCS/Health Extension skill set in recent years. Health Extension efforts bring together programmatic knowledge (e.g., nutrition, food science) and methodological expertise in dissemination and implementation science and community-based participatory research.

Many field-based Extension professionals have great reach and trust within communities that are vulnerable to address poor health outcomes. For example, the SNAP-Ed and EFNEP federal program teams must be comprised of individuals with the cultural expertise, bilingual/multilingual language skills, and community trust to effectively deliver nutrition and physical activity EBIs in diverse settings. As the 2021 National Cooperative Extension Framework for Health Equity and Well-Being gains momentum (Burton et al., 2021), all Extension professionals are responsible for learning community-based strategies to eliminate health disparities and promote health equity.

Examples of Current Health Extension and Health System Partnerships

A set of Health Extension/health system partnerships exists that can offer important guidance for the future. We next offer three examples of these. One relates to a shared responsibility for workforce development; another describes a coalition to implement state-level policy to reduce health disparities; and a third involves an evidence-based intervention to change health behaviors and outcomes.

Example 1. Workforce Development and Training Community Health Workers and Health Care Interpreters

One way that Health Extension programs and payors can partner together is workforce development: specifically, leveraging the expertise of university educators to address gaps in the changing health care workforce. Community health workers (CHWs) are a growing segment of the health care workforce and are also a promising strategy to build a workforce to support Health Extension activities such as implementing evidence-based health interventions, enrolling patients and family members into programs or research studies, and seeking innovative funding. The CHW section of the American Public Health Association defines a CHW as "a frontline public health worker who is a trusted member of and/or has an unusually close understanding of the community served." This trusting relationship enables the worker to serve as a liaison/link/intermediary between health/social services and the community to facilitate access to services and improve the quality and cultural competence of service delivery. A CHW also "builds individual and community capacity by increasing health knowledge and self-sufficiency through a range of activities such as outreach, community education, informal counseling, social support, and advocacy."

For nearly a decade, Oregon State University (OSU) has been partnering with Eastern Oregon Coordinated Care Organization (EOCCO) to train CHWs in Oregon. EOCCO is owned and operated by a set of health care entities and serves a twelve-county, medically underserved rural and frontier region. In 2014, a decision was made by EOCCO and OSU to partner to train CHWs for the purpose of addressing a workforce shortage in the region. EOCCO and OSU share the program goals of increasing the availability of high-quality training for CHWs, improving the Oregon health system, increasing value in the system, and paying for performance with a focus on the social determinants of health and increasing health equity while maintaining sustainable cost growth (Mendez & Myers, 2022).

In Oregon, a CHW is one of five "traditional health worker" types who can be reimbursed for services provided to Oregon Health Plan (Medicaid) beneficiaries (Oregon Health Authority, 2020). Reimbursable services include self-care/home management training (code 97535), preventive medicine counseling and/or risk factor reduction intervention(s) provided to an individual (codes 99401–99404), skills training and development (code H2014), and face-to-face education and training for patient self-management using a standardized curriculum (code 98960) (Oregon Health Authority, 2020). CHWs are required to complete an eighty-five-hour entry-level training before becoming certified and are required to regularly complete continuing education units (CEUs) to maintain their certification. Training programs must be approved by the Oregon Health Authority Equity and Inclusion Division, and approvals are offered in three-year increments.

Since the first cohort began their training in 2016, 389 people have completed OSU's entry-level course, and 115 people have completed one or more of OSU's CEU modules, which include poverty and social determinants of health; behavioral and mental health; managing chronic diseases; and families and youth with special health needs. Following graduation, CHWs provide person- and community-centered care to connect people with health systems, increase appropriate use of care, advocate for patients, support adherence to care and treatment, and empower individuals to be agents in their own health (Mendez & Myers, 2022). CHWs do this work in a variety of care settings, including hospital systems, mental and behavioral health clinics, community health centers, and specialty health clinics, as well as for community-based organizations, local public health authorities, or Medicaid payors themselves (Patil et al., 2020).

The CHW training program was funded with gifts from EOCCO, with the intention that the program would become self-sustaining over time by charging student fees. The cost of the course is $850 for students who live in the eastern Oregon region and $1,200 for students who do not live in the eastern Oregon region. Training program leaders have sought additional funding to expand the program. For example, in 2022 and 2023, a grant from the Oregon Higher Education Coordinating Commission was used to train two cohorts of veterans to become entry-level CHWs and to prepare a CEU model to train non-veteran CHWs about available services and supports for veterans. The training program has benefited from the bilingual and bicultural expertise of a dedicated lead instructor with significant experience as a CHW; a second instructor who is both a CHW and a veteran; partnerships with Extension offices statewide as both recruiting hubs and training locations; partnerships with county-level workforce boards, health systems and payors, and community-based organizations as student recruiters; and the self-paced and remote delivery format. The team expects to secure future grant funding for the purposes of expanding English- and Spanish-language capacity to meet demand for both the entry-level foundational training and current and future CEU courses, and to support students with scholarships, stipends, and practical work experience.

The OSU/EOCCO partnership expanded in 2021 to launch a Spanish-language health care interpreter (HCI) program. HCIs enable spoken or signed communication between language-minority patients and health care personnel with whom they do not share a language. HCI services mitigate disparities in access to care, quality of care, and health outcomes for language-minority patients, furthering the Quintuple Aim (Ratway et al., 2022). As for CHWs, there are shortages of certified and qualified HCIs in the state of Oregon, and as a result, HCI services are not consistently available for patients in Oregon. In addition, Medicaid insurers (payors) like EOCCO are incentivized financially for offering "meaningful language access to culturally responsive health care services," a metric that measures the provision of quality interpreter services and is based on the proportion of member visits with spoken or sign language interpreter needs that were provided with Oregon Health Authority (OHA) qualified or certified HCIs.

The initial goal of the EOCCO and OSU partnership was to design and launch an HCI training that fulfilled OHA requirements for credentialing and responded to the unique needs of rural Spanish-English interpreters (Ratway et al., 2022). Over the near term, additional shared goals are to build and maintain a skilled workforce of Spanish-English interpreters to serve rural Oregon, and to create a professional development opportunity for rural, bilingual Oregonians interested in pursuing a career in interpreting or taking on interpreting in addition to other health care responsibilities. Over the longer term, the EOCCO/OSU partnership plans to develop a more robust workforce of interpreters in rural Oregon to meet the language access needs of language minorities living in rural communities, and to improve health outcomes for rural language minorities.

After an initial year to develop the Spanish-language HCI curriculum and secure approval as a training program by Oregon Health Authority, the first two cohorts of HCI students were trained in winter (twenty-four students) and spring 2023 (six students). The sixty-four-hour blended-model training program combines self-paced work online with in-person sessions where students can practice their skills with instructor feedback, learn to use interpreting equipment, and evaluate themselves and their peers. Already, the team is considering launching a language-neutral HCI program in addition to the Spanish-language program.

Given CES expertise in nonformal/noncredit education, training CHWs has been a productive partnership. CHWs have demonstrated the capacity to improve access to health care and the cultural appropriateness of care. It is also notable that CHWs are equipped to deliver individual-level evidence-based interventions that are known to improve status. In the future, CES can continue to partner with health systems and payors to offer noncredit education that leads to CHW or other traditional health worker certifications. CES can also lead the conceptualization and writing of workforce development grants intended to mitigate shortages and improve health outcomes particularly among disparate populations. Given their many skills and effectiveness at partnering with and serving diverse populations, CES would also do well to employ CHWs in communities.

Example 2. Coalition to Pass a Policy to Support AgriStress Helpline Implementation in Oregon

Another opportunity for partnerships between Health Extension and health systems and payors is through the shared pursuit of policies with the potential to promote health equity. An example of this is the 2023 passage of Oregon Senate Bill 955 "relating to providing for mental health needs of the agricultural workforce; and declaring an emergency," which was signed in to law by Oregon Governor Tina Kotek on July 18, 2023 (Oregon Legislative Information Service, 2023). Political theorist John Kingdon (2011) describes the passage of a policy as occurring only during a window of opportunity when "three streams" come together: the problem stream, the policy stream, and the political stream. In the next few paragraphs, we use Kingdon's theory as a framework to describe the passage of SB 955 and launch of the AgriStress Helpline for Oregon.

THE PROBLEM

The "problem" stream, according to Kingdon, involves public acceptance that a documented problem exists and can be solved (Kingdon, 2011). The severity of Oregon's mental health challenges is known and requires an "all hands on deck" collaborative approach, including from stakeholders like Extension who have not historically been involved with mental health promotion efforts. Oregon is ranked nearly worst in the nation (fiftieth out of fifty-one in 2023) for a higher prevalence of mental illness and lower rates of access to care, according to a composite fifteen-item measure publicized by the national nonprofit advocacy organization Mental Health America (Reinert et al., 2022). According to the Oregon Violent Death Reporting System (2020), deaths by suicide in Oregon have been higher than the national average since at least 2001, and they are increasing. Populations frequently served by the CES are also at greater risk. Suicide rates are higher in rural areas than they are in urban areas (Pettrone & Curtin, 2020), and people within the agriculture, forestry, fishing, and hunting industry group have among the highest rates of suicide, according to data (2016) from thirty-two states within the National Violent Death Reporting System (Peterson et al., 2020).

Oregon's farming, ranching, fishing, and forestry communities have long experienced disparities in suicide rates. Public conversations about the issue were elevated beginning in November 2022, when an eastern Oregon county commissioner and president of the Oregon Cattlemen's Association invited the OSU Health Extension program leader to discuss suicide in the agricultural community on his weekly videocast on the Oregon Cattlemen YouTube channel. Over the winter, OSU Extension's mental health and suicide prevention teams were present in a sponsored booth at the Oregon Cattlemen's Association annual meeting. These two events—the podcast in November 2022 and the meeting in January 2023—served as focusing events for addressing the problem of agricultural suicide in Oregon.

THE POLICY

The "policy" stream, according to Kingdon (2011), involves identifying a policy solution for the problem. A team at the OSU Extension Service became aware of the AgriStress Helpline through their work with the Western Regional Agricultural Stress Assistance Program. The AgriStress Helpline is a twenty-four/seven call-or-text crisis and referral line developed by a national nonprofit, AgriSafe Network. Confidential telephone helplines are an evidence-based strategy and are used to support people at risk as part of a comprehensive public health approach to prevent suicide (Centers for Disease Control and Prevention, 2022). AgriStress Helpline offers a conversation that is known to decrease suicide risk due to the interpersonal connection. Crisis lines work to help a caller feel less depressed, less overwhelmed, less suicidal, and more hopeful (Gould et al., 2013). The AgriStress Helpline is unique because it is completely dedicated to serving the agriculture community. All calls are answered in thirty seconds or less, and all callers are screened for suicidality. Intervention occurs for people at imminent risk (i.e., deescalation, dispatch first responders). Others are offered relevant resources, tailored to the agriculture community and by state/region. In winter 2023, AgriStress Helpline was available and working in six other states (Connecticut, Missouri, Pennsylvania, Texas, Virginia, and Wyoming), but was not yet available in Oregon.

At the January 2023 annual meeting of the Oregon Cattlemen's Association in Pendleton, Oregon, members of the Extension Family and Community Health faculty introduced the AgriStress Helpline to Oregon Senate District 29 Senator Bill Hansell. They explained the problem of suicide in the agricultural community, and the possibility for a telephone crisis and referral line, which could save lives. At that meeting, Senator Hansell agreed to sponsor a piece of legislation to fund the AgriStress Helpline for Oregon. On February 22, 2023, SB 955 was introduced into the Oregon legislature.

THE POLITICS

The "politics" stream, according to Kingdon (2011), involves generating the political will to enact the policy as a solution to the problem. After its introduction, SB 955 was referred to the Senate Judiciary committee on February 23, 2023, which was not perceived by supporters as a natural location given the content. A next step was to secure a public hearing and work session within the Judiciary committee, and this is where health system partnerships came into play. Two professional lobbyists, one supporting the Oregon Cattlemen's Association and another supporting Moda Health and Eastern Oregon Coordinated Care Organization, were instrumental in securing broad bipartisan support for SB 955. Together, they secured a total of twenty-seven endorsements from health care providers and payors and from agricultural organizations (Branam, 2023). It was the support of so many organizations that secured a public hearing for SB 955 on March 16, 2023, and a work session on March 22, where the bill passed out of committee and was sent to the Joint Ways and Means Committee. Following a public hearing, for which some health care providers offered written testimony in support of the bill, coalition supporters kept up pressure. People from the agricultural community who have experienced losses from suicide and other supporters of the legislation acted as sources in six news articles describing the opportunity to pass SB 955 and bring the AgriStress Helpline to Oregon. In the last days of the regular session, on June 23, 2023, a second work session was held in the Joint Ways and Means committee, and a "do pass" recommendation was made for SB 955. The bill was carried to the Senate floor and passed, and was then carried to the House floor and passed with unanimous "aye" votes.

Taking these aspects together, SB 955 was passed with the support of the people and organizations who are most affected by the problem of suicide, and who are best poised to offer solutions: members of the agricultural community, health care providers and payors, and Health Extension. Addressing mental health has become a shared goal for each stakeholder. With regard to health system partners, Oregon's CCOs are incentivized according to the extent to which their provider networks are able to avoid emergency department utilization among beneficiaries with diagnosed mental illness. As such, any evidence-based initiative that can reduce the stigma and improve help-seeking behaviors, contribute to prevention or treatment, and keep Oregonians out of the emergency room is a welcome support. The AgriStress Helpline for Oregon launched on September 1, 2023. In 2023, the OSU Extension Service is leading efforts to educate Oregon's rural and agricultural communities and supporters about the AgriStress Helpline and will leverage the CES network of people, physical places, and strong partnerships in each Oregon county.

Example 3. The National Diabetes Prevention Program

The National Diabetes Prevention Program (NDPP) provides an excellent example of how Extension can partner with the health system by increasing the reach of EBIs. The NDPP was created by the Centers for Disease Control and Prevention (CDC) in 2010 through congressional authorization with a goal of reducing the burden of type 2 diabetes (T2D) and prediabetes (Centers for Disease Control and Prevention, 2023). Evidence for the effectiveness of the NDPP was established through the Diabetes Prevention Program (DPP), a randomized controlled trial with the goal of evaluating a year-long, intensive lifestyle intervention and the use of metformin, as compared to a control group, for treating adults at high risk for T2D. More than three thousand participants were involved in the DPP, which included goals of losing 7 percent of body weight and getting, on average, 150 minutes of activity per week. During a three-year follow-up period, the incidence of T2D was reduced by 58 percent in the lifestyle group and by 31 percent in the metformin group as compared to the control group. Furthermore, follow-up studies showed that the effect of the intervention could be sustained for fifteen or more years and that adapting delivery to occur in a group setting was effective in achieving a 5–7 percent weight loss (Burd et al., 2020). These positive results established the DPP as an EBI that is worthwhile to disseminate broadly to reduce the burden of T2D.

If the NDPP were operationalized through all of CES nationwide, the impact would be substantial. The CDC estimates that more than thirty-seven million people in the United States have diabetes and that 90–95 percent of them have T2D. In addition, an estimated ninety-six million U.S. adults have prediabetes and most are not aware that they have diabetes (CDC, 2022). The annual estimated cost of diabetes is $327 billion annually. As of January 2019, NDPP programs were available in all fifty states and about 28 percent of counties in the United States; still, it is estimated that it reaches less than 0.4 percent of the U.S. adults with prediabetes (Gorczyca et al., 2022). Health Extension is well positioned to help deliver this EBI to communities, given their geographic reach and connection with hard-to-reach and rural populations.

Seeing the potential, CES was encouraged to adopt and provide the CDC-led NDPP lifestyle change program (CDC LCP) in 2009 (Ariel-Donges et al., 2020). The CDC LCP includes sixteen weekly, one-hour core sessions that are delivered in a group-based, classroom setting. The content of the program focuses on skill building around eating a healthy diet, increasing levels of physical activity, and weight reduction. After the intensive period, monthly sessions for eight additional months are held to support participants and improve maintenance. This program can be delivered in person, asynchronously online (no group meetings), with synchronous distance learning, or using a combination of in-person and distance learning (Gorczyca et al., 2022; Wilson et al., 2022). In 2020, it was reported that more than a dozen states were currently offering or planning to offer the NDPP as an Extension program (eXtension, 2020).

In 2022, an online toolkit was published with the goal of helping Extension professionals across the country establish NDPP to meet the needs of their community (Da Silva, 2022). The toolkit offers help in finding funding for the training and other support needed to implement the NDPP. The toolkit was also designed to help increase the number of Extension professionals applying to be Medicaid suppliers for the DPP and to encourage teams to gather quantitative and qualitative data on the effectiveness of Extension-delivered DPP programs. The current toolkit (available at https://preventdiabetes.extension.org) includes program startup checklists, webinars to help Extension professionals promote diabetes prevention classes, sample surveys to evaluate the effectiveness of the program, guidelines for delivering the program remotely, and a discussion board to help connect those delivering the DPP. In addition, there is a hope that extension involvement in bringing DPP programs to communities might facilitate deeper partnerships with county and state health departments, the CDC, and the USDA (Da Silva, 2022).

Despite general agreement across CES that diabetes-related programming is needed and potentially beneficial to their counties, significant challenges have been faced with the delivery of the NDPP by CES. For example, recruiting participants into the program has been a significant challenge. One state reported that recruitment through newspapers, radio, or social media and through health care providers was not very productive (Breazeale et al., 2021). Other challenges included excessive administrative demands for documenting the delivery of the NDPP to health agencies, Extension professionals' lack of confidence in their own ability to teach the content related to diabetes control, and uncertainty with regard to the strength of community relationships and roles of community partners in program implementation (Breazeale et al., 2021). Perceived unproductive competition between community partners on what organization should deliver the program has also been a disincentive for some CES.

Difficulties related to applying for and receiving compensation from health system payors for delivering the program is an ongoing challenge. The CMS's 2022 Physician Fee Schedule final rule adapted policies related to a set of diabetes services, including beneficiary eligibility criteria, payment structure, and supplier enrollment requirements and compliance standards. Work is ongoing to better understand how CES may be able to tap into those funds, which would create a strong incentive to expanding the offering of the NDPP (CMS, 2023). However, setting up an infrastructure for CES to receive third-party reimbursement is quite complex and involves making sure that there is a perceived need for the CES to provide the medical services in a community, that the organization has sufficient staffing and resources to provide high quality health education on an ongoing basis, and that the organization has the capacity and resources to bill third-party payers (Contreras & Anderson, 2020). Realistically, getting systems in place to allow CES to become a medical supplier would require radical changes in the current systems.

In one of the few articles to date that have reported on the effectiveness of the NDPP when delivered by Extension programs, investigators from Kansas State University evaluated the feasibility and comparative effectiveness of two delivery methods of the NDPP designed specifically for a rural population (Gorczyca et al., 2022). Two extension offices in Kansas participated in this pilot work, which enrolled thirty-one participants to participate in a six-month intervention. Two methods for delivering lifestyle coaching for the NDPP were compared: one was delivered by CES personnel to groups of rural residents with prediabetes using one-hour weekly structured sessions by Zoom, and the other was delivered by a research staff member via a private Facebook group where modules from the NDPP curriculum were posted for the group to self-administer. The training for those delivering the intervention was extensive, totaling more than twenty-five hours and including the CDC-NDPP training conducted by Telligen, Inc., with problem-based learning, motivational interviewing, and group facilitation, and also a follow-up training conducted by the research team (Gorczyca et al., 2022).

At the end of the six-month period, both groups had lost weight. Those in the Zoom condition experienced, on average, a 5.4 percent weight loss, as compared to a 1.6 percent weight loss in the Facebook group. Significantly more people in the zoom group (44 percent) lost at least 5 percent or more of their weight as compared to those in the Facebook group (7 percent). Both groups reported being very satisfied with their experience and more than 85 percent in both groups said they would recommend the program to a friend or family. This pilot experience suggests that the NDPP can efficiently and effectively be delivered by Extension professionals and that a face-to-face classroom approach, even delivered via Zoom, may result in significantly more participants losing at least 5 percent of their body weight. The need for careful training and the amount of time for training should not be underestimated (Gorczyca et al., 2022). The Kansas State pilot did not report on any attempt to seek reimbursement for services from a health insurer or from Medicare or Medicaid (Gorczyca et al., 2022).

A Reimagined Future for Health Extension

The purpose of this chapter has been to articulate why and how Health Extension could and should become a health promotion and disease prevention partner of choice for health care providers and payors, and to offer examples of current health system and Health Extension partnerships that can be replicated and evaluated across the United States. In order to optimize the future of Health Extension and health system collaboration, there is a set of actions that must be taken.

The first action has already begun, and that is for both health system and Health Extension partners to learn as much as they can about one another, for the purpose of identifying shared goals and opportunities for collaboration. At the state level, each health-related Extension "program leader" should identify the leaders of the state Medicaid program, the state public health authority, local or regional health systems, and the like, for in-depth conversations about populations of shared priority and overarching health improvement goals. It is vital for health leaders outside of Extension to understand the geographic placement of Extension offices, the size and skills of the current Health Extension workforce, a comprehensive list of ongoing health promotion programming with evaluation metrics, and any opportunities for expansion. Health Extension leaders can also make connections between health system partners and health-related academic programs within each state's land-grant university. Frequently, health system partners benefit from working with experiential learning leaders for both physical and mental health care programs, from nursing or physical therapy to public health, clinical psychology, counseling, or human development and family science. Along the same lines, it is important for Health Extension leaders and their teams of Extension professionals to have a general understanding of trends within the health system, particularly those that overlap with the work of Health Extension. Building strong interpersonal relationships—"successful interactions with diverse individuals and groups to create partnerships, networks, and dynamic human systems"—is a core competency of Extension professionals (Maddy et al., 2002). Intentional relationship building between Health Extension and the health system is expected to be a valuable investment in future shared population health improvements.

Others have written about opportunities for health system and Health Extension collaboration that should continue to be pursued because of the potential for collaborative impact. Referral networks are one example. A paper in the *West Virginia Medical Journal* by Fitch et al. (2013) described opportunities to optimize partnerships between health care providers in West Virginia and the West Virginia University (WVU) Extension Service, namely, by acquainting themselves with health education and chronic disease self-management offered by Extension and referring their patients accordingly. WVU Extension offices are located in each county, and all have staff members who deliver programming to "promote diabetes self-management, physical activity, healthier food choices, stress management, fall prevention, and financial competency." Fitch and colleagues noted that Extension agents are sustainably funded with legislative investments at the state and federal levels (rather than by grants), serve as well-trained community-based health educators, are known in the community, and offer culturally relevant messages to meet local needs. The Rx for Health Referral toolkit from Michigan State University Extension is an example of developing intentional connections with health providers, so they can refer patients to Health Extension programming (Tiret et al., 2019). In a Michigan pilot, providers were educated about the variety of CES health programs and were offered a single point of contact and a simple referral tool that resulted in fifty-six new participant referrals. Examples of topics for referral included healthy eating and active living, cooking skills, healthy aging, preventing and living well with diabetes, dealing with stress and anger, and healthy relationships (Tiret et al., 2019). A survey conducted with Michigan-based physicians found that providers may not be familiar with existing CES health programming (Khan et al., 2020), and family and internal medicine physicians recommended Extension staff members form interpersonal relationships with providers to enhance health program referral networks. For example, when CES professionals and health system actors have a working knowledge of one another, and what each can offer, patients and communities will also benefit.

Another example involves optimizing relationships with clinical and translational science awards (CTSAs) at academic medical centers. The National Center for Advancing Translational Sciences (NCATS) at the National Institutes of Health has been funding a set of CTSAs since 2006, for the purpose of "improving the quality, safety, efficiency, and speed of clinical and translational research nationally" (NCATS, 2015). According to NCATS, translation is "the process of turning observations in the laboratory, clinic and community into interventions that improve the health of individuals and the public—from diagnostics and therapeutics to medical procedures and behavioral changes" (NCATS, 2021). One goal of the CTSA program is to engage communities in every phase of the translational process; therefore, community engagement and collaboration are core function of each CTSA (Zhang et al., 2020). Scientists in all of the more than sixty CTSA biomedical research institutions in the United States are tasked with working with community partners "to prevent disease, promote health, and respond to emergencies among different communities" (NCATS, 2022). Engagement with community partners is meant to result in improved trust in research and participation in clinical trials; expanded outreach from medical centers to community members for priority health challenges; improved identification of community needs; identification of relevant research priorities; and improving access to specialty care, including early detection and treatment (NCATS, 2022; Zhang et al., 2020). Gutter et al. (2020) suggested that CTSA partnerships with Health Extension could focus on meeting health equity goals in rural places, a priority that has been articulated within Healthy People indicators and by the CTSAs themselves. A decade-long partnership between Purdue Extension and Indiana's Clinical and Translational Sciences Institute has resulted in a set of health-promoting initiatives in the state—for example, establishing community health coalitions and ensuring that Extension professionals are trained to implement policy, systems, and environmental interventions for health in a team science model with shared governance (Savaiano et al., 2017). Partnerships between CTSAs and Extension are an important avenue for shared effort toward particular health outcomes or among priority populations. An opportunity exists to ensure that Extension is an integral partner in translational science, akin to the Purdue model. Care should be taken to avoid seeing Health Extension as a recruitment service for clinical trials, which would erode community trust over time.

A second action must be to equip Extension professionals with the training, tools, and technical assistance needed to serve as health promotion and disease prevention partners to the health system. Extension professionals must become experts in the development, dissemination, and implementation of evidence-based interventions that impact health behaviors, outcomes, and populations of shared priority between Extension and health payors and providers. The term "EBI" is used to identify an intervention that has been found to achieve practically important changes in behavioral or environmental conditions using a rigorous evaluation approach (Bartholomew-Eldredge et al., 2016). Demonstrating the effectiveness of an intervention is a very important objective, but effective interventions must be disseminated to other communities and population groups in order to have a meaningful impact on population health.

CES professionals bear responsibility both for developing new interventions and for disseminating existing interventions. CES professionals who create their own programs and interventions must do so with the highest possible levels of methodological rigor. Designing community-level interventions is a complex task and requires a multidisciplinary team that understands epidemiology, behavior change approaches, how to engage audiences, and how to evaluate the effectiveness of the program (Lytle, 2022). Too frequently, Extension programs are evaluated based on outputs, rather than outcomes—in other words, by the number of people who attend a session rather than by the behavior changes (or their antecedents) that result from participation in a program. Extension professionals are expert in working with community and have the potential to co-create powerful, relevant interventions for health behavior change. If Extension is to engage in developing and evaluating new interventions, partnership with academicians or others who bring expertise in many of the technical aspects of intervention design and process and impact evaluation is warranted.

Extension professionals who are working to disseminate EBIs, rather than designing and evaluating new interventions, must know how to identify existing EBIs that are appropriate to the communities they serve and each community's health needs. As behaviorally based health risks are identified, the community, health professionals, funders, and other stakeholders often prioritize the need for a program to help remediate the risk. EBIs are sought out as possible program options. Some EBIs may have already established external validity and are ready to disseminate with very little or no adaptation. Other EBIs may require some adaptation because communities, populations, and intervention settings differ, sometimes in subtle ways, but other times in more substantial ways. EBIs may be identified through several sources, including a health agency, funder, supervisor, or through recommendation by a colleague. They may be learned about through a conference or continuing education. Often professional groups or societies will create guidelines for specific health threats, and those guidelines include recommended EBIs. While there is a recognized need to adapt interventions to increase their potential for dissemination (Castro et al., 2004) and models of adaptation have been proposed (Yu & Seligman, 2002; Lau, 2006; Bartholomew-Eldredge et al., 2016), there is not an established approach for adapting EBIs. The book *Designing Interventions to Promote Community Health: A Multilevel, Stepwise Approach* (Lytle, 2022) offers a stepwise approach for adapting interventions with both researchers and practitioners as potential audiences. This approach stresses the importance of connecting with community at each phase of the design process and how to maintain the "active ingredients" of an intervention that must be maintained in order to sustain effectiveness. In sum, for Extension professionals to optimally partner with the health system, they must be fluent in the language and practice of EBIs: what they are, where to find them, how to create or adapt them to meet community needs, how to evaluate their effectiveness, and how to report on their impact.

Conclusion

The purposes of this chapter have been to describe promising trends in health care that move the system toward becoming one that is health promoting; articulate why and how Health Extension could and should become a health promotion and disease prevention partner of choice for health care providers and payors; offer examples of current health system and Health Extension partnerships that can be replicated and evaluated across the United States; and recommend a set of actions that must be taken to optimize the future of Health Extension and health system collaboration. Our vision for the future of Health Extension is to move beyond the current set of theoretical possibilities and promising practices, to scaling and adopting what we know works, and can work, in community. In order for the vision to become a reality, we must first lean on the principles that we hold dear in Extension: to intentionally build relationships, and to ensure that, together with our partners, we develop the capacity to succeed.

REFERENCES

Alcaraz, K. I., Wiedt, T. L., Daniels, E. C., Yabroff, K. R., Guerra, C. E., & Wender, R. C. (2020). Understanding and addressing social determinants to advance cancer health equity in the United States: A blueprint for practice, research, and policy. *CA: A Cancer Journal for Clinicians, 70*(1), 31–46.

Ariel-Donges, A. H., Gordon, E. L., Dixon, B. N., Eastman, A. J., Bauman, V., Ross, K. M., & Perri, M. G. (2020). Rural/urban disparities in access to the National Diabetes Prevention Program. *Translational Behavioral Medicine, 10*(6), 1554–1558.

Andrasfay, T., & Goldman, N. (2022). Reductions in U.S. life expectancy during the COVID-19 pandemic by race and ethnicity: Is 2021 a repetition of 2020? *PLoS ONE, 17*(8), e0272973.

Bartholomew-Eldredge, L. K., Markham, C., Ruiter, R. A., Fernandez, M.E., Kok, G., & Parcel, G. (2016). *Planning Health Promotion Programs: An Intervention Mapping Approach,* 4th ed. Hoboken, NJ: Jossey-Bass.

Berwick, D. M., Nolan, T. W., & Whittington, J. (2008). The Triple Aim: Care, health, and cost. *Health Affairs, 27*(3), 759–769.

Bodenheimer, T., & Sinsky, C. (2014). From triple to quadruple aim: Care of the patient requires care of the provider. *Annals of Family Medicine, 12*(6).

Bradley, E. H., & Taylor, L. A. (2013). *The American health care paradox: Why spending more is getting us less.* New York: Public Affairs.

Branam, C. (2023, September 8). *Crisis helpline for Oregon's agricultural and forestry communities is now open.* Oregon State University Newsroom. https://extension.oregonstate.edu/news/crisis-helpline-oregons-agricultural-forestry-communities-now-open

Breazeale, N., Norman-Burgdolf, H., Counts, K., & Williams, L. B. (2021). Process evaluation of the early implementation stages of the National Diabetes Prevention Program through Kentucky Cooperative Extension: Perceptions of adopters and potential adopters. *Journal of Human Sciences & Extension,* 9(3).

Burd, C., Gruss, S., Albright, A., Zina, A., Schumacher, P., & Alley, D. (2020). Translating knowledge into action to prevent type 2 diabetes: Medicare expansion of the National Diabetes Prevention Program lifestyle intervention. *Milbank Quarterly* 98(1), 172–196.

Burton, D., Canton, A., Coon, T., Eschbach, C., Gunn, J., Gutter, M., Jones, M., Kennedy, L., Martin, K., Mitchell, A., O'Neal, L., Rennekamp, R., Rodgers, M., Stluka, S., Trautman, K., Yelland, E., & York, D. (2021). *Cooperative Extension's national framework for health equity and well-being.* Washington, DC: Extension Committee on Organization and Policy.

Castro, F. G., Barrera, M., & Martinez, C. R. (2004). The cultural adaptation of prevention interventions: Resolving tensions between fit and fidelity. *Prevention Science* 5(1), 41–45.

Centers for Disease Control and Prevention. (2018). Current cigarette smoking among the adults—United States, 2017. *Morbidity Mortal Weekly Report,* 67, 1225–1232.

Centers for Disease Control and Prevention. (2022, October 11). *Suicide prevention strategies.* https://www.cdc.gov/suicide/prevention

Centers for Disease Control and Prevention. (2023, August 1). *National diabetes prevention program, Key national DPP milestones.* https://www.cdc.gov/diabetes/prevention/milestones

Centers for Disease Control and Prevention, National Center for Chronic Disease Prevention and Health Promotion. (2022, September 6) *Diabetes and prediabetes.* https://www.cdc.gov/chronicdisease/resources/publications/factsheets/diabetes-prediabetes.htm#prediabetes

Centers for Medicare & Medicaid Services. (2011). *Improving quality of care for Medicare patients: Accountable care organizations.* https://www.cms.gov/newsroom/fact-sheets/improving-quality-care-medicare-patients-accountable-care-organizations-0

Centers for Medicare & Medicaid Services. (2023, July 23). *Medicare diabetes prevention program (MDPP) expanded model.* https://www.cms.gov/priorities/innovation/innovation-models/medicare-diabetes-prevention-program

Contreras, D. A., & Anderson, L. A. (2020). Approach to establishing an infrastructure for delivering third-party-reimbursable community-based health education. *Journal of Extension, 58*(3), article 4.

Da Silva, V. (2022). *A template for better health: Diabetes prevention program toolkit designed to make extension health education more effective.* Kansas City, MO: Extension Foundation.

Diez-Roux, A. V., Nieto, G. J., Muntaner, C., Tyroler, H. A., & Comstock G. W. (1997). Neighborhood environments and coronary heart disease: A multilevel analysis. *American Journal of Epidemiology, 146*, 48–63.

Escarce, J. J. (2019, December). *Health inequity in the United States: A primer.* Penn Leonard Davis Institute of Health Economics. https://ldi.upenn.edu/our-work/research-updates/health-inequity-in-the-united-states-a-primer

eXtension. (2020). *Cooperative Extension national diabetes prevention interest group.* https://preventdiabetes.extension.org

Fitch, C., Donato, L., & Strawder, P. (2013). Extending the university into the community to address healthcare disparities. *West Virginia Medical Journal, 109*(4), 7.

Gorczyca, A. M., Washburn, R. A., Smith, P., Montgomery, R. N., Koon, L. M., Hastert, M., Suire, K. B., & Donnelly, J. E. (2022). Feasibility and comparative effectiveness for the delivery of the National Diabetes Prevention Program through Cooperative Extension in rural communities. *International Journal of Environmental Research and Public Health, 19*(16), 9902.

Gunja, M. Z., Guma. E. D., Williams, R. D. (2023, January 31). *U.S. health care from a global perspective, 2022: Accelerating spending, worsening outcomes.* The Commonwealth Fund. https://www.commonwealthfund.org/publications/issue-briefs/2023/jan/us-health-care-global-perspective-2022

Gutter, M. S., O'Neal, L. J., Riportella R., Sugarwala L., Mathias, J., Vilaro, M. J., Paige, S. R., Szurek, S. M., Navarro, G., Baralt, C., & Rhyne, R. (2020). Promoting community health collaboration between CTSA programs and Cooperative Extension to advance rural health equity: Insights from a national un-meeting. *Journal of Clinical and Translational Science, 4*, 377–383.

Gould, M. S., Cross, W., Pisani, A. R., Munfakh, J. L., & Kleinman, M. (2013). Impact of applied suicide intervention skills training on the national suicide prevention lifeline. *Suicide Life Threat Behavior, 43*, 676–691.

Institute of Medicine. (1988). *The future of public health*. Washington, DC: National Academies Press.

Institute of Medicine. (2003). *Unequal treatment: Confronting racial and ethnic disparities in health care*. Washington, DC: National Academies Press.

Itchhaporia, D. (2021). The evolution of the quintuple aim: Health equity, health outcomes, and the economy. *Journal of the American College of Cardiology, 78*(22), 2262–2264.

Kaufman, A., Boren, J., Koukel, S., Ronquillo, F., Davies, C., & Nkouaga, C. (2017). Agriculture and health sectors collaborate in addressing population health. *Annals of Family Medicine, 15*(5), 475–480. https://doi.org/10.1370/afm.2087

Kaufman, A., Dickinson, W. P., Fagnan, L. J., Duffy, F. D., Parchman, M. L., & Rhyne, R. L. (2019). The role of health extension in practice transformation and community health improvement: Lessons from 5 case studies. *Annals of Family Medicine, 17*(S1), 567–572.

Kaufman, A., Powell, W., Alfero, C., Pacheco, M., Silverblatt, H., Anastasoff, J., Ronquillo, F., Lucero, K., Corriveau, E., Vanleit, B., Alverson, D., & Scott, A. (2010). Health extension in New Mexico: An academic health center and the social determinants of disease. *Annals of Family Medicine, 8*(1), 73–81. https://doi.org/10.1370/afm.1077

Khan, T., Eschbach, C., Cuthbertson, C. A., Newkirk, C., Contreras, D., & Kirley, K. (March 2020). Connecting primary care to community-based education: Michigan physicians' familiarity with extension programs. *Health Promotion Practice, 21*(2), 175–180. https://doi.org/10.1177/1524839919868980

Kingdon, J. W. (2011). *Agendas, alternatives, and public policies*. New York: Longman.

Lau, A. S. (2006). Making the case for selective and directed cultural adaptations of evidence-based treatments: Examples from parent training. *Clinical Psychology-Science and Practice, 13*, 295–310.

Lopez, L., Hart, L. H., & Katz, M. H. (2021). Racial and ethnic health disparities related to COVID-19. *Journal of the American Medical Association, 325*(8), 719–720.

Lytle, L. A. (2022). *Designing interventions to promote community health: A multilevel, stepwise approach*. Washington, DC: American Psychological Association.

Maddy, D. J., Niemann, K., Lindquist, J., Bateman, K., & Engel, E. (2002, July 8). *Core competencies for the Cooperative Extension System*. https://apps.msuextension.org/careers/forms/Core_Competencies.pdf

Matoba, N., & Collins, J. W. (2017). Racial disparity in infant mortality, *Seminars in Perinatology, 41*(6), 354–359.

Marvasti, F., & Stafford, R. S. (2012). From sick care to health care-reengineering prevention into the U.S. system. *New England Journal of Medicine, 367*(10), 889–891.

McCarthy, D., & Klein, S. (2010) *The triple aim journey: Improving population health and patients' experience of care, while reducing costs*. The Commonwealth Fund. https://www.commonwealthfund.org/publications/case-study/2010/jul/triple-aim-journey-improving-population-health-and-patients

Mendez, O., & Myers, A. E. (2022, March 2). *Certified community health worker training program from Oregon State University*. Invited testimony to Health Care Committee of North Dakota Legislature, Bismarck.

Molgaard, V. K. (1997). The Extension Service as key mechanism for research and services delivery for prevention of mental health disorders in rural areas. *American Journal of Community Psychology*, *25*(4), 515–544.

Institute of Medicine (US) Committee on Understanding and Eliminating Racial and Ethnic Disparities in Health Care; Smedley, B. D., Stith, A. Y., & Nelson, A. R. (Eds.). (2003). *Unequal Treatment: Confronting Racial and Ethnic Disparities in Health Care*. Washington, DC: National Academies Press (US).

National Center for Advancing Translational Sciences. (2015). *Clinical and translational sciences awards program*. https://ncats.nih.gov/files/CTSA-factsheet.pdf

National Center for Advancing Translational Sciences. (2021, November 10). *Translation science spectrum*. https://ncats.nih.gov/translation/spectrum

National Center for Advancing Translational Sciences. (2022, May). *The healing power of community engagement*. https://ncats.nih.gov/files/NCATS_Community-Engagement-Fact-Sheet.pdf

Nwando Olayiwola, J., & Rastetter, M. (2020). Aiming for health equity: The bullseye of the quadruple aim. *Journal of Hospital Management and Health Policy*, *5*(11). http://dx.doi.org/10.21037/jhmhp-20-101

Office of Disease Prevention and Health Promotion, Office of the Assistant Secretary for Health, Office of the Secretary, U.S. Department of Health and Human Services. (n.d.) *Healthy people 2030 leading health indicators*. https://health.gov/healthypeople/objectives-and-data/leading-health-indicators

Oregon Health Authority. (2020). *Oregon Medicaid reimbursement for community health worker services*. https://www.oregon.gov/oha/HSD/OHP/Tools/CHW_Billing%20Guide.pdf

Oregon Health Authority. (2021). *Coordinated care organization measures matrix*. https://www.oregon.gov/oha/HPA/ANALYTICS/CCOMetrics/CCO-All-Measures-Matrix.pdf

Oregon Health Authority. (2022). *Coordinated care organization incentive measures*. https://www.oregon.gov/oha/HPA/ANALYTICS/CCOMetrics/2023-CCO-incentive-measures_7.15.2022.pdf

Oregon Legislative Information Service. (2023). *2023 Regular session, Senate bill 955 enrolled*. https://olis.oregonlegislature.gov/liz/2023R1/Measures/Overview/SB955

Oregon Violent Death Reporting System (2020). *Suicide deaths*. https://visual-data.dhsoha.state.or.us/t/OHA/views/ORVDRS/Suicide?%3Aembed=y&%3AisGuestRedirectFromVizportal=y

Parisi, L. M., & Gabbay, R. A. (2015). What providers want from the Primary Care Extension Service to facilitate practice transformation. *Family Medicine*, *47*(3), 210–216.

Patil, V., Mendez, O., & Myers, A. E. (2020, October). *Who is getting trained as a community health worker in Oregon? Understanding the first-four-years of a blended (online + in-person + live virtual) entry-level program*. Poster presentation at Oregon Public Health Association annual meeting, Corvallis, OR.

Peterson C., Sussell, A., Li, J., Schumacher P. K., Yeoman, K., & Stone, D. M. (2020, January 24). Suicide rates by industry and occupation—National Violent Death Reporting System, 32 states, 2016. *Morbidity and Mortality Weekly Report, U.S. Centers for Disease Control and Prevention.* https://www.cdc.gov/mmwr/volumes/69/wr/mm6903a1.htm

Pettrone, K., & Curtin, S. C. (2020, August). *Urban-rural differences in suicide rates, by sex and three leading methods: United States, 2000–2018.* Data Brief No. 373. Hyattsville, MD: National Center for Health Statistics.

Ratway, F., Mendez, O., Mendez, A., Myers, A. E., Phibbs, S., & Whidden-Rivera, C. (2022, October). *Toward rural language access: Developing a health care interpreter training curriculum.* Poster presentation at Oregon Public Health Association annual meeting, Corvallis, OR.

Reinert, M., Fritze, D., & Nguyen, T. (2022, October). *The state of mental health in America 2023.* Mental Health America. https://mhanational.org/sites/default/files/2023-State-of-Mental-Health-in-America-Report.pdf

Savaiano, D. A., Lynch, K. H., Vandergraff, D. J., Wiehe, S. E., Staten, L. K., & Miller, D. K. (2017). The Purdue Extension and Indiana CTSI's Community Health Partnerships collaboration: An innovative, generalizable, state-wide model to help communities build a culture of health. *Journal of Clinical and Translational Sciences 1*(5).

Schneider, E. C., Shah, A., Doty, M. M., Tikkanen, R., Fields, K., & Williams II, R. D. (2021). *Mirror, mirror: Reflecting poorly: Health care in the U.S. compared to other high-income countries.* The Commonwealth Fund. https://www.commonwealthfund.org/publications/fund-reports/2021/aug/mirror-mirror-2021-reflecting-poorly

Tiret, H., Eschbach, C., & Newkirk, C. (2019). Rx for health referral toolkit to promote Extension programs. *Journal of Human Sciences and Extension, 7*(3),173–185.

Tucker, K. L., Bermudez, O., & Castanada, C. (2000). Type 2 diabetes is prevalent and poorly controlled among Hispanic elders. *American Journal of Public Health, 90*, 1288–1293.

U.S. Department of Agriculture, Food and Nutrition Service. (2023, May 19). *Supplemental Nutrition Assistance Program Education (SNAP-Ed).* https://www.fns.usda.gov/snap/snap-ed

U.S. Department of Agriculture, National Institute of Food and Agriculture. (2022). *Expanded Food and Nutrition Education Program (EFNEP).* https://www.nifa.usda.gov/grants/programs/capacity-grants/efnep/expanded-food-nutrition-education-program

Warnecke, R. B., Oh, A., Breen, N., Gehlert, S., Paskett, E., Tucker, K. L., Lurie, N., Rebbeck, T., Goodwin, J., Flack, J., Srinivasan, S., Kerner, J., Heurtin-Roberts, S., Abeles, R., Tyson, F. L., Patmios, G., & Hiatt, R. A. (2008). Approaching health disparities from a population perspective: The National Institutes of Health Centers for Population Health and Health Disparities. *American Journal of Public Health, 98*, 1608–1615. https://doi.org/10.2105/AJPH.2006.102525

Wilson, H. K., Averill, B., Cook, G., & Campbell, C. L. (2022). Implementation of the national diabetes prevention program in FCS Extension during the COVID-19 pandemic: Participant experiences, lessons learned. *Journal of Family and Consumer Sciences, 114*(3), 11–19.

Yu, D. L., & Seligman, M. E. P. (2002). Preventing depressive symptoms in Chinese children.

Prevention and Treatment, 5(1), article 9.

Zhang, X., Kurilla, M. G., & Austin, C. P. (2020). The CTSA program's role in improving rural public health: Community-engaged disease prevention and health care innovation. *Journal of Clinical and Translational Science, 4*(5), 373–376. https://doi.org/10.1017/cts.2020.541

Dissemination and Implementation Science for Health Extension: Getting Back to Our Roots

Elizabeth H. Weybright, Laura E. Balis, Lauren E. Kennedy,
Brittany Rhoades Cooper, Kathryn E. Bruzios, and Samantha M. Harden

The Cooperative Extension System (CES) has been successful in supporting individuals, families, and communities in doing what works for more than a century, especially when it comes to agriculture. This system was developed on the premise of delivering educational outreach, or "diffusing . . . useful and practical information," to the United States public (Smith-Lever Act, 1914).

> The first concept of agricultural extension in the United States is that it is an educational organization designed to carry to rural people the studies, teaching, and the results of research by the State agricultural colleges, State experiment stations, and the United States Department of Agriculture and to help them apply these teachings and research findings in the improvement of the farm, the home, the rural community, rural institutions, and rural life. (Smith, 1944, 1–2)

This quote is taken from a leaflet containing an address by Dr. C. B. Smith at the annual conference of Extension staff, U.S. Department of Agriculture (USDA), in January 1944. Dr. Smith served as the chief of the Office of Cooperative Extension Work and later assistant director of Extension at the USDA during 1912–1938 (National 4-H News, 2016). Although Dr. Smith's address focused on agricultural Extension, the process of disseminating research evidence to communities remains today. Despite Extension's long-standing role as a dissemination system and growth of health-related programming, there is little knowledge of and integration with the fields of dissemination and implementation science (DIS).

Understanding and engaging with the fields of DIS are critical in advancing Health Extension as a national movement and partner in community-based health. Clinical and community health systems and providers are already engaging in DIS. This means researchers and practitioners at land-grant universities and in the CES wanting to partner within and across allied health fields, academic medical centers, and community-based clinical sites will also need to be fluent in DIS. Being fluent in the theories, frameworks, and terms within DIS will facilitate deeper relationships with and for communities, development of new partners interested in community-based health, and funding of DIS research and programmatic efforts. CES is unique in that it serves as fertile training ground for testing out innovations in a practical, realistic context with local collaborators and partners in the form of Extension professionals. Working in community settings is much needed in DIS, as existing research predominantly comes from clinical health services (Mazzucca et al., 2021). Ultimately, this intentional merging with DIS is how the nature and scale of CES will transform and how state Extension efforts can fill community-based health needs. We advocate that DIS is the future of CES in health spaces. This chapter provides an overview of DIS and provides examples from researchers and practitioners who are already working at the intersection of DIS and CES.

What Is Dissemination and Implementation Science?

DIS can bridge the gap between Health Extension research and practice. As a growing field, DIS focuses on how evidence-based programs, policies, and practices (EBPs) can be shared, adopted, implemented, and sustained over time. Dissemination uses an active approach to seeking and sharing information or knowledge about EBPs to specific audiences (e.g., health promotors) to impact the adoption of knowledge or an intervention (Brown et al., 2017; Strayer et al., 2022). Implementation research and practice aim to understand the research-to-practice gap and to identify strategies that best promote the adoption and continued high-quality implementation of EBPs (Durlak & DuPre, 2008). Specifically, implementation research seeks to understand the processes and strategies that work best to help translate and integrate EBPs into practice in real-world settings. This informs implementation practice, which in turn promotes the uptake and adaptation of processes and strategies across settings to achieve desired participant outcomes associated with EBPs (Curran, 2020; Peters et al., 2014; Ramaswamy et al., 2019). For a more detailed introduction to the field of DIS, see descriptions by Bauer et al. (2015) and Shelton et al. (2020).

DIS is a complex and multidimensional concept that often leads to inconsistencies and challenges with definitions and terminology. While DIS continues to receive critique based on its taxonomy and evolving language, we hope that this chapter provides examples and guidance to create "clarity out of chaos" (Damschroder, 2020). In the table, we define some of the key terms that are commonly used in DIS that are operationalized in the context of Health Extension in the remaining sections of this chapter.

Key Dissemination and Implementation Science Terms

TERM	DEFINITION
DISSEMINATION	"An active approach of spreading evidence-based interventions to the [specific] audience via determined channels using planned strategies" (Rabin & Brownson, 2017, 22).
IMPLEMENTATION	"The process of putting to use or integrating evidence-based interventions within a setting" (Rabin & Brownson, 2017, 22).
EVIDENCE-BASED PROGRAMS	"D&I activities . . . with proven efficacy and effectiveness" including "programs, practices, processes, policies, and guidelines" (Rabin & Brownson, 2017, 20).
KNOWLEDGE TRANSLATION	"The dynamic and iterative process that includes the synthesis, dissemination, exchange and ethically sound application of knowledge to improve health, provide more effective health services and products, and strengthen the health care system" (Canadian Institutes & of Health Research, 2016; Straus et al., 2009).
CAPACITY BUILDING	"Activities (e.g., training, identification of alternative resources, building internal assets) that build durable resources and enable the recipient setting or community to continue the delivery of an evidence-based intervention after the external support from the donor agency is terminated" (Rabin & Brownson, 2017, 23).
READINESS	"The extent to which an organization is both willing and able to implement a particular [EBP]" (Dymnicki et al., 2014).
FIDELITY	"The degree to which program components are implemented as intended by program developers" (Carvalho et al., 2013, 349).
CORE ELEMENTS	"The active ingredients of the intervention that are essential to achieving the desired outcomes of the intervention" (Rabin & Brownson, 2017, 31).
ADAPTATION	"The degree to which an evidence based intervention is changed or modified by a user during adoption and implementation to suit the needs of the setting or to improve the fit to local conditions" (Rabin & Brownson, 2017, 30).
IMPLEMENTATION STRATEGIES	"The systematic processes or methods, techniques, activities, and resources that support the adoption, integration, and sustainment of evidence-based interventions into usual settings" (Rabin & Brownson, 2017, 31).
SUSTAINABILITY	"To what extent an evidence-based intervention can deliver its intended benefits over an extended period of time after external support from the donor agency is terminated" (Rabin & Brownson, 2017, 23).

Moving Evidence-Based Programs into Real-World Practice

The translational pipeline described in Brown and colleagues' (2017) overview of DIS research and evaluation designs depicts the history of how EBPs traditionally move from research into practice. During the preintervention phase, etiological research is conducted to inform the development of interventions that target modifiable risk and protective factors associated with a mental, emotional, or behavioral outcome of interest (Wight et al., 2016). They then are tested under controlled conditions in efficacy trials to determine whether the intervention works. The next stage is effectiveness trials, which test the program in "real-world" contexts to determine whether it works outside of controlled conditions. After the EBP makes it through these rigorous trials, the next stage is dissemination and implementation into the applicable setting (e.g., schools, healthcare, community). At this juncture, implementation researchers use implementation theories, models, or frameworks (TMFs) to guide the knowledge translation process, understand determinants of high-quality implementation, intervene to improve implementation outcomes (e.g., fidelity), and evaluate these efforts. Calls have been made for DIS to be considered throughout the translational pipeline rather than once an EBP has been identified or tested (Zullig et al., 2023).

Using Theories, Models, or Frameworks (TMFs)—Too Many to Choose

To guide the implementation process of translating and applying EBPs in real-world settings, implementation researchers use implementation TMFs to "describe and/or guide the process of translating research into practice" (i.e., process models), "understand and/or explain what influences implementation outcomes" (i.e., determinant frameworks, classic theories, and implementation theories), and "evaluate implementation" (i.e., evaluation frameworks) (Nilsen, 2015, 2).

There are many TMFs to choose from. In this chapter, we select two that have been applied within Extension to use as examples and a third to guide the structure of the chapter. We recommend use of the D&I Models in Health webtool (https://dissemination-implementation.org/), an interactive platform to support users in identifying and using DIS TMFS.

Example 1. Consolidated Framework for Implementation Research

Determinant frameworks are used to identify predictors at multiple levels (e.g., organization, external environment, individuals) that may impact successful implementation and participant outcomes. The Consolidated Framework for Implementation Research (CFIR) is one example of a determinant framework and provides a menu of constructs (i.e., determinants) across five domains (intervention characteristics, outer setting, inner setting, characteristics of individuals, and process) that have been established to impact implementation outcomes (Damschroder et al., 2022). To achieve the desired participant outcomes, we must first achieve desired implementation outcomes. Implementation outcomes are separate from service outcomes (e.g., safety, timeliness) and participant outcomes (e.g., satisfaction, symptomatology) and include things like acceptability feasibility, fidelity, and sustainability (see Proctor et al., 2011). CFIR has a robust website to guide implementation evaluation and design available online at cfirguide.org. Examples of research conducted using CFIR within Extension are found in Balis and Vincent (2023), King et al. (2019), and Washburn et al. (2022).

Example 2. Reach, Effectiveness, Adoption, Implementation, Maintenance

RE-AIM is a planning and evaluation framework that has expanded its focus recently to determine implementation success (Glasgow et al., 1999, 2019). RE-AIM was updated to include PRISM, the Practical, Robust, Implementation and Sustainability Model, in 2008. PRISM expands RE-AIM to incorporate contextual factors such as readiness, sustainability plan, and organizational culture that influence RE-AIM outcomes (Feldstein & Glasgow, 2008). Taken together, PRISM contextual factors help evaluate how a "program or intervention interacts with the recipients to influence program adoption, implementation, maintenance, reach, and effectiveness" (Feldstein & Glasgow, 2008, 228). RE-AIM and PRISM have a website with guidance and resources (https://re-aim.org). Examples of RE-AIM within Extension are given by Balis and Strayer (2019) and Downey and colleagues (2017).

Updating TMFs to Address Health Equity

Although DIS is primarily concerned with addressing gaps between EBP and priority population benefits, health equity has not historically been an explicit focus. This is changing. Health equity is the fair and just opportunity for everyone to be as healthy as possible, despite the context, and it is dependent on addressing upstream causes (Office of Disease Prevention and Health Promotion, n.d.). Inequities are not randomly occurring disparities in health outcomes. Inequities are preventable, avoidable, and unjust and are perpetuated via the systems, institutions, policies, and environments that structure our lives. Structural oppression and power disparities, like anti-Black racism, ableism, and sexism, are contributors to inequities in health outcomes. Oppression is the result of unjust allocations of power to some groups, severe restrictions on power for other groups, and the maintenance of this status quo by the groups who have power. This leads to health benefits and protections for some and poor health (up to and including premature death) for others.

Many TMFs in DIS lack attention to power, historical context, or producing equitable outcomes, even if that is an incidental outcome of many DIS-informed interventions. Yousefi Nooraie et al. (2020) shared an EQ-DI (equity-focused dissemination and implementation) framework that depicts the interactions between two major overlapping domains of health equity and DIS: sensitizing and operationalizing. Sensitizing planning and evaluation processes can improve the equitable dissemination and implementation of EBPs, whereas DIS can guide operationalizing of strategies, toolkits, adaptations, or methodologies focused on health equity. Therefore, some TMFs are adaptable to health equity approaches. For example, i-PARIHS (integrated-Promoting Action on Research Implementation in Health Services) was integrated with the Health Care Disparities Framework to develop the Health Equity Implementation Framework (HEIF; Woodward et al., 2019). Such integration of frameworks can inform how existing programs can best be adapted for different contexts and build the evidence base for effective adaptations to promote health equity.

Given the abundance of existing TMFs, some researchers are opting to update existing TMFs with new constructs or guidance for users, rather than to create new ones. CFIR was updated in 2022, and the authors not only updated constructs and explanations to better encompass social and political determinants of health, but they also provided some guidance on how to move beyond individual-level determinants (Damschroder et al., 2022). For example, they suggest using a combination of both equity-focused frameworks and deeper engagement with critical theoretical approaches (e.g., critical race theory, public health critical race praxis) in DIS. This is in alignment with other proposals from DIS scholars to adopt theories of postcoloniality, reflexivity, structural violence, intersectionality, policy, and governance as a way to generate evidence and programs that have the capacity to advance health equity (Snell-Rood et al., 2021).

The Phases of Implementation

Exploration, Preparation, Implementation, Sustainment (EPIS) is an implementation framework that defines four phases of the implementation process (Moullin et al., 2019). Implementing systems or organizations (e.g., schools, community-based organizations, faith-based organizations, etc.) begin by examining and evaluating the health needs of the individuals, families, or other groups within a community during the exploration phase. Once these health needs are identified, the implementing organization and other invested parties work together to identify an EBP that best fits the context and resources to address those needs. Preparation begins once implementers decide to adopt an EBP. With the increasing number of EBPs available, sometimes more than one EBP may be agreed upon, and during the preparation phase implementers determine which EBP is more feasible. During this phase, time is spent identifying potential barriers and facilitators to implementation. Other activities during preparation include capacity building and determining which implementation strategies are needed, such as coaching or training.

Implementation begins when the EBP use is initiated by the organization. Time is spent assessing whether the EBP is having the desired impact on the preidentified health needs (participant outcomes) and on whether the EBP is being delivered with fidelity (implementation outcome). During this phase, organizations may need to monitor and address additional barriers/facilitators that were not planned for during the preparation phase. As the implementation process is refined, and the EBP becomes embedded within an organization, the sustainment phase begins. During sustainment, implementers begin focusing on what monitoring and funding is needed to continue implementation over the long term. At this phase, implementers may consider whether adaptations to the EBP need to be made to better fit the context or individuals being served. It is important to note that these phases are not linear but rather an iterative process. Across these four phases, three key components are considered: (1) outer system context and inner organizational context, (2) factors relating to the EBP, and (3) relationships between inner and outer contexts, or "bridging factors." Like the other TMFs highlighted, EPIS has a dedicated website including resources (e.g., measures, tools) to support users (https://episframework.com). This chapter uses the phases of implementation in EPIS to organize and highlight the DIS work in Extension.

Applying Dissemination and Implementation to Health Within Extension

To ensure EBP integration, implementation laboratories have emerged as a relatively stable way to explore the inner and outer context for implementation strategies and ongoing adaptations (Ivers & Grimshaw, 2016). CES has been an exemplar community-engaged implementation laboratory for more than a hundred years (Estabrooks et al., 2018; Franz & Townson, 2008; Rogers, 1962). As noted previously, this work was predominantly in the dissemination and implementation of agricultural advancements. Then, in the early 2000s, two pioneers within the Kansas State Extension system used participatory action research at the core of the development, adaptation, delivery, and evaluation of health promotion programs (Dzewaltowski et al., 2002, 2004; Estabrooks et al., 2004; Harden et al., 2020). They were also trained in the RE-AIM framework (Glasgow et al., 1999, 2019) that had been recently introduced as a way to balance internal (can the outcome of a study be explained by other factors?) and external (can a study be generalized to other contexts?) validity factors of public health interventions. As the field of DIS emerged, its application for health promotion in CES developed in tandem. However, much of this work continued in silos. Some reasons for this include that although the infrastructure of the national system touts replicability and generalizability, each state has different priorities, policies, and people (Harden et al., 2020).

These contextual nuances provide opportunities to investigate ways to integrate EBPs within states and across the nation (Balis & Strayer, 2019; Strayer et al., 2020). One of the key advantages of CES is that it employs, trains, and supports both the implementers and the researchers across multiple environments simultaneously. This provides a novel opportunity to inform the advancement of "what works" (Fernandez et al., 2019; Lengnick-Hall et al., 2021) by engaging community to understand key facilitators of intervention uptake and creating bidirectional communication between community-based delivery personnel and university-based researchers (Harden et al., 2018, 2020). Next, this chapter explores where and how Extension has been a vehicle for development and promotion of health-focused EBPs. Organized by phases of implementation as outlined in the EPIS Framework, we share brief case studies within each EPIS phase highlighting work in Extension. The chapter concludes with next steps related to the role of DIS in Health Extension.

Exploration

The first EPIS phase is exploration. We share examples related to ensuring contextual fit in the needs assessment and program planning process, including balancing research evidence with community needs.

Needs Assessment and Program Planning Using the Hexagon Tool

A common thread in Extension from its beginning to today is a focus on understanding local needs and how to best meet them. The process of conducting a needs assessment and planning programming to address those needs is not a new process for Extension professionals. However, with increasing community-based health providers (e.g., community health workers, Health Extension) and greater access to epidemiological data, the needs assessment process can now broaden from individual Extension personnel conducting a local survey to an integrated partnership of resource and data sharing making use of nontraditional data collection approaches. This may be a shift for some Extension professionals but is an important step toward more rigorous needs assessments (Kennedy et al., 2022).

Numerous resources exist on how to conduct an Extension needs assessment. A sample of these include

- University of Tennessee's Needs Assessment Guidebook for Extension Professionals: https://extension.tennessee.edu/publications/documents/pb1839.pdf
- Rutger's New Jersey Agricultural Experiment Station Program Evaluation resources: https://njaes.rutgers.edu/evaluation/resources/needs-assessment.php
- North Carolina Cooperative Extension (a strategic partnership of North Carolina State University and North Carolina A&T State University) Needs Assessment resources, including surveys, protocols, and reports: https://evaluation.ces.ncsu.edu/needs-assessment
- University of Florida's Extension publication on using needs assessments in Extension programming: https://edis.ifas.ufl.edu/publication/WC347
- University of Nevada, Reno's annotated bibliography on needs assessment processes and methods: https://extension.unr.edu/publication.aspx?PubID=3557

Rather than focus on the importance of or general process for a needs assessment, which is so familiar to Extension professionals, this chapter focuses on the process of exploring evidence-based programs and practices for implementation using the National Implementation Research Network (NIRN) Hexagon Tool (Metz & Louison, 2019).

The Hexagon Tool (Metz & Louison, 2019) is a resource for planning to ensure fit and feasibility between a given program and the context in which the program is implemented. This is done by assessing six indicators, which are three programs and three sites (i.e., contextual), as follows. Program indicators include understanding program evidence to identify program effectiveness, strength of supporting data, theoretical and conceptual foundation, and translation within and across demographic groups. The second program indicator is level of program support, or components including having access to formalized curricula, available training, coaching, data management plan, and availability of administrative policies, procedures, and systems. The third program indicator is program usability or operationalized principles, including core components and fidelity assessment. Site indicators include need and whether the program can or has the potential to best meet the site level identified need and the rigor of evidence to determine this. The second site indicator is capacity to implement, including availability of qualified staff, organizational capacity (e.g., financial, structural), and guidance on facilitating buy-in from key individuals and partners. Finally, fit with current initiatives is assessed at the site level and includes alignment with site priorities, organizational history and values, and organizational structure, as well as potential impact on other site-level programs or efforts.

Multiple resources exist to support use of the Hexagon Tool, including interactive lessons, critical reflection on use of the tool, and templates used by state agencies. These resources are available through the active implementation hub of the State Implementation and Scaling-up of Evidence-based Practices Center and NIRN. Using these resources, Washington State University Extension specialists have provided trainings to audiences including prevention professionals at a state prevention conference and to health-focused Extension personnel at an annual meeting on the importance and use of the Hexagon Tool in determining program fit and feasibility at the local level (Weybright & Cooper, 2020, 2021).

The Role of Evidence: What Counts as an Evidence-Based Program?

One aspect of the program planning process, and the Hexagon Tool, is understanding what "evidence-based" is and is not, which is typically driven by classifications based on strength of evidence for a given program and available in online inventories (e.g., registries, clearinghouses) or listings of EBPs. However, determining the level of evidence for an EBP is challenging due to the confusion around what is and is not deemed "evidence-based" and by whom. This is, in part, because popular EBP inventories differ in how they review and rate programs and how they assess the degree of evidence required to label something as an EBP (Walker et al., 2017). As a result, these inventories are useful for quickly identifying what works to achieve a given health outcome and should be used as one tool in a broader decision-making context (Horne, 2017). Articles such as those by Horne and Walker and colleagues list popular EBP registries. However, some registries, such as SAMSHA's National Registry of Evidence-Based Programs and Practices, are no longer updated or supported, illustrating the challenge of maintaining such resources. Inclusion in inventories and registries as an EBP is often an unreachable bar for community-developed programs that struggle to achieve a rigorous level of evidence due to factors such as a narrow priority population (e.g., youth who identify as Native American) or lack of "gold-standard" research design (e.g., randomized controlled trial). This illustrates the tension of balancing rigorous evidence while best meeting the contextual needs and the importance of valuing promising practices and research-based programs alongside EBPs, including addressing issues of health equity (Buckley et al., 2023; Hirsch et al., 2023). Resources such as the Hexagon Tool and the National Cancer Institute's (2019) Implementation Science at a Glance" workbook and associated website (https://cancercontrol.cancer.gov/is/tools/practice-tools) guide how individuals and communities balance research evidence with community needs in decision making.

Preparation

The second EPIS phase is preparation. We share two examples, including how CES has evaluated the capacity and readiness for implementation of an EBP and a structure for supporting delivery of EBPs through training and technical assistance.

Determining Organizational Capacity and Readiness

Although the CES's delivery model centers on sharing research-based information with communities, successful implementation of EBPs requires continuous planning and preparation. During the preparation phase, implementation climates that cannot support or reward EBP implementation are addressed (i.e., barriers) and enabling factors (i.e., facilitators) are accentuated and protected. Identifying barriers and facilitators can inform detailed plans to support implementation and sustainment through activities such as continuous training and coaching, process evaluation or auditing, and planned adaptations (discussed later in this chapter; Moullin et al., 2019).

Addressing such barriers and facilitators requires an understanding of the readiness and capacity for furthering use of EBPs. One relevant example from CES is the shift away from direct education to more policy, systems, and environment (PSE) work (Washburn et al., 2022). Providing group-based direct education is the hallmark of the CES. Since the publication of the original National Framework for Health and Wellness in 2014, CES has expanded its health and nutrition educational program options. However, education tends to have the smallest impact on health outcomes, whereas changing contextual factors has the greatest impact (Frieden, 2010). Consequently, there have been calls for CES to focus on PSE change work, in addition to education.

Widespread adoption of PSE change work at the local level is often limited to Extension professionals who deliver nutrition education funded by the Supplemental Nutrition Assistance Program—Education (SNAP-Ed), due to SNAP-Ed's requirement that implementing agencies develop PSE change plans and the emphasis on training and technical assistance for their workforce. Much of the research on acceptability of PSE change work in ces has focused on these professionals' perspectives (Derrick et al., 2023; Draper & Younginer, 2021; Haynes-Maslow et al., 2018; Pope et al., 2020). With updates to the National Framework in 2021 and increasing investments into ces's community health infrastructure, there is a need to understand the readiness and capacity professionals have to implement PSE changes beyond SNAP-Ed.

In response, researchers developed a survey using CFIR constructs that assessed professionals' perceptions, attitudes, and readiness to implement PSE change strategies (Washburn et al., 2022). CFIR domains were selected based on relevance to the research questions and the system/adopters, and corresponding questions were formulated. Extension professionals were surveyed in two states, Tennessee and Kentucky, that have similar state CES structures and are made up primarily of rural counties. Overall, respondents indicated that professionals perceived value in PSE changes and they mostly agreed there was adequate organizational support. However, they were less confident in Extension's long-term commitment to PSE change work, which is understandable given that there have been few changes to organizational structures like evaluation and reporting systems, job descriptions, or training opportunities. Professionals reported barriers to PSE change work such as funding or grants and time. For those who have begun implementing PSE change work, they cited relationships and trust as resources important to their success.

Similar studies have been done in four other states, with results elucidating that barriers and facilitators to PSE integration vary by state system (Balis & Grocke-Dewey, 2022; Balis & Vincent, 2023). Future work should use rapid processes to determine contextual factors in additional state systems and match these factors to specific implementation strategies. Thus, efforts are underway to collect data that are more representative of a national sample of professionals and the state systems in which they work. Additionally, attention to how PSE change implementation advances health equity and, ultimately, health justice, is paramount. The 2021 National Framework for Health Equity and Well-Being instructs state systems to consider health equity a national goal. However, there is little evidence that Extension has the capacity or readiness to advance health equity through PSE change (Kennedy et al., 2022). Without significant investments in capacity building, Extension runs the risk of further marginalizing and perpetuating harm on individuals, families, and communities we purport to serve.

Planning for Implementation Support

Implementation support includes activities or processes that assist personnel in delivery, sustainment, and scale-up of EBPs (Albers et al., 2020). This can include delivery of training and technical assistance (TTA). TTA supports the implementation of evidence-based, culturally and linguistically relevant interventions by offering guidance, training, or expertise to build community and practitioner capacity. The provision of TTA bridges gaps in capacity, experience, and training for communities and practitioners for improved self-efficacy and likelihood to select appropriate evidence-based practices, implement and adapt them, and ultimately achieve intended outcomes (Katz & Wandersman, 2016). Starting in 2018, the Substance Abuse and Mental Health Services Administration funded Rural Opioid Technical Assistance efforts open to the entire land-grant university system and CES. The intent was to leverage the CES for delivery of opioid-focused training and technical assistance to support rural communities. As this funding was released, research on delivery of TTA was being published.

In 2019, Dunst and colleagues identified core elements of TTA by conducting a scoping review of related models and frameworks. Five main categories emerged that organized twenty-five core elements, including:

- preparing for delivery of TTA (e.g., conducting a needs assessment),
- developing a TTA plan (e.g., creating a logic model),
- provision of TTA (e.g., offering coaching or mentoring),
- evaluating TTA (e.g., process evaluation), and
- sustainability of TTA-related change (e.g., ongoing TTA provider support).

Across these core elements, relationships are a critical link when providing TTA (Le et al., 2016). It is these relationships that have been leveraged to facilitate uptake of EBPs—in this case, those addressing substance use (Hagaman et al., 2023). An additional important factor in delivery of TTA is the intensity of training received. Educational trainings alone are generally not sufficient to facilitate uptake of EBPs. However, multisession trainings paired with ongoing technical assistance via mentoring or coaching are effective (Edmunds et al., 2013).

Implementation

The third EPIS phase is implementation. Given the rich history of CES in delivering programming, we share four examples covering topics of fidelity, adaptation, and community-level strategies and support for implementation.

Balancing Fidelity and Adaptation

After Extension personnel select an evidence-based health promotion program to meet the needs of their community, there is still more work to do. DIS shows us that some degree of adaptation is needed to effectively implement EBP in community settings (Barrera et al., 2017; Chambers & Norton, 2016). Yet DIS also tells us that maintaining fidelity to the core elements and functions of the EBP is critical to achieving positive program

Model of five best practices for balancing program fidelity and adaptation. Cooper et al. (2019).

and participant outcomes (Kirk et al., 2020). In other words, Extension professionals must engage strategies to maintain a delicate balance between delivering the program with fidelity and adapting it to fit their specific context, given their available resources and knowledge of the community.

Cooper et al. (2019) outline five best practices to guide Extension professionals in how to achieve this balance (see the figure). The first best practice—selecting an EBP that meets community needs—has already been covered in the Exploration section above and is based in the logic that implementers should consider issues around possible adaptation when first exploring and comparing EBPs. Also, whenever possible, one should select an EBP that closely meets the community's needs and available resources and thus will require the fewest adaptations. The second best practice guides Extension professionals in determining the core elements and functions that make the EBP effective. This is an important step because it provides implementers with a deep understanding of how the EBP works—and therefore which components are the "active ingredients" that should be delivered with fidelity and should not be adapted. The third best practice involves assessing the need for adaptation by identifying mismatches between the original program model and the community context. This provides program deliverers with the information needed to inform the fourth best practice, determining whether adaptations are necessary and if so, how to adapt the program while still maintaining fidelity to core components.

This best practice draws heavily from DIS that specifies the levels of risk posed by certain types of adaptations—green light adaptations are minor changes that mostly aim to improve audience reach, receptivity, and participation (e.g., tailored language, picture, examples), yellow light adaptations usually include adding or modifying rather than deleting content to enhance fit with the priority population (e.g., adding activities), and red light adaptations include changes to the core components of the EBP (e.g., deleting core components, reducing program dosage) (Balis, Kennedy, et al., 2021; National Cancer Institute, 2019). DIS research tells us that green light adaptations are usually acceptable to make and likely will not interfere with the core components and functions of the EBP. Yellow light adaptations should be made with caution and their impacts on program quality and participant outcomes should be monitored. Red light adaptations are strongly discouraged and should be avoided. Once adaptation decisions have been made and the EBP is being implemented in the community, the final best practice encourages Extension professionals to develop a continuous quality improvement system that monitors program fidelity and adaptations—especially in terms of how they influence participant engagement and outcomes. This information should be collected and discussed regularly to assure the program is being delivered with high quality and meeting the needs of the community. Fidelity checklists, also called class profile forms, are often used to assess a program's core components and may be available from the program developer (Balis et al., 2022).

Adaptation of Evidence-Based Programs

While some program adaptations are unplanned or reactive (e.g., adjusting or removing content to account for reduced program time), others are planned and intentionally developed to alter the program using a strategic framework or process. This is often to better meet community needs. In fact, most programs delivered in community settings end up being adapted during implementation (Moore et al., 2013). Planned adaptations are one approach to tailor an EBP for greater contextual fit while retaining the core program elements (Moore et al., 2021).

In Washington State, CES professionals have delivered the family-focused, evidence-based program Strengthening Families Program for Parents and Youth 10–14 (years old; SFP 10–14) since the late 1990s. With state legislation legalizing cannabis (both recreational and nonrecreational), parents were voicing to CES professionals a need to develop skills around talking with their youth about cannabis. In response, a team from Washington State University (WSU) comprised of CES specialists, researchers, and county-based faculty and staff convened to intentionally adapt SFP 10–14 for a context of legalized cannabis. With extramural support from USDA, National Institute of Food and Agriculture (NIFA; Children, Youth, and Families at-Risk [CYFAR] mechanism), the WSU team systematically adapted SFP 10–14 to include cannabis content and followed key adaptation steps (Escoffery et al., 2019) that included

- understanding the intervention,
- consulting with experts and partners,
- deciding what needs adaptation,
- adapting the original program,
- training staff,
- testing adapted materials,
- implementing, and
- evaluating.

The Framework for Reporting Adaptations and Modifications—Expanded (FRAME; Stirman et al., 2019) and Model for Adaptation Design and Impact (MADI; Kirk et al., 2020) were used to document and make decisions about adaptations, both in a planful way to inform initial adaptations and in a reactive way after piloting the adapted program and conducting a process evaluation. In addition to tracking the adaptation process, FRAME and MADI served to push the team to thoughtfully consider each element of the adaptation, alignment with program core components, and anticipated intended and unintended outcomes.

Pilot evaluation indicated significant increases in key caregiver and youth outcomes of interest (e.g., attachment, family harmony, communication), as well as increased caregiver confidence in speaking to youth about behaviors suggestive of substance use and increased awareness of substance use prevention resources in the community (Hampilos et al., 2023). Collectively, evaluation data suggested the SFP 10–14 + Cannabis adaptation was a feasible and acceptable family-focused intervention with initial promising outcomes. It also serves as a model for conducting community-driven content adaptations to existing EBPs.

Use of Community-Based Implementation Strategies

Once a program has been selected, or adapted, to best meet contextual fit, it is time to implement. One of the biggest obstacles to integrating EBPs for health promotion in Extension is the lack of systems-level supports for its skilled and motivated delivery professionals. One solution from DIS is the use of implementation strategies (i.e., methods or techniques used to move evidence-based programs into practice; Balis et al., 2022; Leeman et al., 2017; Powell et al., 2015). These strategies are typically used at the staff or setting level to build capacity, increase interventions' usability, or change organizational practices to support intervention uptake. For example, implementation strategies include combining funding sources to support adoption of a new intervention, conducting observations and providing feedback to improve fidelity, using program champions to better reach the priority population, and providing TTA to delivery agents (Balis, 2023). Implementation strategies can also be considered multilevel interventions (Fernandez et al., 2019). At the first "level" of intervention, the implementation strategies have outcomes at the system level (e.g., improved adoption or implementation of new healthy eating or active living interventions). At the second "level," healthy eating or active living interventions (e.g., healthy food retail, crosswalks to enhance walkability) are delivered at the community member level, with outcomes of improved fruit and vegetable intake or physical activity levels (Balis & Grocke-Dewey, 2022; Balis & Vincent, 2023).

One challenge in using implementation strategies is that one must ensure the selected strategies are a good fit for overcoming barriers and capitalizing on facilitators. For example, CES professionals may be challenged to adopt a new program because it does not align with their job description or community members' perceptions of their role (Balis et al., 2018; Balis et al., 2021). TTA is commonly used in community settings (Wolfenden et al., 2019) and is appropriate for addressing staff-level barriers, but using TTA to build CES professionals' capacity will likely not resolve barriers and improve this situation. However, an implementation strategy that targets barriers by changing job descriptions or engaging community members would be more appropriate (Balis & Grocke-Dewey, 2022; Balis & Vincent, 2023).

Planning for Implementation Support

To assist in selecting relevant implementation strategies, multiple compilations of strategies exist (Leeman et al., 2017; Powell et al., 2015). While many of these compilations were developed in health care fields using clinical terminology, a team of researchers recently developed a new compilation, Implementation Strategies Adapted for Communities, through input from both researchers and practitioners in community settings (Balis, 2023). CES researchers and professionals are encouraged to consider barriers faced in integrating health interventions, review strategy compilations, and collaboratively select implementation strategies that address barriers and fit with state system values and resources. This exploration can simultaneously advance health promotion within CES and methods and measures for DIS in a national system.

Sustainment

The fourth and final EPIS phase is sustainment. We share an example of an assessment tool to understand and inform program sustainability.

Using the Program Sustainability Assessment Tool to Maintain and Expand Program Impact

The continued delivery of EBPs across time and settings to extend reach and health impacts is known as program sustainability (Rabin & Brownson, 2017). Because Extension professionals aim to continue meeting the needs of their community by delivering effective health promotion programs, once there is evidence that a particular program is effective, the ability to continue delivering that program is critical (Cooper & Betz,

2017). Although sustained funding is one important factor, DIS shows that it often is not sufficient on its own. Instead, research shows organizational capacity and support (i.e., implementation infrastructure needed to manage and successfully deliver programs across time and locations), community capacity and support (i.e., community relationships that create a supportive implementation climate), and sustainability planning may play an even bigger role in determining program sustainability success (Shelton et al., 2018; Wiltsey Stirman et al., 2012).

Sustainability of health-related programs has been a focus of Extension and funders, such as USDA, NIFA, for decades. For example, the CYFAR funding mechanism has sought to understand and support program sustainability through research and as a funding priority. CYFAR grantee data and reports on sustainability were instrumental in development of sustainability theories, frameworks, and measures, including the Program Sustainability Index (Mancini & Marek, 2004). Grantees reported the importance of the CYFAR Professional Development and Technical Assistance model for program sustainability even after funding had concluded. This model included funding for a full-time project director role, opportunities for networking and learning at an annual professional development conference, and access to an online repository of resources (Marek et al., 2003). Eventually, CYFAR moved to having grantees administer the PSAT, or Program Sustainability Assessment Tool that is available online at sustaintool.org (Luke et al., 2014).

Based on available research, the PSAT was designed to assess and develop a plan to systematically build capacity in areas that influence EBP sustainability. The PSAT is a concrete product from DIS that can be used by Extension professionals to enhance their ability to secure the resources and support needed to keep EBPs going in their community (Calhoun et al., 2014). Calhoun and colleagues provide detailed steps on how to use the PSAT to develop an action plan (e.g., assemble a team, prioritize areas of sustainability) and take action (e.g., implement, reassess sustainability capacity).

Ways Forward for Integrating Dissemination and Implementation Science and Health Extension

In concept, doing more of what we know works in communities is the foundation of the land-grant mission and the CES. For Health Extension to advance, we need to build from the existing efforts bridging DIS and CES to address community health in an equitable way. The current chapter provides examples, framed by EPIS, of existing efforts. We now identify practical recommendations for both researchers and Extension professionals to move forward.

Health Equity as a Core Value

The pursuit of health equity as a national outcome for CES is relatively new. CES's National Framework for Health Equity and Well-Being recommends health equity advanced as a "systemwide core value" and provides activities to move in this direction (Burton et al., 2021, 14). While this may help some states to begin conceptualizing new ways of working, the recommendations lack robust dissemination and implementation guidance that could aid local efforts. In response, this framework should be paired with health equity focused DIS frameworks. Infusing Health Extension with DIS is an opportunity to improve our efforts with advancing health equity, but any efforts to address health equity by CES must be done carefully and intentionally. We outline three considerations for bridging this gap for Health Extension—trust, reflexivity, and accountability.

In DIS, trust is seen as a critical component for effectiveness, yet is often not assessed (Metz et al., 2022). One strength of the CES is the foundation of engaging communities in relationships based on mutual trust. In many communities these trusted relationships work well and are the key to effective engagement. However, the CES's origins, history, and even contemporary structure and resource allocation demonstrate the potential for harm (e.g., use of stolen Indigenous land for land-grant universities (LGUs), differential funding for historically Black universities and tribal colleges; Lee & Keys, 2013; Lee & Ahtone, 2020). As a result, many communities do not view CES as trustworthy.

The process of building trust would benefit from Extension professionals creating individual reflexivity practices. Locating oneself in the context—socially, politically, economically, and so on—and analyzing the power dynamics present are essential parts to building trust. This practice can reveal biases, assumptions, contradictions, and possibilities that we might not have been aware of previously. Masuda and colleagues (2014) offer detailed practice-based guidelines and suggest using an approach that encourages consideration of "how we know" what we know and use of that to transform our reality in relation to others. Reflexivity can be and should be an ongoing practice for Extension professionals, particularly if they are working in communities where they do not share identities or backgrounds of the people being reached.

As reflexivity is being cultivated, authentically engaging with communities is another important step. We can find that awareness by listening to community members' stories, believing and affirming their experiences, and consistently offering repair and accountability to them (Braveman et al., 2018). These behaviors and practices can look like use of participatory approaches and formal agreements to equalize partnerships, facilitate trust, and value other ways of knowing.

Measuring our progress toward health equity is one element of being accountable to the communities we serve (Braveman et al., 2018). Metrics for promoting health equity in DIS can focus on sources of data (community-defined vs. public health surveillance), assessments of organizational and staff capacity, process (e.g., coalition-building activities, small wins, changes in individual staff capacities), and outcome (e.g., changes in disparities). For example, process metrics related to adaptations and implementation strategies can be used to demonstrate best practices in implementation for various contexts while also revealing implementation failures, which may necessitate deimplementation or further refinement of strategies or adaptations. Communities change over time and how we deliver EBPs likely will change alongside them.

Building Capacity

To bridge DIS and CES, additional capacity will be needed with regard to staffing and competencies. Increased staffing capacity for DIS is needed among both local Extension professionals and state specialists. This can include hiring folks with DIS expertise who may be new to the CES or supporting DIS professional development among existing Extension professionals. In addition to additional staffing, increasing Extension professionals' competencies within DIS is an important step. Many community-based CES professionals are already doing DIS work but without common TMFs. For example, those in CES and other community settings have a long history of using implementation strategies but not labeling them as such, which limits the extent to which they can be identified and used to build the evidence of what works, for whom, and why. Suggestions for reporting implementation strategies exist, and include detailing the involved personnel, dose and duration, and outcomes affected (Proctor et al., 2011). In the future, better reporting of implementation strategies can lead to improved tools for matching barriers to strategies to streamline the selection process.

Increasing knowledge and skill in DIS can facilitate a shared language for communicating, evaluating, and justifying Health Extension. Tabak and colleagues (2017) engaged both researchers and practitioners to identify nine competencies for trainees of DIS that can serve as a starting point for CES. These broad categories include

- communicating research findings,
- improving practice partnerships,
- making research more relevant,
- strengthening communication skills,
- considering and enhancing fit,
- developing research methods and measures,
- building capacity for research,
- ensuring research is meaningful, and
- understanding multi-level context.

Tabak and colleagues (2017) provide examples within each category of specific competencies. Training opportunities in DIS are available (see review of training opportunities by Davis and D'Lima [2020]; some are available online). Resources such as the professional organization Society for Implementation Research Collaboration (https://societyforimplementationresearchcollaboration.org/) provide a listing of open-access training and opportunities, as well as degree programs and certificates. Health Extension will benefit from seeking out such opportunities to build knowledge and skill in DIS while learning from leaders within CES who are engaged in this work.

Getting Back to Our Roots

Thinking back to the agricultural roots of CES, one approach to controlling the impact of pests on crops is by using push-pull technology, or the simultaneous use of approaches to "pull" pests in to a desired place paired with approaches to "push" pests out (e.g., Eigenbrode et al., 2016). Moving Health Extension forward to promote community-based health requires a conceptually similar push and pull, where theory and research developed within DIS (and related fields) are "pulled," or adopted, tested, and refined within the real-world community context CES provides, and findings are "pushed" out to advance the fields of DIS into much-needed areas of community focus. Estabrooks and colleagues (2018) outlined broad approaches for public health professionals to engage in DIS work—approaches that also apply to work within CES. One suggestion is to leverage the efforts already underway in CES to advance DIS. The descriptions of CES work in this chapter provide an example and foundation to build from. An initial step toward this "push and pull" is using DIS TMFs to describe processes used and successes, as well as failures, of delivering EBPs in community settings. The potential for using the CES to bridge the research practice gap cannot be understated. For Health Extension to be successful, we need to connect with our roots in the original mission of the CES while integrating with the science of dissemination and implementation.

REFERENCES

Albers, B., Metz, A., & Burke, K. (2020). Implementation support practitioners—A proposal for consolidating a diverse evidence base. *BMC Health Services Research, 20*(1), 368. https://doi.org/10.1186/s12913-020-05145-1

Balis, L. E. (2023, September 21). *Implementation strategies adapted for communities: Enhancing health equity through a new compilation*. National Cancer Institute, Division of Cancer Control & Population Sciences, Virtual. https://cancercontrol.cancer.gov/is/training-events/webinars

Balis, L. E., & Grocke-Dewey, M. (2022). Built environment approaches: Extension personnel's preferences, barriers, and facilitators. *Frontiers in Public Health, 10*. https://www.frontiersin.org/articles/10.3389/fpubh.2022.960949

Balis, L. E., Houghtaling, B., & Buck, J. H. (2022). Evaluating fidelity to the National Extension Dining with Diabetes Program: Challenges and opportunities. *Journal of Human Sciences and Extension*. https://doi.org/10.54718/LAKR5242

Balis, L. E., Houghtaling, B., & Harden, S. M. (2022). Using implementation strategies in community settings: An introduction to the Expert Recommendations for Implementing Change (ERIC) compilation and future directions. *Translational Behavioral Medicine, 12*(10), 965–978. https://doi.org/10.1093/tbm/ibac061

Balis, L. E., Kennedy, L. E., Houghtaling, B., & Harden, S. M. (2021). Red, yellow, and green light changes: Adaptations to Extension health promotion programs. *Prevention Science, 22*(7), 903–912. https://doi.org/10.1007/s11121-021-01222-x

Balis, L. E., & Strayer, T. (2019). Evaluating "Take the stairs, Wyoming!" Through the RE-AIM framework: Challenges and opportunities. *Frontiers in Public Health, 7*. https://www.frontiersin.org/articles/10.3389/fpubh.2019.00368

Balis, L. E., Strayer, T. E., III, & Harden, S. M. (2021). First things first: Assessing needs, comfort, and role clarity for physical activity promotion. *Journal of Human Sciences and Extension.* https://doi.org/10.54718/HBHV1111

Balis, L. E., Strayer, T. E., Ramalingam, N., & Harden, S. M. (2018). Beginning with the end in mind: Contextual considerations for scaling-out a community-based intervention. *Frontiers in Public Health, 6*, 357. https://doi.org/10.3389/fpubh.2018.00357

Balis, L. E., & Vincent, J. (2023). Implementation strategies to support built environment approaches in community settings. *Health Promotion Practice, 24*(3), 502–513. https://doi.org/10.1177/15248399221081835

Barrera, M., Berkel, C., & Castro, F. G. (2017). Directions for the advancement of culturally adapted preventive interventions: Local adaptations, engagement, and sustainability. *Prevention Science, 18*(6), 640–648. https://doi.org/10.1007/s11121-016-0705-9

Bauer, M. S., Damschroder, L., Hagedorn, H., Smith, J., & Kilbourne, A. M. (2015). An introduction to implementation science for the non-specialist. *BMC Psychology, 3*(1), 32. https://doi.org/10.1186/s40359-015-0089-9

Braveman, P., Arkin, E., Orleans, T., Proctor, D., Acker, J., & Plough, A. (2018). What is health equity? *Behavioral Science & Policy, 4*(1), 1–14. https://doi.org/10.1177/237946151800400102

Brown, C. H., Curran, G., Palinkas, L. A., Aarons, G. A., Wells, K. B., Jones, L., Collins, L. M., Duan, N., Mittman, B. S., Wallace, A., Tabak, R. G., Ducharme, L., Chambers, D. A., Neta, G., Wiley, T., Landsverk, J., Cheung, K., & Cruden, G. (2017). An overview of research and evaluation designs for dissemination and implementation. *Annual Review of Public Health, 38*(1), 1–22. https://doi.org/10.1146/annurev-publhealth-031816-044215

Buckley, P. R., Murry, V. M., Gust, C. J., Ladika, A., & Pampel, F. C. (2023). Racial and ethnic representation in preventive intervention research: A methodological study. *Prevention Science*. https://doi.org/10.1007/s11121-023-01564-8

Burton, D., Canto, A., Coon, T., Eschbach, C., Gunn, J., Gutter, M., Jones, M., Kennedy, L., Martin, K., Mitchell, A., O'Neal, L., Rennekamp, R., Rodgers, M., Stluka, S., Trautman, K., Yelland, E., & York, D. (2021). *Cooperative Extension's national framework for health equity and well being.* Extension Committee on Organization and Policy.

Calhoun, A., Mainor, A., Moreland-Russell, S., Maier, R. C., Brossart, L., & Luke, D. A. (2014). Using the Program Sustainability Assessment Tool to assess and plan for sustainability. *Preventing Chronic Disease, 11*, 130185. https://doi.org/10.5888/pcd11.130185

Canadian Institutes of Health Research. (2016). *About us.* https://cihr-irsc.gc.ca/e/29418.html

Carvalho, M. L., Honeycutt, S., Escoffery, C., Glanz, K., Sabbs, D., & Kegler, M. C. (2013). Balancing fidelity and adaptation: Implementing evidence-based chronic disease prevention programs. *Journal of Public Health Management and Practice, 19*(4), 348–356.

Chambers, D. A., & Norton, W. E. (2016). The adaptome: Advancing the science of intervention adaptation. *American Journal of Preventive Medicine, 51*(4, Suppl. 2), S124–S131. https://doi.org/10.1016/j.amepre.2016.05.011

Cooper, B. R., & Betz, D. (2017). *How can we keep it going? Key ingredients for evidence-based program sustainability*. Washington State University Extension. https://pubs.extension.wsu.edu/how-can-we-keep-it-going-key-ingredients-for-evidencebased-program-sustainability

Cooper, B. R., Parker, L., & Martinez, A. D. (2019). *Balancing fidelity & adaptation: A best practices guide for evidence-based program implementation*. Washington State University Extension. https://pubs.extension.wsu.edu/balancing-fidelity-adaptation-a-best-practices-guide-for-evidence-based-program-implementation

Curran, G. M. (2020). Implementation science made too simple: A teaching tool. *Implementation Science Communications, 1*(1), 27. https://doi.org/10.1186/s43058-020-00001-z

Damschroder, L. J. (2020). Clarity out of chaos: Use of theory in implementation research. *Psychiatry Research, 283*, 112461. https://doi.org/10.1016/j.psychres.2019.06.036

Damschroder, L. J., Reardon, C. M., Widerquist, M. A. O., & Lowery, J. (2022). The updated Consolidated Framework for Implementation Research based on user feedback. *Implementation Science, 17*(1), 75. https://doi.org/10.1186/s13012-022-01245-0

Davis, R., & D'Lima, D. (2020). Building capacity in dissemination and implementation science: A systematic review of the academic literature on teaching and training initiatives. *Implementation Science, 15*(1), 97. https://doi.org/10.1186/s13012-020-01051-6

Derrick, B., Griffin, N., Moreschi, J., Ramirez-Prado, V., Allison, T., & McCaffrey, J. (2023). Addressing SNAP Education training and program implementation needs within a land grant university system. *Journal of Nutrition Education and Behavior, 55*(7, Suppl.), 7–8. https://doi.org/10.1016/j.jneb.2023.05.018

Downey, L., Peterson, D., Donaldson, J., & Hardman, A. (2017). An Extension application of the RE-AIM Evaluation framework. *Journal of Extension, 55*(3). https://doi.org/10.34068/joe.55.03.25

Draper, C. L., & Younginer, N. (2021). Readiness of SNAP-Ed implementers to incorporate policy, systems, and environmental approaches into programming. *Journal of Nutrition Education and Behavior, 53*(9), 751–758. https://doi.org/10.1016/j.jneb.2021.05.004

Dunst, C. J., Annas, K., Wilkie, H., & Hamby, D. W. (2019). Scoping review of the core elements of technical assistance models and frameworks. *World Journal of Education, 9*(2), 109. https://doi.org/10.5430/wje.v9n2p109

Durlak, J. A., & DuPre, E. P. (2008). Implementation matters: A review of research on the influence of implementation on program outcomes and the factors affecting implementation. *American Journal of Community Psychology, 41*(3), 327–350. https://doi.org/10.1007/s10464-008-9165-0

Dymnicki, A., Wandersman, A., Osher, D., Grigorescu, V., & Huang, L. (2014). *Willing, able → ready: Basics and policy implications of readiness as a key component for implementation of evidence-based interventions*. ASPE Issue Brief. Department of Health & Human Services.

https://aspe.hhs.gov/report/willing-able-ready-basics-and-policy-implications-readiness-key-component-scaling-implementation-evidence-based-interventions

Dzewaltowski, D. A., Estabrooks, P. A., & Glasgow, R. E. (2004). The future of physical activity behavior change research: What is needed to improve translation of research into health promotion practice? *Exercise and Sport Sciences Reviews, 32*(2), 57.

Dzewaltowski, D. A., Estabrooks, P. A., Gyurcsik, N. C., & Johnston, J. A. (2002). Promotion of physical activity through community development. In J. L. Van Raalte & B. W. Brewer (Eds.), *Exploring sport and exercise psychology (2nd ed.)* (pp. 209–223). Washington, DC: American Psychological Association. https://doi.org/10.1037/10465-010

Edmunds, J. M., Beidas, R. S., & Kendall, P. C. (2013). Dissemination and implementation of evidence-based practices: Training and consultation as implementation strategies. *Clinical Psychology: Science and Practice, 20*(2), 152–165. https://doi.org/10.1111/cpsp.12031

Eigenbrode, S. D., Birch, A. N. E., Lindzey, S., Meadow, R., & Snyder, W. E. (2016). Review: A mechanistic framework to improve understanding and applications of push-pull systems in pest management. *Journal of Applied Ecology, 53*(1), 202–212. https://doi.org/10.1111/1365-2664.12556

Escoffery, C., Lebow-Skelley, E., Udelson, H., Böing, E. A., Wood, R., Fernandez, M. E., & Mullen, P. D. (2019). A scoping study of frameworks for adapting public health evidence-based interventions. *Translational Behavioral Medicine, 9*(1), 1–10. https://doi.org/10.1093/tbm/ibx067

Estabrooks, P. A., Bradshaw, M., Fox, E., Berg, J., & Dzewaltowski, D. A. (2004). The relationships between delivery agents' physical activity level and the likelihood of implementing a physical activity program. *American Journal of Health Promotion, 18*(5), 350–353. https://doi.org/10.4278/0890-1171-18.5.350

Estabrooks, P. A., Brownson, R. C., & Pronk, N. P. (2018). Dissemination and implementation science for public health professionals: An overview and call to action. *Preventing Chronic Disease, 15*, E162. https://doi.org/10.5888/pcd15.180525

Feldstein, A. C., & Glasgow, R. E. (2008). A Practical, Robust Implementation and Sustainability Model (PRISM) for integrating research findings into practice. *Joint Commission Journal on Quality and Patient Safety, 34*(4), 228–243. https://doi.org/10.1016/S1553-7250(08)34030-6

Fernandez, M. E., Ten Hoor, G. A., Van Lieshout, S., Rodriguez, S. A., Beidas, R. S., Parcel, G., Ruiter, R. A. C., Markham, C. M., & Kok, G. (2019). Implementation mapping: Using intervention mapping to develop implementation strategies. *Frontiers in Public Health, 7*, 158. https://doi.org/10.3389/fpubh.2019.00158

Franz, N. K., & Townson, L. (2008). The nature of complex organizations: The case of Cooperative Extension. *New Directions for Evaluation, 2008*(120), 5–14. https://doi.org/10.1002/ev.272

Frieden, T. R. (2010). A framework for public health action: The Health Impact Pyramid. *American Journal of Public Health, 100*(4), 590–595. https://doi.org/10.2105/AJPH.2009.185652

Glasgow, R. E., Harden, S. M., Gaglio, B., Rabin, B., Smith, M. L., Porter, G. C., Ory, M. G., &

Estabrooks, P. A. (2019). RE-AIM planning and evaluation framework: Adapting to new science and practice with a 20-year review. *Frontiers in Public Health, 7*, 64. https://doi.org/10.3389/fpubh.2019.00064

Glasgow, R. E., Vogt, T. M., & Boles, S. M. (1999). Evaluating the public health impact of health promotion interventions: The RE-AIM framework. *American Journal of Public Health, 89*(9), 1322–1327. https://doi.org/10.2105/AJPH.89.9.1322

Hagaman, A., Roark, K., & Washburn, L. T. (2023). U.S. Cooperative Extension's response to substance misuse: A scoping review. *Frontiers in Public Health, 11*, 1127813. https://doi.org/10.3389/fpubh.2023.1127813

Hampilos, K., Pascoe, K., Weybright, E. W., Martinez, A. D., Cooper, B. R., Doering, E., & Purser, E. (2023, April). *Addressing youth cannabis use in a legalized context: Pilot evaluation of an adapted substance use prevention program for youth and families.* San Diego, CA: Society for Research on Adolescence.

Harden, S. M., Balis, L. E., Strayer, T. E., Prosch, N., Carlson, B., Lindsay, A., Estabrooks, P. A., Dzewaltowski, D. A., & Gunter, K. B. (2020). Strengths, challenges, and opportunities for physical activity promotion in the century-old national Cooperative Extension System. *Journal of Human Sciences & Extension, 8*(3). https://doi.org/10.54718/WIIV1194

Harden, S. M., Gunter, K. B., & Lindsay, A. R. (2018). How to leverage your state's land grant Extension system: Partnering to promote physical activity. *Translational Journal of the American College of Sports Medicine, 3*(15), 113–118. https://doi.org/10.1249/TJX.0000000000000066

Haynes-Maslow, L., Osborne, I., & Jilcott Pitts, S. (2018). Best practices and innovative solutions to overcome barriers to delivering policy, systems and environmental changes in rural communities. *Nutrients, 10*(8), 1012. https://doi.org/10.3390/nu10081012

Hirsch, B. K., Stevenson, M. C., & Givens, M. L. (2023). Evidence clearinghouses as tools to advance health equity: What we know from a systematic scan. *Prevention Science, 24*(4), 613–624. https://doi.org/10.1007/s11121-023-01511-7

Horne, C. S. (2017). Assessing and strengthening evidence-based program registries' usefulness for social service program replication and adaptation. *Evaluation Review, 41*(5), 407–435. https://doi.org/10.1177/0193841X15625014

Ivers, N. M., & Grimshaw, J. M. (2016). Reducing research waste with implementation laboratories. *Lancet, 388*(10044), 547–548. https://doi.org/10.1016/S0140-6736(16)31256-9

Katz, J., & Wandersman, A. (2016). Technical assistance to enhance prevention capacity: A research synthesis of the evidence base. *Prevention Science, 17*(4), 417–428. https://doi.org/10.1007/s11121-016-0636-5

Kennedy, L. E., Strayer, T. E., & Balis, L. E. (2022). Addressing health inequities: An exploratory assessment of Extension educators' perceptions of program demand for diverse communities. *Family & Community Health, 45*(4), 228–237. https://doi.org/10.1097/FCH.0000000000000332

King, E. S., Moore, C. J., Wilson, H. K., Harden, S. M., Davis, M., & Berg, A. C. (2019). Mixed methods evaluation of implementation and outcomes in a community-based cancer prevention intervention. *BMC Public Health, 19*(1), 1051. https://doi.org/10.1186/

s12889-019-7315-y

Kirk, M. A., Moore, J. E., Wiltsey Stirman, S., & Birken, S. A. (2020). Towards a comprehensive model for understanding adaptations' impact: The Model for Adaptation Design and Impact (MADI). *Implementation Science, 15*(1), 56. https://doi.org/10.1186/s13012-020-01021-y

Le, L. T., Anthony, B. J., Bronheim, S. M., Holland, C. M., & Perry, D. F. (2016). A technical assistance model for guiding service and systems change. *Journal of Behavioral Health Services & Research, 43*(3), 380–395. https://doi.org/10.1007/s11414-014-9439-2

Lee, J. M., & Keys, S. W. (2013). *Land-grant but unequal. State one-to-one match funding for 1890 land-grant universities* (3000-PB1). Association of Public and Land-Grant Universities. https://www.aplu.org/wp-content/uploads/land-grant-but-unequal-state-one-to-one-match-funding-for-1890-land-grant-universities.pdf

Lee, R., & Ahtone, T. (2020, March 30). Land-grab universities: Expropriated Indigenous land is the foundation of the land-grant university system. *High Country News, 52*, 4. https://www.hcn.org/issues/52.4/indigenous-affairs-education-land-grab-universities

Leeman, J., Birken, S. A., Powell, B. J., Rohweder, C., & Shea, C. M. (2017). Beyond "implementation strategies": Classifying the full range of strategies used in implementation science and practice. *Implementation Science, 12*(1), 125. https://doi.org/10.1186/s13012-017-0657-x

Lengnick-Hall, R., Proctor, E. K., Bunger, A. C., & Gerke, D. R. (2021). Ten years of implementation outcome research: A scoping review protocol. *BMJ Open, 11*(6), e049339. https://doi.org/10.1136/bmjopen-2021-049339

Luke, D. A., Calhoun, A., Robichaux, C. B., Elliott, M. B., & Moreland-Russell, S. (2014). The Program Sustainability Assessment Tool: A new instrument for public health programs. *Preventing Chronic Disease, 11*, 130184. https://doi.org/10.5888/pcd11.130184

Mancini, J. A., & Marek, L. I. (2004). Sustaining community-based programs for families: Conceptualization and measurement. *Family Relations, 53*(4), 339–347. https://doi.org/10.1111/j.0197-6664.2004.00040.x

Marek, L. I., Mancini, J. A., & Brock, D. J. P. (2003). *National state strengthening program sustainability study: Patterns of early sustainability.* Blacksburg: Virginia Polytechnic Institute and State University.

Masuda, J. R., Zupancic, T., Crighton, E., Muhajarine, N., & Phipps, E. (2014). Equity-focused knowledge translation: A framework for "reasonable action" on health inequities. *International Journal of Public Health, 59*(3), 457–464. https://doi.org/10.1007/s00038-013-0520-z

Mazzucca, S., Arredondo, E. M., Hoelscher, D. M., Haire-Joshu, D., Tabak, R. G., Kumanyika, S. K., & Brownson, R. C. (2021). Expanding implementation research to prevent chronic diseases in community settings. *Annual Review of Public Health, 42*(1), 135–158. https://doi.org/10.1146/annurev-publhealth-090419-102547

Metz, A., Jensen, T., Farley, A., Boaz, A., Bartley, L., & Villodas, M. (2022). Building trusting relationships to support implementation: A proposed theoretical model. *Frontiers in Health Services, 2*, 894599. https://doi.org/10.3389/frhs.2022.894599

Metz, A., & Louison, L. (2019). *The hexagon tool: Exploring context.* National Implementation Research Network, Frank Porter Graham Child Development Institute, University of North Carolina at Chapel Hill.

Moore, G., Campbell, M., Copeland, L., Craig, P., Movsisyan, A., Hoddinott, P., Littlecott, H., O'Cathain, A., Pfadenhauer, L., Rehfuess, E., Segrott, J., Hawe, P., Kee, F., Couturiaux, D., Hallingberg, B., & Evans, R. (2021). Adapting interventions to new contexts—The ADAPT guidance. *BMJ, 373,* n1679. https://doi.org/10.1136/bmj.n1679

Moore, J. E., Bumbarger, B. K., & Cooper, B. R. (2013). Examining adaptations of evidence-based programs in natural contexts. *Journal of Primary Prevention, 34*(3), 147–161. https://doi.org/10.1007/s10935-013-0303-6

Moullin, J. C., Dickson, K. S., Stadnick, N. A., Rabin, B., & Aarons, G. A. (2019). Systematic review of the Exploration, Preparation, Implementation, Sustainment (EPIS) framework. *Implementation Science, 14*(1), 1. https://doi.org/10.1186/s13012-018-0842-6

National 4-H News. (2016, March). *Folks who helped make 4-H great. C.B. Smith.* National 4-H History Preservation Program. http://news.4-hhistorypreservation.com/tag/clarence-beaman-smith

National Cancer Institute. (2019). *Implementation science at a glance: A guide for cancer control practitioners.* NIH Publication Number 19-CA-8055. https://cancercontrol.cancer.gov/sites/default/files/2020-07/NCI-ISaaG-Workbook.pdf

Nilsen, P. (2015). Making sense of implementation theories, models and frameworks. *Implementation Science, 10*(1), 53. https://doi.org/10.1186/s13012-015-0242-0

Office of Disease Prevention and Health Promotion. (n.d.). *Health equity in healthy people 2030.* https://health.gov/healthypeople/priority-areas/health-equity-healthy-people-2030

Peters, D. H., Adam, T., Alonge, O., Agyepong, I. A., & Tran, N. (2014). Implementation research: What it is and how to do it. *British Journal of Sports Medicine, 48*(8), 731–736. https://doi.org/10.1136/bmj.f6753

Pope, H. C., Draper, C., Younginer, N., Whitt, O., & Paget, C. (2020). Use of decision cases for building SNAP-Ed implementers' capacities to realize policy, systems, and environmental strategies. *Journal of Nutrition Education and Behavior, 52*(5), 512–521. https://doi.org/10.1016/j.jneb.2019.09.020

Powell, B. J., Waltz, T. J., Chinman, M. J., Damschroder, L. J., Smith, J. L., Matthieu, M. M., Proctor, E. K., & Kirchner, J. E. (2015). A refined compilation of implementation strategies: Results from the Expert Recommendations for Implementing Change (ERIC) project. *Implementation Science, 10*(1), 21. https://doi.org/10.1186/s13012-015-0209-1

Proctor, E., Silmere, H., Raghavan, R., Hovmand, P., Aarons, G., Bunger, A., Griffey, R., & Hensley, M. (2011). Outcomes for implementation research: Conceptual distinctions, measurement challenges, and research agenda. *Administration and Policy in Mental Health and Mental Health Services Research, 38*(2), 65–76. https://doi.org/10.1007/s10488-010-0319-7

Rabin, B. A., & Brownson, R. C. (2017). *Terminology for dissemination and implementation research* (Vol. 1). New York: Oxford University Press. https://doi.org/10.1093/oso/9780190683214.003.0002

Ramaswamy, R., Mosnier, J., Reed, K., Powell, B. J., & Schenck, A. P. (2019). Building capacity for Public Health 3.0: Introducing implementation science into an MPH curriculum. *Implementation Science, 14*(1), 18. https://doi.org/10.1186/s13012-019-0866-6

Rogers, E. M. (1962). *Diffusion of innovations.* New York: Free Press.

Shelton, R. C., Cooper, B. R., & Stirman, S. W. (2018). The sustainability of evidence-based interventions and practices in public health and health care. *Annual Review of Public Health, 39*(1), 55–76. https://doi.org/10.1146/annurev-publhealth-040617-014731

Shelton, R. C., Lee, M., Brotzman, L. E., Wolfenden, L., Nathan, N., & Wainberg, M. L. (2020). What is dissemination and implementation science?: An introduction and opportunities to advance behavioral medicine and public health globally. *International Journal of Behavioral Medicine, 27*(1), 3–20. https://doi.org/10.1007/s12529-020-09848-x

Smith, C. B. (1944). *What agricultural extension is.* Washington, DC: United States Government Printing Office. https://archive.org/details/CAT10682603

Smith–Lever Act. (1914). 7 U.S. Code § 341 (1914).

Snell-Rood, C., Jaramillo, E. T., Hamilton, A. B., Raskin, S. E., Nicosia, F. M., & Willging, C. (2021). Advancing health equity through a theoretically critical implementation science. *Translational Behavioral Medicine, 11*(8), 1617–1625. https://doi.org/10.1093/tbm/ibab008

Stirman, S. W., Baumann, A. A., & Miller, C. J. (2019). The FRAME: An expanded framework for reporting adaptations and modifications to evidence-based interventions. *Implementation Science, 14*(1), 58. https://doi.org/10.1186/s13012-019-0898-y

Straus, S. E., Tetroe, J., & Graham, I. (2009). Defining knowledge translation. *Canadian Medical Association Journal, 181*(3–4), 165–168. https://doi.org/10.1503/cmaj.081229

Strayer, T. E., Balis, L. E., & Harden, S. M. (2020). Partnering for successful dissemination: How to improve public health with the national Cooperative Extension System. *Journal of Public Health Management and Practice, 26*(2), 184–186. https://doi.org/10.1097/PHH.0000000000001025

Strayer, T. E., Balis, L. E., Ramalingam, N. S., & Harden, S. M. (2022). Dissemination in extension: Health specialists' information sources and channels for health promotion programming. *International Journal of Environmental Research and Public Health, 19*(24), 16673. https://doi.org/10.3390/ijerph192416673

Tabak, R. G., Padek, M. M., Kerner, J. F., Stange, K. C., Proctor, E. K., Dobbins, M. J., Colditz, G. A., Chambers, D. A., & Brownson, R. C. (2017). Dissemination and implementation science training needs: Insights from practitioners and researchers. *American Journal of Preventive Medicine, 52*(3), S322–S329. https://doi.org/10.1016/j.amepre.2016.10.005

Walker, S. C., Lyon, A. R., Aos, S., & Trupin, E. W. (2017). The consistencies and vagaries of the Washington State Inventory of Evidence-Based Practice: The definition of "evidence-based" in a policy context. *Administration and Policy in Mental Health and Mental Health Services Research, 44*(1), 42–54. https://doi.org/10.1007/s10488-015-0652-y

Washburn, L., Norman-Burgdolf, H., Jones, N., Kennedy, L. E., & Jarvandi, S. (2022). Exploring extension agent capacity and readiness to adopt policy, systems and environmental change approaches. *Frontiers in Public Health, 10*, 856788. https://doi.org/10.3389/fpubh.2022.856788

Weybright, E. W., & Cooper, B. R. (2020, February). *Leveraging Extension to implement prevention initiatives promoting individual, family, and community health.* WSU All-Extension Meeting, Spokane, WA.

Weybright, E. W., & Cooper, B. R. (2021, August). *Moving toward the next right thing: Six steps to assess contextual fit & feasibility of opioid-related prevention efforts for community implementation.* Region 10 Opioid Summit, Virtual.

Wight, D., Wimbush, E., Jepson, R., & Doi, L. (2016). Six steps in quality intervention development (6SQuID). *Journal of Epidemiology and Community Health, 70*(5), 520–525. https://doi.org/10.1136/jech-2015-205952

Wiltsey Stirman, S., Kimberly, J., Cook, N., Calloway, A., Castro, F., & Charns, M. (2012). The sustainability of new programs and innovations: A review of the empirical literature and recommendations for future research. *Implementation Science, 7*(1), 17. https://doi.org/10.1186/1748-5908-7-17

Wolfenden, L., Reilly, K., Kingsland, M., Grady, A., Williams, C. M., Nathan, N., Sutherland, R., Wiggers, J., Jones, J., Hodder, R., Finch, M., McFadyen, T., Bauman, A., Rissel, C., Milat, A., Swindle, T., & Yoong, S. L. (2019). Identifying opportunities to develop the science of implementation for community-based non-communicable disease prevention: A review of implementation trials. *Preventive Medicine, 118*, 279–285. https://doi.org/10.1016/j.ypmed.2018.11.014

Woodward, E. N., Matthieu, M. M., Uchendu, U. S., Rogal, S., & Kirchner, J. E. (2019). The health equity implementation framework: Proposal and preliminary study of hepatitis C virus treatment. *Implementation Science, 14*(1), 26. https://doi.org/10.1186/s13012-019-0861-y

Yousefi Nooraie, R., Kwan, B. M., Cohn, E., AuYoung, M., Clarke Roberts, M., Adsul, P., & Shelton, R. C. (2020). Advancing health equity through CTSA programs: Opportunities for interaction between health equity, dissemination and implementation, and translational science. *Journal of Clinical and Translational Science, 4*(3), 168–175. https://doi.org/10.1017/cts.2020.10

Zullig, L. L., Drake, C., Check, D. K., Brunkert, T., Deschodt, M., Olson, M. (S.), & De Geest, S. (2023). Embedding implementation science in the research pipeline. *Translational Behavioral Medicine*, ibad050. https://doi.org/10.1093/tbm/ibad050

Diversity, Equity, and Inclusion: Envisioning Pathways to Health Justice

Courtney Cuthbertson, Lauren E. Kennedy, Lindsey Lunsford, Danielle Y. Hairston Green, Ana Lucia Fonseca, Camaya Wallace Bechard, and Carmen V. Harris

In November 2022, I (Courtney) attended two Extension-related conferences back-to-back: the Professional Agricultural Workers Conference (PAWC) in Montgomery, Alabama, and the Illinois Extension Annual Conference in Champaign, Illinois. PAWC, hosted by Tuskegee University, began in 1942 and is a national conference open to the broad range of people who work in agricultural roles, to share new knowledge, information, and programs, share information with decision makers, facilitate collaborations, and offer professional development and networking opportunities. Within the first twenty-four hours at the 2022 conference, at least two speakers openly and plainly acknowledged the historical legacy and contemporary reality of racialized disparities between predominantly white land-grant institutions (PWLGIs) and historically Black land-grant colleges and universities (HBLGCUs) in the Extension system, where HBLGCUs have been underfunded by more than $12 billion since the 1990s—not taking into account the nearly eighty years prior in which there were federal funding mechanisms for some (mostly PWLGI) Extension institutions. In Extension, we tend to speak using years as shorthand—1862 for PWLGIs, 1890 for HBLGCUs, and 1994 for tribal land-grant colleges and universities (TLGCUs)—where years indicate the year legislation entered a subset of those institutions into the Extension system. Using years as shorthand obscures the racialized history of Extension and I (Courtney) am intentionally using PWLGI, HBLGCU, and TLGCU instead.

The presenters were right. There are multiple legislative mechanisms that fund land-grant universities and Cooperative Extension. The Hatch Act of 1887 established funding to PWLGIs and research funds are allocated to HBLGCUs through the Evans-Allen Act. As recently as fiscal year 2019, Evans-Allen appropriations had been a mere 22 percent of Hatch Act appropriations, even though federal legislation dictates Evan-Allen appropriations not to be less than 30 percent of Hatch appropriations each year (Croft,

2019). Evans-Allen Act appropriations first met and exceeded this threshold in fiscal year 2022 (Croft, 2022). The McIntire-Stennis Act of 1962 established appropriations for forestry research to PWLGIs, yet it was not until 2008 that HBLGCUs were eligible for this funding, and not until 2018 for TLGCUs (Croft, 2019). The Smith-Lever Act of 1914 established Cooperative Extension funding to PWLGIs; HBLGCUs were funded through Smith-Lever through the 1960s, and Section 1444 of National Agricultural Research, Extension, and Teaching Policy Act of 1977 (NARETPA) now funds the HBLGCU Extension system (Croft, 2019; Smith-Lever Act, 1914). HBLGCU funding through NARETPA has been about 15 percent of Smith-Lever appropriations to PWLGIs as recently as fiscal year 2019, failing to meet federal requirements of 20 percent. Prior to 2018, HBLGCUs could carry over 20 percent or less of their annual appropriations while PWLGIs did not have a similar stipulation. Funding for TLGCUs is from only interest accrued on the National American Institutions Endowment Fund. Not all Cooperative Extension is equal.

Later that week, I traveled back to Illinois to attend the Illinois Extension Annual Conference. An enthusiastic Extension speaker from a different PWLGI shared a presentation intended to motivate and impress the audience regarding Extension's promise to serve state residents by talking about the establishment and history of the Extension system overall. Pictures from Extension's early days were included; to my surprise, none of them included Black people or people of color. The speaker's narrative of Extension's history did not acknowledge that the Extension system started at Tuskegee University, T. M. Campbell as the first Extension agent, or the role of HBLGCUs in establishing the Extension concept (Goldenstein, 1989). When I think about diversity, equity, and inclusion in Extension, I think about the stories that are told about the huge potential of the system, about its impressive impacts for communities, and how much the story and storyteller shape our understanding of who has contributed to where Extension is today and where and with whom Extension can be effective.

This Chapter

Diversity, equity, and inclusion (DEI) have increasingly become topics of conversation within Cooperative Extension organizations across the United States. In 2018, for example, Dr. Shatomi Luster-Edward edited the first edition of a DEI e-fieldbook, which is now hosted on the Extension Committee on Organization and Policy's (ECOP) website as a flipping book, along with the second edition, edited in 2022 by Dr. Lindsey Lunsford (a contributor to this chapter). These were intended to provide the curious with ready resources to assist their learning and the integration of DEI into Extension programming. In addition to these e-fieldbooks, ECOP also hosts an online resource repository where Extension professionals can submit publicly accessible DEI materials like fact sheets, logic models, and websites. They list seven DEI competencies in their website: Understanding Implicit Bias, Microaggression Development and Understanding, Cultural Competency, Promotion of Civility, Social Justice Development, Organizational Learning, and Youth

Development (Extension Committee on Organization and Policy, n.d.-a–g). ECOP also suggests its program Coming Together for Racial Understanding is having an impact by fostering important community dialogues that build trust across divides.

The focus of this chapter is to reflect experiences and contemporary perspectives about DEI in the context of Health Extension. Within the group, we have experiences both within and outside of Extension, including historical perspectives of where Extension has been over time. We structured this chapter as a conversation—not as omniscient experts about DEI, but as experts of our own experience to share our situated perspectives. Each co-author was asked to contribute responses to three questions, and we organized the chapter by these questions:

- How do you describe your own positionality?
- From your experience, what do diversity, equity, and inclusion mean in Extension?
- What does Extension need to do to fully take on diversity, equity, and inclusion as strategies to work toward health justice? What will help Extension to adopt your recommendations?

The three questions were worded intentionally to make space for each contributor to share about their personal experiences, expertise, and identities as well as perspectives towards diversity, equity, and inclusion and health Extension. The first question asked contributors to describe their own positionality. The concept of positionality has origins in Black feminist thought, for example, through the works of Audre Lorde (1984, 1997) and bell hooks (2000), both of whom wrote about understanding how lived experiences were shaped by the intersection of power and identity. Positionality is the unique combination of intersecting social locations one individual occupies, and each of their identities may differently inform their perspective. Experiences we have in the world are contingent upon our positionality at an interpersonal level based on assumptions and expectations people have, and at a structural level from institutionalized privilege or marginalization that shape access to opportunity. All knowledge is situated (Haraway, 1988), and each of us has biases in our perspectives because of our positionality (Takacs, 2003). Naming or acknowledging one's social locations is a reflexive tool to recognize the depth and boundaries of our perspectives. Positionality is a key starting point because it situates oneself in context (Qin, 2016), informs how people show up in conversation, may illuminate potential experiences of privilege and marginalization, and helps us to recognize that our one singular viewpoint is not universal.

From each of our unique positions, we can shed light on what diversity, equity, and inclusion in Extension mean. The second question sets a baseline to understand what interacting with diversity, equity, and inclusion has looked like, acknowledging differences in word and action. The popularity of diversity, equity, and inclusion as contemporary buzzwords unfortunately comes at the cost of the terms losing meaning, and people carry individual meanings of diversity, equity, and inclusion based on their own experiences. While DEI is defined in ECOP e-fieldbooks, it is unclear how widely adopted definitions are; without widespread consensus in defining diversity, equity, and inclusion, it becomes all the more important for each contributor to share how they think of these terms.

The third question asks contributors to consider health justice and Extension's movement toward health justice. Where health equity may be defined as achieving the same outcomes for marginalized groups as privileged ones, we see health justice as a fundamentally different approach that fully engages with historical disparities in attention to health programs that help communities thrive (Venkatapuram, 2013). Health justice requires centering diversity, equity, and inclusion as strategies to ensure full access and participation of marginalized and minoritized communities, centering voices that have been silenced, and working collaboratively to achieve thriving. Health justice also requires systems-level change to stop historical legacies of health disparities that are baked into our current systems.

Contributor Positionality

Dr. Lindsey Lunsford (LL): I describe myself as a Black woman. I see myself as a Southern "transplant" (to Alabama), having first been grown in the Midwest (Indiana). As a third-generation graduate and now faculty member of Tuskegee University, I say it has had a firm hand in shaping who I am today. My expertise, which I view as my passion, lies in seeking justice for Black communities especially as it relates to the stories told around our food. I am a storyteller.

Dr. Carmen V. Harris (CVH): I am a Black Southern woman, a child of the civil rights era, an activist both personally and professionally. I am the descendant of enslaved people with recent roots that are blue-collar factory (mostly textiles) and farmers including sharecroppers and renters. I am a scholar (described by my thesis adviser as "young, gifted, and Black") and an academic leader.

Dr. Camaya Wallace Bechard (CWB): As an Afro-Caribbean, first-generation college student, first-generation immigrant, and cisgender woman, I have remained energized through scholarship and personal interest to focus on the social injustices and disparities that affect all aspects of our lives. I found opportunities to learn from others and remain open and curious while reflecting on my biases and assumptions that further perpetuate inequities.

Dr. Ana Lucia Fonseca (ALF): My path to lead diversity, equity, and inclusion started young: defeating patriarchy by being the first woman from my lineage who left home to study instead of to marry, the previous only option for women in my family. As a Mexican immigrant, Extension professional, and feminist scholar, I strive to understand and heal the systems that hurt the full possibilities of humanity.

Dr. Danielle Hairston Green (DHG): As a middle-class African American woman who has pursued and achieved a terminal degree, my positionality is situated at the intersection of various identities and experiences. My educational journey reflects the perseverance and determination it takes to overcome systemic barriers and my race and gender inform the lens through which I view the world, allowing me to empathize with the struggles faced by people of color and women in academia and beyond.

Dr. Courtney Cuthbertson (CC): I am a white, trans/nonbinary, genderqueer, queer, neurodivergent millennial who has worked within two Midwestern predominantly white institutions (PWI) Extension organizations and with Extension Foundation, starting in 2016. My educational background and training are in sociology and psychology, and my work has focused on health, mental health, substance use, and social determinants of well-being. Growing up queer and neurodivergent, I often noticed and was upset by how some groups seemed to be given preferential access and treatment while some were marginalized and not enabled to have the same opportunities. Dr. Angela Davis's quote is a guiding light for me: "I am no longer accepting the things I cannot change. I am changing the things I cannot accept."

Dr. Lauren E. Kennedy (LK): I am a white cis neurodivergent woman who was born and raised in the Appalachian region of southwest Virginia to a working-class family that encouraged me to pursue my education. Because of this, I was part of the first generation in my family to earn a college degree and I went on to earn a Ph.D. in community and behavioral nutrition. I've been an employee of the 1862 PWI Extension system and the 1890 HBCU (historically Black college and university) system, but my experience lies mainly with the 1862. My motherhood, to a Black biracial child, and being a wife, to a Black American man, have irrevocably shaped my politic and my commitment to fight for liberation and healing from dominant systems of oppression—theirs, my own, and everyone's.

Diversity, Equity, and Inclusion in Extension

LL: I find it fascinating how diversity, equity, and inclusion are often viewed as outside constructs or "supplements" that need to be infused into Extension, rather than as vital elements of its DNA or core structure. When we look at the history of Extension, we see that without diversity, equity, and inclusion we would have no Extension. I mean this to say that America's very first Extension agent was a Black man—for it is at Tuskegee University that the first Cooperative Extension program in the United States began, and Thomas Monroe Campbell, a graduate of Tuskegee, was the first Extension agent employed by a Cooperative Extension program. Campbell's ethic and innovations in community outreach set a standard the nationwide Cooperative Extension system uses to this day. Yet this history is often unheard of throughout the national Extension community. We must ask ourselves, why is that?

DHG: Extension, in its inception, was never intended to embody equity, diversity, or inclusivity. The roots trace back to the early 1900s, and with the induction of our pioneer African American Extension agent, Thomas Monroe Campbell, the narrative took a new direction. This era saw our Black professionals/agents grappling with adversity and bias while serving vulnerable families. Notably, prevailing attitudes among white leaders and farmers discounted the capacity of African American agents to effectively articulate research, positioning them as unequal counterparts to their white peers.

Contemporary strides have been more intentional in fostering diversity and inclusiveness, spanning hiring practices, program architecture, delivery methods, and coalition formation. My vantage point, encompassing involvement with both 1862 (PWIs) and 1890 (HBCUs) land-grant institutions, reveals an array of challenges. From an HBCU stance, a presumption of innate comprehension sometimes blinds us to the privileges inherent in our own positionality, potentially obstructing a thorough grasp of the circumstances affecting our racially distinctive and culturally distinctive communities.

Conversely, the PWI perspective discloses aspirations for inclusivity, often hampered by inadequate systemic support to sustain diversity efforts and perpetuating the idealism that "we are here to fix you." These dynamics impel me to bridge the gap, leveraging my insights and experiences to contribute to the holistic transformation of Extension, ensuring that its evolution is both purposeful and truly all-encompassing.

CWB: A commitment to diversity, equity, and inclusion in Cooperative Extension means understanding the needs of individuals and groups within the local communities. It also means examining people's lived experiences, critically reflecting on injustices, adopting culturally responsive and affirming strategies, and conducting ongoing evaluation strategies to determine whether the organization is fulfilling its responsibility to all its diverse communities.

In Cooperative Extension, federal guidelines set the minimum standards for programs reaching underserved and underrepresented audiences. However, Extension has a broader responsibility to foster inclusive excellence in all aspects of its community-based work. A few ways Extension tries to do this are through research, community engagement, training, staff development, and leadership opportunities. The challenge may be to consistently integrate strategic DEI processes that address the changing needs of communities, which may change faster than Extension's response time. Another challenge could be the anti-DEI laws that public land-grant universities and state Extension services have been facing across the United States. Such laws and policies may limit the scope of inclusion work, as well as Extension's accountability to its communities, staff, volunteers, youth, and other stakeholders. Nonetheless, Extension has the capacity to continue community-engaged work through a DEI lens that acknowledges social injustices, environmental justice concerns, and other emerging and existing social problems that affect individual community members.

ALF: In Extension, diversity, equity, and inclusion are fundamental principles shaping our work's essence. From how we think about our role in communities to how we partner and engage with communities to co-create solutions, these principles guide our efforts to address the needs of all community members, especially those historically underserved. By embracing our values and adapting to society's needs, we can create spaces that amplify voices and bring different views together to co-create solutions that require our best thinking and doing. Ultimately, these principles are interwoven in Extension's mission to serve communities. By embracing diversity, equity, and inclusion, we amplify our impact, address systemic inequities, and forge a more just and inclusive path toward collective success. There is no way back; there is only a path forward.

CVH: Given past practices, restorative policies are required to address a long history of the U.S. Department of Agriculture's (USDA) disparate treatment of the diverse farming community. By diverse I not only mean farmers of color who have been historically excluded—this also requires taking account of the needs of noncorporate white farmers as well who aren't agribusinesses masquerading as family farms. It also includes service to urban areas. In the early twentieth century in South Carolina, in addition to working with rural areas, there were extension workers doing work described as "mill projects." Urban work included family farms, home demonstration clubs for urban wives, and 4-H for children. As groups in urban areas work to address food deserts and food insecurity, the extension service needs to reach out to help these groups and even people at the street level develop ways to strategize and maximize their food dollars through innovative farming practices.

DEI in extension practices also requires reparations for farmers—especially nonwhite ones—who have been financially robbed by extension practices that relied on local white control that left these farmers under resourced—for example, when during COVID Donald Trump bought off Midwestern (mostly white) farmers (McCrimmon, 2020). Those farmers took those benefits without consideration of diversity equity and inclusion, but then turned around and sued when the Biden Administration tried to compensate for historic practices that resulted in catastrophic Black land loss (Jordan, 2021). They just can't seem to get it right (see Bustillo, 2023).

CC: First, I think DEI has different definitions between PWIs, HBCUs, and tribal colleges and universities (TCUs), and my experience is limited to PWIs. Within PWIs, I see divisions within Extension between DEI as quantifiable, desirable achievements based on demographic—usually racial or ethnic—characteristics of program participants, partner organizations, and staff, in order to comply with external expectations or laws, and DEI as a set of ongoing practices or strategies to improve Extension programs and modus operandi through digging deep into questions of how things are done, for whom, and how to improve them to meet Extension's mission to serve communities. The two perspectives can be integrated but often seem to conflict with one another. I observe in disbelief the contradiction that goes seemingly unnoticed by others when I hear references to the "And Justice For All" posters that must be visible during programs that say programs are open to everyone, with elisions making it sound like the posters are titled "injustice for all." DEI must not be reduced to compulsory sign posting, literally or metaphorically.

LK: When I reflect on Extension and DEI, I feel disillusioned. Ours is a history that hasn't been accounted for, because if it were, what would the words "diversity, equity, and inclusion" mean for the Indigenous people who were violently dispossessed of their land? If DEI were a primary concern of Extension, we would not have three separate and *unequal* Extension systems. My experiences in PWI Extension are that DEI is one-dimensional. For example, we tend to focus our outreach to rural distressed areas, and we claim that as "DEI." However, alignment with DEI principles should compel us to include intersectionality in our approach, yet our missions, values, programs, and relationships tend to ignore it altogether. This is why "rural" is often code for "white" in PWI Extension. My experience at an HBCU Extension system included being asked to remove any references to historical and contemporary inequities in care and access to health care services for Black individuals and communities from an Extension fact-sheet publication that I authored. The rationale I was provided at the time was that the fact sheet needed to be for a "general audience," which I understood as prioritizing oppressors' feelings over honesty. What is it about being confronted with stark inequities for Black individuals and communities that makes white people so uncomfortable? I reflect on the ways that DEI is (mis)interpreted, intentionally and unintentionally, in Extension—at the expense of real people forced into racialization, discrimination, oppression—always in service of their oppressors. This ongoing reflection informs my commitment to disrupting the Extension system in pursuit of health justice and the liberation of all oppressed people.

Précis

Several common threads emerge across these perspectives. Extension fundamentally relied on DEI in its foundation. Dr. Lunsford reminds us how important it is to remember that without "DEI" in this country, we would not have Extension. It was a Black innovation. But integration of DEI strategies to ensure participation of all people or to assuage disparities is more complicated in Extension. This is reflected in historical work about racial segregation in the Extension system (Harris, 2008). As Dr. Hairston Green points out, white leaders professed disbelief that African Americans had the capacity to understand research, and they used this as rationale for shutting down early Extension work, replacing it with a whites-only system. Dr. Harris goes on to note the long history of USDA's disparate treatment of farmers of color, noncorporate farmers, and urban farmers. As Dr. Cuthbertson described in their reflection at the beginning, this is history that for many PWI Extension systems has been papered over and whitewashed with ahistorical myths generated by white people with vested interests in CES, perpetuated over the years, even in present day. These historical notes are an important foundation for understanding Dr. Hairston Green's assertion that Extension was never intended to embody DEI. Trust cannot be built without this accountability to our history.

A second thread is about the rocky terrain of DEI in Extension today, which may be related to compliance, thinking deeply about how things are done, and differences between PWI, HBCU, and potentially TCU systems. Interestingly, two of our authors' experiences with both the PWI and HBCU systems shared perspectives that have some overlap. Dr. Hairston Green noted that for some HBCU systems, there may be some overlooked privileges in Extension personnel's positionalities that are obscuring their sense of the conditions that shape their communities' health. Dr. Kennedy also noted that as an employee of an HBCU, she was asked to remove mention of racial inequities in an Extension fact sheet prior to publishing it, so that it would be "suitable for a general audience." This may not be a universal experience for employees of HBCU Extension systems, but these two viewpoints do allude to the deep-rooted, multilayered, pervasive influence of and existence of racism and oppression that structure systems like Extension and the institutions that house them. It also reflects the differences in how "DEI" is defined, practiced, and implemented—which is to say, at times "compulsory" as Dr. Cuthbertson notes or also as white savior-ism as Dr. Hairston Green points out. Neither is beneficial.

A third thread is around Extension's responsibilities and needs related to DEI, to be excellent, to more quickly respond to community concerns, to co-create solutions in partnership with communities rather than assuming what appropriate solutions are to "fix" community issues, and the need for restorative policies and strategies. Extension professionals in some states face challenging new laws disallowing DEI work and will have to be creative to engage communities in the spirit of working toward health justice in all communities. Dr. Wallace Bechard mentioned the anti-DEI laws that have passed—some at the federal level, others at state and/or local levels. These laws threaten the capacity that Dr. Wallace Bechard sees in Extension to adopt a DEI lens. Dr. Harris also brought our attention to recent policy decisions, like farmer financial bailouts, that benefited mostly white farmers, one of the most traditional Extension audiences that consistently benefits from the funding allocation disparities between HBCU Extension/TCU Extension and PWI Extension. Policies that support DEI in Extension (and beyond) need our support. This includes policies that have an impact on fundamental, root drivers of health (e.g., oppression) and the resulting social, economic, commercial, environmental, and political determinants of health.

One of the most important insights in this section comes from Dr. Fonseca: "There is no way back, there is only a path forward." This acknowledges our history, complicated by both physical and structural violence, and shines a light toward the future, nudging us along, urging us to take steps toward authentic DEI. This vision is especially important given that this chapter did not receive any contributions from an Indigenous person or a TCU representative. Their relationship with U.S. land-grant universities and, ultimately, CES began with a violent land dispossession. That history has been described in detail through other sources, like the land-grab university project, and Indigenous people have provided detailed instructions on how reparations can be made to their nations, tribes, and communities. Recognizing and accounting for this is part of that forward path for CES and Health Extension.

Health Justice

LL: There is a Western African Adinkra symbol called the "Sankofa." It depicts a bird flying forward with its neck turned backward. It teaches us that to move forward we must be willing to see the past. If Extension wants to reckon with its future, it must honor and celebrate its roots. Macon and Wilcox counties located in Alabama's Black Belt region are among the first counties in the nation to be served by a Cooperative Extension system. Where are they now? What difference has Extension made in the outcomes of the lives of those living in these communities? I think when incoming and seasoned Extension professionals are versed in the history of Extension and its legacy in trying to assist those first generations of people who were rising from the depths of enslavement, we'll have a more equitable and inclusive system.

CWB: Cooperative Extension System in the United States exists in an economic and social structure that has historically created (intentionally or unintentionally) unfair or limited access to the healthcare opportunities or services that all people need to improve health outcomes in their lives. Whether responding to food access needs in local programs or pursuing grant opportunities to develop pilot programs that address health disparities within LGBTQIA+ communities, Extension is situated to reexamine its mission and commitment to the health and wellness of local communities through DEI efforts. Fields and Shaffer (2022) described diversity, equity, and inclusion as an engine of opportunity in Cooperative Extension. This engine provides more energy to understand the health discrepancies in local communities. It also examines systemic inequities and generational injustices that prevent access for all people. Therefore, for Extension to fully utilize DEI as a strategy for health justice, there must be greater focus and responses to the evolving needs of all our community members—for example, recognizing the inequities among racial and ethnic minority groups who have higher rates of poor health and diseases such as hypertension, diabetes, and heart disease (Centers for Disease Control and Prevention, 2023), and going beyond needs assessments to establish reciprocal relationships with community groups to determine how Extension can support health and wellness in ways that we are not extracting from these communities. Considering where Extension is positioned in local communities, here are a few additional thoughts for the broad spectrum of health-related community-based work:

- Examine the uniqueness and intersectionality of people's experiences and the interconnections that exist between the historical and present factors that reduce access to equitable health services and resources. This includes learning about the social determinants of health and generational health injustices that may reduce access to healthy foods and maternal healthcare.

- Update strategies in the hiring processes for health professional staff to include DEI in the competency requirements and expectations.
- Ensure that cultural humility, trauma-informed practices, emotional intelligence, and other thoughtful and affirming principles are integrated throughout all health-related work.
- Promote interdisciplinary approaches to health justice that demonstrate the connections between mental health, financial health, social health, physical health, and others.
- Provide ongoing opportunities for growth and development for staff, volunteers, and community members to learn about Extension's commitment to health justice.

DHG: Health justice stands as a grassroots initiative driven by the imperative to dismantle the intricate obstacles posed by poverty, prejudice, and layered marginalization. These hindrances have intricately thwarted individuals dwelling within low-income households, and communities, including Black enclaves, racial minorities, women, disabled individuals, newcomers to this nation, and LGBTQIA+ members. The consequences of these impediments are acutely pronounced, as they impede access to vital resources encompassing healthcare, occupational prospects, and suitable habitation. Drawing upon Extension's storied history of community engagement, notably with underrepresented and marginalized families, an opportune juncture arises for a more methodical adoption of diversity, equity, and inclusion (DEI) initiatives.

The substantial significance of our outreach lies in its capacity to edify and enmesh stakeholders. Aligned with the tenets of diversity, equity, and inclusivity, the alignment of Extension catapults participants into a paramount position. Realizing this, as Extension professionals, mandates transcendence beyond sterile data and statistics toward a more profound comprehension of our audience. This necessitates fostering an environment that resonates with diverse voices, assimilating their priorities, and orchestrating our discourse and initiatives congruently. This concerted endeavor constructs a trajectory toward an equitable and just landscape, actively acknowledging and addressing the multifaceted requisites of each individual and community.

Amid the United States, Cooperative Extension programs are orchestrating more meticulous, strategic efforts to embrace impactful strategies for engaging with the intricate realm of health justice. A particularly innovative avenue involves harnessing the power of storytelling. As a universal conduit, storytelling surmounts barriers and territorial confines, enabling Extension to hone the art of narrating not only its endeavors but the profound influence these endeavors wield on participants. Thereby, voices advocating for their health justice and communal prerequisites are amplified.

A paradigm shift away from the ethos of fixing or rescuing communities is paramount. The narrative must pivot, centering on individuals, families, and communities as partners and stakeholders, emphasizing their strengths and contributions. Moreover, a critical evaluation of current partnerships is warranted, identifying gaps and cultivating nontraditional alliances. This approach accentuates the imperative of comprehensively understanding the communities and individuals being served. Extension's historical legacy of catalyzing family transformation underscores its uniqueness; however, a risk of obsolescence looms if Extension fails to remain attuned to its beneficiaries' evolving dynamics and the cadence of emerging issues. By strategically aligning with nontraditional collaborators, well versed in the nuanced needs, aspirations, norms, and motivations of our target audiences, Extension fortifies its efficacy and ensures program longevity.

CVH: They need courage, they need commitment, they need to grow diverse leadership. This would require reaching out to the nonwhite land-grant colleges and universities. There likely isn't a critical mass of nonwhite students or faculty at the 1862 land-grant colleges and universities to build capacity of DEI voices to have an impact on local practices. White personnel should do just what Republicans want to outlaw at this point—learn about how administrative structures and policies were designed to disadvantage nonwhite farmers. (While this is the focus of my work, the late Jack Temple Kirby reaches a similar conclusion in his work *Rural Worlds Lost: The American South, 1920–1960.*)

Intersectional education and analysis of rural problems would enlighten personnel on how solutions are not one-size-fits-all. There needs to be inverse financial support. The larger and more sustainable enterprises have already been rewarded by the financial success that has permitted them to grow. Therefore, the "training wheels" need to come off. It is an issue of vital national security that we don't rely on mega farm monopolies to feed us. The nation has a vested interest in ensuring that there is competition between the sources from which we get our food. Imagine an American population put at the mercy of agricapitalists who extort our personal liberties from us in exchange for food.

Would the Extension Service adopt these recommendations at the state or federal level? Doubtful? From my research in agricultural policy it became clear that state and federal Extension services were inherently conservative and an inherently reinforcing echo chamber, partly because many federal (Washington, DC) employees began their careers in state Extension ranks. If they have privileged agricultural backgrounds, this also might contribute to their valuing marginalized farms and their agricultural enterprises as less worthy of their attention than larger agricultural enterprises.

ALF: Key actions are essential for Extension to embrace equity and justice wholeheartedly. First and foremost, we need to articulate what health justice means for us and our priorities. Second, Extension needs to understand how systems of oppression and health disparities work and what Extension´s role is in preventing the perpetuation of health disparities. Third is an honest view of how Extension is equipped to address the needs of historically underserved and/or excluded communities. Extension can grow, develop, and adapt by adopting a proactive and honest approach to be a key partner in achieving health justice across the board.

In my opinion and experience, relevant professional development for Extension professionals is crucial. Understanding power, privilege, oppression, civil rights, communication, civic engagement, and discourse is crucial to equip them with the tools to understand and address the unique needs of diverse populations. Collaborative partnerships with community leaders and organizations are also vital, as they provide insights and guidance for tailoring programs that resonate with diverse audiences.

Extension must also commit to allocating resources to support initiatives prioritizing health equity. This includes funding research projects and interventions targeting marginalized communities to address health disparities.

In addition, prioritizing the voices and perspectives of affected groups is crucial to building partnerships and creating effective and culturally relevant solutions. Moreover, leadership's commitment to fostering a culture of diversity, equity, and inclusion is essential. This can be demonstrated through policies that hold everyone accountable for promoting these values and create spaces for open dialogues that address challenges and promote ongoing learning.

Ultimately, as an extension, we are well positioned to be conveners of empowering conversations that support the co-creation of solutions to attain health justice and create lasting positive impacts by weaving diversity, equity, and inclusion into the fabric of Extension's strategies.

CC: Working toward health justice would require dreaming beyond our current system to imagine what health justice looks like, planning steps to get there, doing the work, and engaging in active processing to ensure direction, sustainability, and, most importantly, centering of marginalized voices. Health justice means people have access to care and support that enables them to thrive; that care and support will look different for each person based on their identities and social history of oppression and marginalization that shapes health risks. I don't know if health justice is possible in a country that does not guarantee healthcare for all; this is a limitation Extension cannot overcome.

To fully take on DEI to work toward health justice would require fundamentally questioning (and changing) the basis of Cooperative Extension and how different institutions are funded. It would also require intentional consideration of the shape of Extension programs. Many times, Extension programs teach participants how to cope with inhospitable circumstances without attention to what creates such circumstances—for example, budgeting meager wages in attempts to afford more food, rather than organizing efforts toward a minimum wage that is a living wage. Working toward health justice in Extension would require shifting at least some focus to policies, systems, and environments creating and sustaining health privilege, including social determinants of health that include things like the War on Drugs that disproportionately impacted Black communities. Extension could start this work by creating a policy, systems, and environments (PSE) framework for all health programs that centers DEI in every part, by having open conversations about how oppression (e.g., racism, sexism, cissexism, heterosexism, ableism) shapes health, and being a force to dismantle such oppression. The benefit of the Extension system is in being research based, and we have access to information about how oppressions result in health disparities that carry across generations. We must make the choice to act, and recognize that not to act is also a choice.

LK: Health justice requires the abolition of punitive systems and institutions and the reimagining of our society to be in alignment with everyone's needs and their liberation. In order to attain this, we must seek out new ways of being in community with communities and demand an end to punishment, surveillance, and incarceration that leads to poor health and premature death. We are positioning ourselves in Health Extension as the choice partner. In order to fulfill that role, we must be prepared to assess and intervene within our partnerships when racism and other forms of oppression are present. Medical racism and ableism must be confronted in all Extension partnerships with health care. Standards for partnerships and competencies of all staff and partners should be adhered to, rather than just talked about.

With Extension's mission to extend knowledge being generated at the university into communities, we should be questioning the connections and commitments to the communities for the scholars and researchers whose work we share and adopt. As Kaston Anderson-Carpenter writes (2021), the limitations of the ontology, epistemology, and axiology that guides most public health approaches, including Health Extension, must be critically appraised and adapted for collective lived experiences, core values, and ideals of marginalized individuals, families, and communities. Adopting approaches that center different ways of knowing and valuing knowledge is essential to adopting an approach for health justice.

Extension professionals must be able to consistently and authentically present themselves as committed to principles of DEI, belongingness, accessibility for all, and so on, so that we become known for this in our work and sought after as a true partner and accomplice. This will require structural changes to CES that contrast with the "apolitical" Extension myth that is really a smokescreen for upholding whiteness as the norm. And although structural changes are desperately needed, Extension can also no longer be a safe haven for anyone not committed to health justice.

Précis

This may be an auspicious moment for CES and Health Extension, as Dr. Hairston Green expressed. Several of our contributors have expressed doubt, wariness, or uncertainty about Extension's capacity to "get it right," as Dr. Harris stated. Still, other contributors see glimmers of hope in our capacity, in the possibility that we can change our systems to demonstrate inclusive excellence. This is what Dr. Cuthbertson refers to as "dreaming beyond what we have" or what Dr. Kennedy calls a "reimagining." But how do we do that? How can we push a system rooted in tradition toward change?

Collectively, numerous recommendations for Extension flow from the preceding section. A baseline recommendation is for Extension professionals to know and understand history, in at least three senses: the history of Extension, social and political history impacting health, and social structures impacting health. A unanimous thread in this chapter is the need to know, understand, acknowledge, and repair our history. Dr. Lunsford gifted us with her powerful evocation of a Western African Adinkra symbol, the Sankofa. This is a fitting image for a system founded on Black Americans' innovation and their love for their community, but with its own troubled history of white supremacy that is often disregarded, even as it bleeds into the present. What would our system be like today if we did not disregard the violent past of CES and, instead, honored and celebrated the true roots of Extension, the legacy of trying to realize justice for formerly enslaved people? Importantly, Dr. Harris notes that white Extension personnel especially need to know their history, and we believe this extends beyond the history of Extension, into the full history of this country, and how it has been structured to systematically disadvantage some and benefit and protect others. An important example of this in Dr. Harris's statement is the symbiosis between affluent white farmers and the USDA wherein the farmers received financial incentives and then reciprocated political support. Still, there are currently national political divides over whether or not knowing accurate history is a worthy goal, but make no mistake about our position—history is essential to our future. Understanding the generational experiences of people in our communities, as Dr. Wallace Bechard reminds us, will take courage, commitment, diverse leadership, and *honesty*. And as Dr. Hairston Green points out, without the Sankofa reflected in our endeavors, there is a looming threat of obsolescence on the horizon. We can ensure our longevity, and thereby our relevance, by adopting the recommendations outlined in this chapter. Choosing not to or choosing a state of inaction is no longer viable for CES or Health Extension.

Our mission in CES is to extend the university to the people, sharing the knowledge and research being generated there, to improve people's lives. This lacks a critical awareness of what forms of knowledge are being valued most and which forms are being discounted. Dr. Kennedy suggests adoption of approaches that center different ways of knowing. Many of our authors mentioned prioritization of community voices and the inclusion of storytelling—a rich cultural tradition reflected in the positionalities of our contributors and their words so carefully prepared for this chapter. Storytelling is a powerful tool for healing, community development, and celebrating relationships (Beltrán & Begun, 2014; Toliver, 2021).

A key ingredient to systems change that is often overlooked is accountability. Dr. Fonseca suggests implementation of policies that insist on accountability and restructure our systems to provide that. A complementary solution is to make the system inhospitable for those who reject or decline DEI, as Dr. Kennedy describes. Either way, accountability will afford us credibility, it will build trust, and it will fundamentally change who we are and what we do.

A second recommendation is to diversify Extension's workforce, especially leadership. Many authors mentioned the need for changes to our workforce. Strategies suggested were updated competencies and expectations, hiring practices, and ongoing professional development. This is particularly important given that many federal leaders began their careers in state Extension offices, as Dr. Harris notes. Part of this includes honestly assessing the capability for Extension to address health justice and provide professional development opportunities.

In CES, our programs are technically open to all, but as Dr. Cuthbertson described, this is sometimes contradicted by the actual reach of our efforts or how welcome people feel (or do not feel) at programs. Dr. Kennedy noted the ways that we limit our potential, especially in rural areas, by eschewing intersectionality. To be clear, intersectionality refers to the interwoven social systems of power that create privilege and marginalization, with attention to how for each next marginalized identity one holds, oppression is not additive but exponential (Collins, 2002; Crenshaw, 1989). Dr. Harris advises us that intersectional education is critical to doing DEI in Extension. This should be part of the workforce development previously mentioned and should be reflected in the hiring of marginalized workers, especially from Black and tribal institutions, in addition to the materials, programs, and reporting that our systems do.

A third recommendation is to disrupt the way things have been done, including rectifying existing partnerships that may work counter to health justice and building new partnerships. The way Extension works must evolve with communities. Collaboration is a hallmark of community engagement, and Extension surely has a diverse network of partners from state to state. Authors suggest evaluating the nature and the quality of our partnerships and quality of the partners themselves. Dr. Kennedy believes that quality partners should mirror the commitments and authentic connections that we aspire to have with our communities. This can thwart the extraction that Dr. Wallace Bechard cautions us against. Partnerships also need to be explored among the PWI, HBCU, and TCU systems. This was also recommended in Extension's new National Framework for Health Equity and Well Being (Burton et al., 2021), but it lacked any accountability or guidelines for engagement, and, most importantly, it contained zero examination of the readiness of the PWI system to be a suitable, trustworthy partner to the HBCU or TCU systems. Given our history, this assessment seems to be a pertinent first step.

A fourth recommendation is to collaborate with communities in ways that center community voices. This includes using community-specific strategies and programs instead of one-size-fits-all approaches. Still, Dr. Cuthbertson questions whether or not health justice is even possible for a nation that doesn't ensure quality, accessible, affordable health care for everyone. They also point out that our efforts are too often focused on teaching people to adapt to oppressive conditions, rather than changing the conditions themselves. Dr. Kennedy echoes this, calling our attention to the ways the punitive systems accelerate poor health and premature death. Adoption of healing frameworks, like C-HeARTS (Chioneso et al., 2020), will assist us in pivoting toward culturally relevant healing traditions and centering community voices in our collaborations.

Several contributors pointed out the need for CES to have the agility to respond to rapidly shifting and evolving community needs. It is impossible to do that if our stance is predicated on "fixing" or "rescuing" communities from their circumstances, as Dr. Hairston Green notes. Dr. Cuthbertson recommends "fundamental changes" and Dr. Kennedy "structural changes" that disallow people, programs, and funders that are not centered on DEI. There was also the suggestion to integrate trauma-informed community care—recognizing historical trauma and identity-based traumas like racism. These traumas are not just relegated to adversity in childhood, but are ongoing, compounding traumas that must be accounted for, particularly by those inflicting the trauma (Bernard et al., 2021).

This may be understood by others as a part of accountability, but I (Dr. Kennedy) believe financial reparations deserves its own space, given the severity of inequitable resource allocation, funding, theft, and the lack of attention that these have received over the years. Dr. Fonseca explains that allocation of resources must be a *commitment* of CES leaders and funders. Dr. Harris suggests "inverse financial support" as appropriate. There is some history of this with USDA (e.g., the 2023 Discrimination Financial Assistance Program [DFAP], a financial assistance program for farmers who have experienced discrimination at USDA). However, it remains to be seen whether programs like DFAP will be low-barrier and have widespread participation or whether they will be like past attempts that resulted in continued disenfranchisement (e.g., *Pigford v. Glickman*, 1999; Cowan & Feder, 2013). On top of resource allocation and financial supports, more attempts could be made by PWI Extension on behalf of the HBCU and TCU systems to restore and repair decades of disinvestment by state and federal legislatures. Finally, Indigenous leaders have long called for financial reparations for the violent dispossession that took place to create the land-grant university system and CES. Their reparations requests include returning stolen lands, allowing Indigenous people to attend land-grant universities for free, cash payments to repay stolen wealth, and more (Red Shirt-Shaw, 2020). CES should be at the front of the line advocating to university leaders, state lawmakers, and federal officials for these reparations.

Finally, as part of changing approaches, using a PSE change approach to health justice would enable Extension to work at root causes of health disparities. At the moment, PSE change work is not widespread in Health Extension. Recent research has revealed critical gaps in readiness and capacity at multiple levels for implementation of PSE change efforts in Extension (specifically, within family and consumer science; Washburn et al., 2022). But macro-level problems require macro-level solutions, and PSE changes that do not account for DEI are doomed to perpetuate discrimination and harm to individuals, families, and communities. We should incorporate policy, systems, and environmental change frameworks that center DEI, apply this to Health Extension across all program areas, and support it with resources, professional development, and rewards for adoption. Widespread integration of PSE change work can also assist with revealing the interdisciplinary nature of Health Extension and communicating to new and traditional partners that we are earnest in our commitment to DEI.

Conclusion

Diversity, equity, and inclusion are complex topics within Extension, and at times with contradictory meaning. Diversity, equity, and inclusion are core values that guide Extension's work, yet the history of Extension through T. M. Campbell's work at Tuskegee is often erased from historical storytelling in contemporary Extension organizations. The shape of DEI across 1862, 1890, and 1994 Extension systems is different. For Extension to fulfill its mission of providing research-based information to communities across the country, Extension professionals must engage in critical reflection about the shape of local communities, as well as social, political, and historical forces that created disparities and injustices we see today. The future of Extension is in working in community-driven and community-collaborative processes to co-create goals, co-identify processes to meet goals, and engage together to meet those goals; in one way, it is paying attention to and taking seriously the *cooperative* nature of Cooperative Extension. Moving forward, it will be crucial to do community-engaged work that goes beyond federal minimum compliance expectations, to engage in restorative practices that can help achieve health justice across communities.

REFERENCES

Anderson-Carpenter, K. D. (2021). Black Lives Matter principles as an Africentric approach to improving Black American health. *Journal of Racial and Ethnic Health Disparities, 8*(4), 870–878. https://doi.org/10.1007/s40615-020-00845-0

Beltrán, R., & Begun, S. (2014). "It is medicine": Narratives of healing from the Aotearoa Digital Storytelling as Indigenous Media Project (ADSIMP). *Psychology and Developing Societies, 26*(2), 155–179. https://doi.org/10.1177/0971333614549137

Bernard, D. L., Calhoun, C. D., Banks, D. E., Halliday, C. A., Hughes-Halbert, C., & Danielson, C. K. (2021). Making the "C-ACE" for a culturally-informed adverse childhood experiences framework to understand the pervasive mental health impact of racism on Black youth. *Journal of Child & Adolescent Trauma, 14*(2), 233–247. https://doi.org/10.1007/s40653-020-00319-9

Burton, D., Canto, A., Coon, T., Eschbach, C., Gutter, M., Jones, M., Kennedy, L., Martin, K., Mitchell, A., O'Neal, L., Rennekamp, R., Rodgers, M., Stluka, S., Trautman, K., Yelland, E., & York, D. (2021). *Cooperative Extension's national framework for health equity and well-being*. Extension Committee on Organization and Policy.

Bustillo, X. (2023, February 19). In 2022, Black farmers were persistently left behind from the USDA's loan system. *NPR*. https://www.npr.org/2023/02/19/1156851675/in-2022-black-farmers-were-persistently-left-behind-from-the-usdas-loan-system

Centers for Disease Control and Prevention. (2023, March 21). *What is health equity?* https://www.cdc.gov/healthequity/whatis/index.html

Chioneso, N. A., Hunter, C. D., Gobin, R. L., McNeil Smith, S., Mendenhall, R., & Neville, H. A. (2020). Community healing and resistance through storytelling: A framework to address racial trauma in Africana communities. *Journal of Black Psychology, 46*(2–3), 95–121. https://doi.org/10.1177/0095798420929468

Collins, P. H. (2002). *Black feminist thought: Knowledge, consciousness, and the politics of empowerment*. New York: Routledge.

Cowan, T., & Feder, J. (2013). *The Pigford cases: USDA settlement of discrimination suits by Black farmers*. Washington, DC: Congressional Research Service.

Crenshaw, K. (1989). Demarginalizing the intersection of race and sex: A Black feminist critique of antidiscrimination doctrine, feminist theory and antiracist politics. *University of Chicago Legal Forum, 1*(8), 139–167.

Croft, G. E. (2022). *The U.S. land-grant university system: Overview and role in agricultural research* (R45897). Washington, DC: Congressional Research Service.

Croft, G. K. (2019). *The U.S. land-grant university system: An overview* (R45897). Washington, DC: Congressional Research Service.

Extension Committee on Organization and Policy. (n.d.-a). *Implicit bias.* Diversity Equity and Inclusion. https://dei.extension.org/implicit-bias/

Extension Committee on Organization and Policy. (n.d.-b). *Microaggression development and understanding.* Diversity Equity and Inclusion. https://dei.extension.org/microaggression/ Extension

Committee on Organization and Policy. (n.d.-c). *Cultural competency.* Diversity Equity and Inclusion. https://dei.extension.org/cultural-competency

Extension Committee on Organization and Policy. (n.d.-d). *Promotion of civility.* Diversity Equity and Inclusion. https://dei.extension.org/promotion-of-civility

Extension Committee on Organization and Policy. (n.d.-e). *Social justice development.* Diversity Equity and Inclusion. https://dei.extension.org/social-justice

Extension Committee on Organization and Policy. (n.d.-f). *Organizational learning.* Diversity Equity and Inclusion. https://dei.extension.org/organizational-learning

Extension Committee on Organization and Policy. (n.d.-g). *Youth development.* Diversity Equity and Inclusion. https://dei.extension.org/youth-development

Fields, N. I., & Shaffer, T. J. (2022). *Grassroots engagement and social justice through Cooperative Extension.* East Lansing: Michigan State University Press.

Goldenstein, E. H. (1989). Booker T. Washington and Cooperative Extension. *Negro Educational Review, 40*(2), 4–14.

Haraway, D. (1988). Situated knowledges: The science question in feminism and the privilege of partial perspective. *Feminist Studies, 14*(3), 575–599. https://doi.org/10.2307/3178066

Harris, C. V. (2008). "The Extension Service is not an integration agency": The idea of race in the Cooperative Extension Service. *Agricultural History, 82*(2), 193–219. https://doi.org/10.1215/00021482-82.2.193

hooks, b. (2000). *Feminist theory: From margin to center.* London: Pluto Press.

Jordan, M. (2021, June 22). Black US farmers dismayed as white farmers' lawsuit halts relief payments. *The Guardian.* https://www.theguardian.com/us-news/2021/jun/22/black-farmers-loan-payments

Kirby, J. T. (1986). *Rural worlds lost: The American South, 1920–1960.* Baton Rouge: Louisiana State University Press.

Lorde, A. (1984). *Sister outsider.* Berkeley, CA: Crossing Press.

Lorde, A. (1997). The uses of anger. *Women's Studies Quarterly, 25*(1/2), 278–285.

McCrimmon, R. (2020, July 14). "Here's your check": Trump's massive payouts to farmers will be hard to pull back. *Politico.* https://www.politico.com/news/2020/07/14/donald-trump-coronavirus-farmer-bailouts-359932

Pigford v. Glickman (U.S. District Court April 14, 1999).

Qin, D. (2016). Positionality. In *The Wiley Blackwell encyclopedia of gender and sexuality studies*. https://onlinelibrary.wiley.com/doi/abs/10.1002/9781118663219.wbegss619

Red Shirt-Shaw, M. (2020). *Beyond the land acknowledgement: College "LAND BACK" or free tuition for native students*. Hack the Gates. https://www.communitycommons.org/entities/53f92e12-94e1-4286-9e8b-58cc3ad34986

Smith–Lever Act. (1914). H.R. 7951, 63rd Congress.

Takacs, D. (2003). How does your positionality bias your epistemology? *Thought & Action, 27*. https://repository.uclawsf.edu/faculty_scholarship/1264

Toliver, S. R. (2021). *Recovering Black storytelling in qualitative research: Endarkened storywork*. New York: Routledge.

Venkatapuram, S. (2013). *Health justice: An argument from the capabilities approach*. Hoboken, NJ: John Wiley & Sons.

Washburn, L., Norman-Burgdolf, H., Jones, N., Kennedy, L. E., & Jarvandi, S. (2022). Exploring Extension agent capacity and readiness to adopt policy, systems and environmental change approaches. *Frontiers in Public Health, 10*. https://doi.org/10.3389/fpubh.2022.856788

The Transformation of Extension Family and Consumer Science Programs to Health Extension

Erin L. Martinez

The land-grant university (LGU) system and the Cooperative Extension Service (CES) have continuously evolved since the late nineteenth century, yet the overall premise has remained the same—to translate research into action by extending the university to individuals and communities. To an extent, this mission has been successful. Within the Extension field of family and consumer sciences (FCS), one of four historical program areas (agriculture, community development, and 4-H youth development are the others), CES has contributed to the advancement of rural homemakers, revolutionized food safety practices and techniques, improved individual and community nutrition, assisted in the extension of early learning programs, enhanced financial literacy, and partnered to develop healthier communities. However, dynamic community needs, global challenges and advancements, and policy and funding shifts demand that CES engage in a reimagining of how it contributes to community health. It is apparent that FCS is at a critical turning point, and timing is crucial to ensure that CES programs remain relevant, effective, and responsive to the changing landscape of public health and community well-being.

This chapter guides readers through an exploration of what has shaped the history and purpose of CES, home economics, FCS, and the evolution of programming as it relates to human health. Several calls to action encourage readers to pursue culturally appropriate, rigorous, and upstream interventions and programs that address the social determinants of health (SDOH) and vital conditions for health and well-being. This historical review sets the stage for the proposed recommendations that can assist in the transformation of FCS programs to Health Extension.

Extension Beginning: Home Economics and Family and Consumer Sciences

From "movable school" stagecoaches and home demonstration kitchens to food pantry development and vaccination campaigns, the implementation of education within CES has undeniably transformed. By the early twentieth century, scholars noted that CES professionals exhibited varying relationships and styles of engagement with the public. Smith and Wilson (1930) characterized three stages, with the first being the expert model in which CES presumed to know what topics were important and taught consumers to follow their lead. Next, a process of program development based on the needs of the local community was developed, where "farmers, for the first time in their experience, were given an opportunity by the extension service to gather around to study and plan action on their problems" (Morris, 1937, 3). The third phase emphasized collaborative and research-driven decision making in which CES and consumers "together made the analysis of conditions, together selected the outstanding needs, and together made a program to make those needs" (Smith & Wilson, 1930, 132). Today, CES is a blend of these stages, serving both as the expert and as a community-needs-driven organization that is heavily influenced by stakeholders (Lindemann et al., 2022; Meendering et al., 2023; Vines, 2017). Yet CES needs to be self-critical about serving only as experts and to be careful with partners who tell individuals how to be healthy. Instead, to be more effective, CES should shift to improving community health via the model of Health Extension. The context of human health is the space in which to enrich communication and vision for CES's effectiveness and success.

Home Economics in Academia and the Land-Grant Institution

Home economics, an academic field of study that precipitated the FCS program area within CES, is believed to date back to 1873, when a "radical" for-credit domestic economy department was developed by Kansas State University (Gunn, 1995, 2). The curriculum courses related to nutrition and food preservation, which were deeply rooted in the sciences of chemistry, nutrition, and sanitation. Additional fields of study in the curriculum included sewing, clothing and textiles, housekeeping, and home management. Despite the innovative nature of "the Kansas plan," the curriculum was often denounced as "a conservative attempt to keep educated women locked into domesticity" and "dismissed as offering little more than a sewing and cooking course for women" (Gunn, 1995, 3). Still, others believed the program to be "radical for its day in that it successfully encouraged women to prepare for self-supporting careers as well as traditional roles" (3), thus giving women the opportunity to become an "industrialist instead of a butterfly" (6). Overwhelmingly, however, home economics was viewed as a way to "enrich the daily lives of *women* . . . to make meaningful to them the tasks which were theirs to perform, by the creative use of the experiences which the average women's environment supplies" (New York State College of Home Economics, 1942, 129).

With the passage of the Smith-Lever Act of 1914, LGUs became a natural fit for home economics, as its applied approaches to learning (and content complementary to agriculture) fit well within the CES vision. National funding for CES established a platform for disseminating science-based information, and home economists needed academic growth and innovation for practices they were already doing in local communities (Heggestad,

2023). More academic programs emerged as LGU leaders began to acknowledge, or at least tolerate, the significant contribution that advanced knowledge and skills in home economics could have on the safety and well-being of individuals, families, and communities (Vincenti, 1997).

Despite the need and an ideological academic fit, home economics faced significant early challenges integrating into LGUs (Dreilinger, 2021; Stage & Vincenti, 1997). Home economics was regarded as a less prestigious, "soft science" discipline primarily associated with women's roles in domesticity. Many argued that the needs of the country, and ultimately human success, were dependent upon a "deep, sturdy science and technology foundation," the base of which is "education in science and mathematics" (National Commission on Excellence in Education, 1983, 33). Gendered biases have persisted and made it difficult for home economics scholars to assert the field's academic contributions and relevance, especially within disciplines that are both male-dominated and centered on agriculture. A bidirectional connection between home economics and agriculture has, over time, embraced food as a common opportunity and challenge. Within CES, food has been a hallmark of its work in a myriad of contexts, including food production and sustainability, farm productivity, agricultural marketing, food safety, and nutrition.

There is a clear opportunity to unite the efforts of agriculturalists and home economists in the realm of public and community health, or Health Extension. For instance, there have been strategic efforts in some states to partner agricultural safety programming, typically offered by agriculture-focused educators (e.g., AgrAbility and farm safety), with mental health, falls prevention, and chronic disease prevention and management education, all of which are typically led by FCS educators (K. Funkenbush, personal communication, November 2022). These have been effective, in part, because colleagues in agriculture facilitated FCS access to audiences that they have worked with for decades. On a national scale, collaboration between the academic fields is evident in the 2009 establishment of the U.S. Department of Agriculture (USDA). One Health Joint Working Group, an effort to coordinate the sciences of health, people, plants, environment, and animals to improve health outcomes for humans and animals (USDA, 2016). Still, the value of FCS within CES continues to be questioned by some, and it has been a challenge for many agriculture educators to "see themselves fitting into" health-focused work, particularly when the terms "public health" and "community health" are used. Conversely, nonagricultural Extension professionals have also been excluded or underrepresented in historically agricultural programming areas, even when the initiatives require, or would benefit from, cross-program collaborations (Bloom et al., 2020).

Home Economics in Communities and Its Growing Relevance: Early to Mid Twentieth Century

Into the early twentieth century, home economics outreach was recognized for focusing on needs such as food preservation and conservation, cookery, textiles, homemaking, and home management, which were often implemented through home demonstrations with groups of women. Early programming focused on food preservation and safety through girls' canning clubs, gardening, and sanitation demonstrations (Hart et al., 1996). Over time, the work of home economics agents, volunteers, and homemaker groups expanded to include "hot school lunch programs, home and community sanitation, physical fitness, communicable disease, home care of the sick, home improvement, landscape gardening, and control of household pests" (Hart et al., 1996, 4). The field pursued a rapid response strategy during the flu epidemic in 1917 and World War II, in which CES addressed food shortages and rationing, increased production of foodstuffs, aided in the remodeling and repairing of clothing, and built victory gardens. Here, home economics began to stretch its priorities from traditional domesticity and homemaking to more purposefully addressing individual and community health. Notably, the World War II response was funded by various government entities (i.e., Temporary Emergency Relief Administration, U.S. Office of Education, USDA, and the War Production Board) and was one of the early significant funding accomplishments for the field of Home Economics outside of the Smith-Lever Act. Postwar programming efforts resulted in home economics within CES gaining visibility.

Even with this increased recognition, there was considerable instability in human capital within home economics endeavors, as women were typically hired as summer staff (coinciding with the canning and gardening season), with little resources for supplies and equipment, or were needed only temporarily for rapid-response efforts. Women and home economics were often at a capacity disadvantage, and the agriculture sector remained white male dominant and patriarchal. It took powerful movements by large groups of enthusiastic women to push back against the exclusionary leadership of white males.

Early advances in the field were primarily accomplished through collaborative national organizations, including the following: the International Federation for Home Economics (1908), the American Home Economics Association (1909), the Home Economics section of the American Association of Land-Grant Colleges (1920), the Family and Consumer Sciences Education Association (1927), the USDA Bureau of Home Economics (1927), the National Extension Association of Family and Consumer Sciences (1933), Future Homemakers of America (1945), and the Council of Administrators of Family and Consumer Sciences (1966). There are even more examples from early efforts, and many of these listed organizations still operate today under revised names.

Home Economics and Its Growing Relevance: Mid to Late Twentieth Century

Transformations in the field's foci and identity sparked divergences in the historical composition of home economics, particularly within academia. Over time, nutrition, commonly perceived as the more scientific aspect of home economics, was often parceled out to form its own unique department of nutritional sciences or merged with agricultural food science programs (Brandt, 2022; Rossiter, 1995). Other fields of study that stemmed from traditional home economics, such as chemistry (e.g., household cleaning chemicals, pH of cleaning products) and engineering (e.g., household appliance development and repair, energy efficiency), remained male dominated, associated with the "hard sciences," and were also purposefully distanced from the field of home economics. Many of the remaining home economics disciplines shifted to what are now human development and family science, an intriguing shift as those departments were primarily dominated by men yet largely considered a "soft science." Many of these changes occurred simply because more men had the opportunity (and college scholarship funding) to earn doctoral degrees in these fields, were hired into faculty positions, and advanced their way to deanships and various leadership positions (e.g., Dreilinger, 2021; Rossiter, 1995). Concurrently, early funding from federal agencies (e.g., the National Institutes of Health, National Science Foundation), often led by men, continued to provide significant opportunities to the "hard sciences," with only very modest increases for home economics in the late 1960s, early 1970s, and early 2000s. At the same time, federal funding for home economics (as measured by the term "social sciences") decreased by 23.4 percent between 2007 and 2017, while engineering and environmental sciences saw increases of 23.6 percent and 20.7 percent, respectively (American Association for the Advancement of Science, 2022). As gendered redefinitions, conceptualizations, and reorganizations of home economics continued, the field evolved into what is now known as FCS.

Although the field seemed to continue its struggle within academia, Home Economics Extension—today's FCS Extension—moved beyond the scope of "the home" to meet changing societal needs and gender roles (Hart et al., 1996). The Civil Rights and Feminist movements in the 1960s, advancement of science linking diet, exercise, and disease, and calls to advocate for environmental preservation all provided bases for disrupting the traditional nature of the field (Clancy, 1999). Women working outside of the home and shifting domestic responsibilities provided the opportunity for FCS to embrace personal leadership and organizational development, adult literacy, modern technologies, emergency preparedness, money management, and bookkeeping (Clancy, 1999; Hart et al., 1996).

The ever-evolving identity of home economics and FCS is evident in the names. One of the earliest reported names for the field was "domestic economy" (1844–1899), which was then followed by "home economics" (1899–1993), the name that is commonly used to refer to the field's history. It was not until the early 1990s, when attendees at the Scottsdale Initiative came together to explore the field's purpose and values, that a name change to family and consumer sciences was ultimately recommended (Simerly et al., 2000). Today, that term is very much alive in academic departments, CES divisions or units, and the job titles of Extension professionals. Even so, many FCS programs are reimagining descriptors and position titles such as Family and Community Wellness (e.g., North Dakota State University Extension), Health and Nutrition (e.g., Michigan State University Extension), Community Health Extension (e.g., Washington State University Extension, Kentucky State University Extension), Health and Well-Being (e.g., University of Delaware Extension), and Family and Community Health Extension (e.g., Oregon

State University Extension, Prairie View A&M Extension, Texas A&M AgriLife Extension). A similar progression has occurred at the national level. In 1966, the Association of Public and Land-Grant Universities (APLU) started a Board on Home Economics, and in 1995 the APLU changed the name to Board on Human Sciences (APLU, n.d.). In 2022, the APLU again updated the name to reflect health (now known as the APLU Board on Health and Human Sciences).

Interestingly, there is a powerful connection between job title and a person's professional identity and how others perceive their professional responsibilities (Neary, 2014). This suggests that what the field calls itself has considerable impact on the work it does and how community health partners may view FCS Extension. Perhaps adopting a systemwide name for the field, such as Health Extension, would assist in the professional identity of CES staff, while also generating more visibility for the field among health-focused private, state, and federal partners and funders. Further, the purposeful pursuit of Health Extension provides the means to reframe and differentiate FCS within the LGU academic structure that can result in enhanced partnerships, education, funding, and research.

A Shift to Health: The Twenty-First Century

Human health has experienced a significant and damaging decline in the past two decades, as measured by outcomes such as lowering life expectancy, the devastating effects of COVID-19, skyrocketing rates of chronic disease, high mortality rates, increasing rates of substance use disorders, declining self-rated physical and mental well-being, and more. Health is threatened by dynamic national and global crises such as emerging infectious diseases and potential pandemics, climate change, natural disasters, and global food security (e.g., Ansah & Chiu, 2023; Arias et al., 2022; Case & Deaton, 2017). An underlying threat to equitable health for all is racism. For CES to transform yet again, it is imperative to address racism as a public health issue and to pursue health equity and justice as a means toward liberation.

Forming Cooperative Extension's Role in Contemporary Public Health: SNAP-Ed and EFNEP

SNAP (Supplemental Nutrition Assistance Program), which began as the Food Stamp Program in 1939 (USDA, 2018), provides food assistance benefits to low-income individuals and families, helping them meet essential grocery and nutritional needs that are vital to their health. This antihunger initiative is a lifeline for the more than forty-two million families served (USDA, 2023a), many of which include vulnerable populations such as families with children (65 percent), older adults, and individuals with disabilities (36 percent combined). The critically under-resourced individuals and families who receive SNAP benefits are eligible to engage in and benefit from the resources of SNAP-Education (SNAP-Ed). SNAP-Ed is a federally appropriated program that evaluates community needs to offer tailored interventions that encourage healthy eating habits, an uptake of physical activity, and a reduction of obesity and chronic disease rates among low-income individuals and families of all ages. SNAP-Ed engages with its clientele in various forms, including direct evidence-based education, behavior change interventions, social marketing, and policy, systems, and environmental (PSE) changes.

EFNEP (the Expanded Food and Nutrition Education Program) is a federally appropriated program operated through 1862 and 1890 LGUs that utilizes education to support individual's efforts toward self-sufficiency, nutritional health, and well-being. Like SNAP recipients, EFNEP families are significantly deprived of equitable community resources, and more than 80 percent report living at or below the poverty line (USDA, 2023b). Conversely, the intended audience for EFNEP resources is low-income families, youth, and children (including those responsible for feeding young children), whereas SNAP-Ed is intended to support lower income individuals across the life span. An additional legislative characteristic of EFNEP is the use of a peer educator (paraprofessional) model. That is, the paraprofessionals who provide the services typically come from the communities they serve, and share lived experiences with their clientele (e.g., economic level); this is not a requirement for SNAP-Ed educators and instructors.

These programs represent significant, long-standing efforts that have cemented CES as a vehicle for nationwide health efforts, funding investments, and federal and state commitments. CES has received funding to implement EFNEP education since the late 1960s, and as EFNEP funds became more constrained, CES leveraged its expertise in nutrition education with lower income audiences to seek additional funding. In 1988, CES professionals in Brown County, Wisconsin, capitalized on the opportunity to secure additional federal dollars by committing state and local funds via a contract with the state's food stamp agency. These state and local contributions resulted in an equal amount of federal Food Stamp Program (SNAP) dollars from the U.S. Department of Agriculture's (USDA) Food and Nutrition Service (FNS) being allocated for additional nutrition education. Given CES's grassroots presence in communities and its successful history with nutrition education, LGUs became the primary contractors for SNAP-Ed. In 1992, seven LGUs were engaged in SNAP-Ed using $661,000 in federal funds. By 2004, SNAP-Ed and EFNEP were core CES programs in all fifty states and accounted for most state and local SNAP-Ed funding nationally, nearly $460 million (USDA, 2023c). Today, seventy-six LGUs conduct SNAP-Ed and EFNEP through CES in all fifty states. The FNS estimates fiscal year 2024 allocations for SNAP-Ed at $516 million (USDA, 2023d), and USDA reports a $90 million budget for EFNEP in fiscal year 2024 (USDA, 2023e).

SNAP-Ed National Framework

USDA's evolving funding requirements for community nutrition education programs have expanded CES's role to move beyond expert-model education to also include conducting PSE changes with sites and partners, indirect activities (e.g., mass communication, social media, material distribution, health fairs), and providing farm-to-institution education (e.g., schools). Specifically, SNAP-Ed identifies three distinct yet complimentary approaches, namely, individual or group-based direct nutrition education, health promotion, and intervention strategies; comprehensive, multilevel interventions at multiple complementary organizational and institutional levels; and community and public health approaches to improve nutrition and obesity prevention (USDA, 2023c). The fundamentals of these approaches mirror those recommended by CES at a national level (via the 2021 Cooperative Extension National Framework for Health Equity and Well-Being; see Burton et al., 2021) with one critical caveat—receiving SNAP-Ed and EFNEP funding requires the implementation and evaluation of these research-based approaches, whereas for the broader FCS programming area, these only serve as recommendations.

Because of the federal guidelines and requirements for SNAP-Ed and EFNEP to which CES is held accountable, there stems an interesting implication for contemporary CES efforts—tensions between compliance and the workforce. For one, "People simply do not like being told what to do." A statewide SNAP-Ed and EFNEP coordinator reported in 2023 (anonymous personal communication) that "recruiting" generalized CES FCS professionals to take on SNAP-Ed or EFNEP responsibilities (programming and/or supervisory roles) is nearly impossible because there exists a false perception that it requires them to relinquish creativity or control of their work while taking on a burdensome set of mandated responsibilities, programming, evaluation, and reporting. There is a considerable reliance on paraprofessionals (47 percent of personnel FTEs nationwide; Yetter & Tripp, 2020) to carry out SNAP-Ed and EFNEP initiatives, but workforce and hiring practices have not kept up with what the federal legislation requires of these programs. Historically, job descriptions for SNAP-Ed and EFNEP paraprofessionals focused primarily on the candidate's ability to provide education on nutrition-focused topics. As funding guidelines have changed to include PSE approaches, job descriptions and pay rates for paraprofessionals have generally not been updated to reflect the experience and skills required to effectively implement this work. Further, broad-scale standards for core competencies and upskilling paraprofessionals are limited and prove to be another major challenge for the SNAP-Ed and EFNEP workforce (Baker et al., 2023). Given persistent and growing staffing considerations, the 2022 SNAP-Ed Needs Assessment Toolkit (Gleason et al., 2022) draws particular attention to workforce readiness and training and suggests that strengthening the workforce's capacity to implement health equity frameworks should be considered a primary goal. In November 2023, the Association of SNAP Nutrition Education Administrators (ASNNA) Race, Health, and Social Equity Committee published a collection of essays in a position paper, "A Roadmap to Equity in SNAP-Ed" (ASNNA, 2023). This roadmap calls on "practitioners to be better partners, for funders to expand guidance, and for administrators to envision and implement projects that are shaped, planned, implemented, and evaluated with the guidance of people who experience nutrition insecurity most acutely and who have historically been excluded, exploited, underserved, and under-resourced" (7).

These workforce and administrative considerations are only exacerbated by mismatched funding and values that some SNAP-Ed and EFNEP programs within CES experience when compared to the broader scope of FCS. SNAP-Ed and EFNEP allocations typically bring in the largest proportion of grant dollars within a state's FCS program area. For example, 52.6 percent of FCS funding across the North Central Extension twelve-state region in 2014 was SNAP-Ed and EFNEP, as cited in the Battelle Report (2015). Despite this contribution in funding, some state program leaders report a persistent undervaluation of SNAP-Ed and EFNEP in terms of their states' staffing priorities, resource allocations, technical assistance, and base CES budget allocations. There is also notable separation between state administrators/specialists and local SNAP-Ed and EFNEP educators or paraprofessionals. Local staff (i.e., county-based) are often supervised and trained at the local level, rather than a state FCS level (or other core CES program area) that could provide more comprehensive training and professional development. State-level specialist support outside of SNAP-Ed and EFNEP varies among disciplines such that 74 percent of SNAP-Ed and EFNEP coordinators report external support from nutrition specialists or faculty, versus 52 percent in general FCS, and 28 percent in 4-H youth development program areas (Schneider, 2014). This disconnect across program areas leaves significant opportunity for bidirectional relationships and collaborative program growth.

The programming and intervention framework of SNAP-Ed and EFNEP can serve as a roadmap for the larger FCS programming area, with successes and pain points serving as valuable learning opportunities for the system's necessary transformation to Health Extension. SNAP-Ed and EFNEP have the closest alignment with the goals and outcomes of Health Extension and are among the most impactful programs implemented by the broader FCS system in the last few decades. Annually, SNAP-Ed engages with 1.7 million participants through direct education, reaches 27.6 million via social marketing campaigns, and affects nearly three million individuals via PSE changes that prioritize nutritional support (Yetter & Tripp, 2020). EFNEP reaches five hundred thousand low-income adults and families each year, of whom 70 percent self-report being of minority status and 75 percent live at or below the poverty line (USDA, 2022). Although obtaining recent data on the reach of generalized FCS programs proves to be challenging, a 2015 report indicated that 89 percent of the 5.3 million total direct contacts in a twelve-state CES region were in food, nutrition, and health, 63 percent of which was attributable to SNAP-Ed and EFNEP (Battelle, 2015). When SNAP-Ed and EFNEP are excluded, the remaining FCS provides services to a small portion of the population. Considering the achievements of SNAP-Ed and EFNEP, along with their contemporary evidence-based approaches and extensive outreach to individuals and families, it becomes apparent that FCS should emulate the transformative strategies employed by these successful and important community nutrition education programs.

Transforming Family and Consumer Sciences to Health Extension

FCS has adapted continuously to respond to the ever-changing needs of individuals, families, and communities. To an extent, those served by CES have benefited. However, these historic organizations find themselves in a different place now. Monumental challenges lie ahead, and there is an urgent need to confront global threats to human health. CES is primed for transformation, and the moment has arrived to empower systems to address the SDOH and vital conditions for health and well-being in the pursuit of equity and health justice.

Cooperative Extension's First National Framework for Health and Wellness

Dr. Daryl Buchholz (former chair of the Extension Committee on Organization and Policy) made a now well-known statement in 2014 that called upon CES to "do for the nation's health what it did for American agriculture" (Braun et al., 2014, 2). This statement was a systemwide call to action for health in CES and sparked awareness and debate about possible roles CES could play within public health. The first attempt at a national framework to guide CES's health work was completed in 2014 (Braun et al., 2014). The model centered on increasing the number of Americans who are healthy at every stage of life via the identification of partners and priorities utilizing a social ecological lens. This was CES's first national document that introduced the SDOH and a complementary approach to CES's direct education work: PSE. Buy-in to the framework, however, varied widely depending on geographic location, role within CES, length of time working within the system, and administrative support or views. Some state administrators and program leaders led mini-conferences, traveled to share strategies and models, and touted the recommendations at every opportunity. Other state systems largely ignored the movement or viewed it as a national push for something that would negatively "change Extension as we know it."

Added variability with buy-in occurred among perhaps the most vital stakeholders in this effort—local, grassroots CES professionals. Some early adopters embraced the notion that CES can engage in true, meaningful change and look at issues larger than those that can be presented at noontime lunch-n-learns. Other, often more seasoned, professionals were staunchly opposed, with one CES professional saying (anonymous personal communication), "If this is the way Extension is going, I'm out of here." Still others were indifferent or simply did not understand—or care to understand—the model and its purpose.

Regardless, the 2014 national framework sparked momentum to change the scope of health work within CES. Some state systems formally restructured their identity and name, changing from FCS to an iteration of Family and Community Wellness or Community Health. Since 2014, more FCS professionals have been hired with public health backgrounds, the National Health Outreach Conference gained traction, the lexicon of "health" flourished, and awareness of CES among larger-scale funders began to increase (Burton et al., 2021).

Importantly, larger scale, evidence-based efforts emerged and were successfully implemented in some states. Readers should seek out the 2018 (volume 6) special series in the *Journal of Human Sciences Extension* for a collection of articles that used the 2014 national framework. Another example is the Michigan State University (MSU) Health

Extension Model that was and continues to be a groundbreaking effort that builds sustainable community infrastructure that supports human health promotion and research (Dwyer et al., 2017). This model built fruitful partnerships with the MSU College of Human Medicine and identified strategies to improving health outcomes via building partnerships, preparing CES educators for participation in research, increasing primary care patient referrals and enrollment in CES health programs, and exploring innovative funding opportunities (Dwyer et al., 2017). Efforts across CES have been impressive, resulting in hundreds of partnerships, increased awareness of CES professionals and programs, collaborative connections with campus researchers, increased grant funded projects, and more. These early successes generated opportunities for considerable grant funding in the areas of opioid misuse, farm stress, and mental health literacy.

Other institutions have seen meaningful programming successes since the release of the 2014 national framework. Notably, as of 2022, there were nineteen Rural Opioid Technical Assistance grantees from LGUs—a program supported by the Department of Health and Human Services that develops and disseminates programming and training for rural opioid issues (Substance Abuse and Mental Health Services Administration, 2022). In addition, an interagency agreement between the Centers for Disease Control and Prevention and the National Institute of Food and Agriculture (NIFA) funded CES nationally to provide immunization education and engagement through EXCITE—the Extension Collaboration on Immunization Teaching and Engagement (Extension Foundation, 2023). Though there are many other examples that could be shared, CES has continued to prove its capacity to influence the development of healthy individuals, families, and communities. However, this work of transforming traditional FCS to Health Extension is only beginning, and there are vast challenges and opportunities ahead.

Embracing Shortcomings

Despite the successes of health initiatives and investment from large-scale state and federal partnerships to date, CES must continue to revolutionize its work to better address emerging needs in real time by engaging in purposeful health outreach on a much broader scale. To successfully accomplish this—with more than just lip service—there needs to be critical reflection, discussion, and change. CES can provide educational programs all day, every day, and still have little influence on public health if there is no effort to challenge its shortcomings. The critique that follows examines a few key aspects of foundational and programmatic considerations that, if embraced together, can challenge existing conventions within CES and steer the system toward Health Extension.

Where We've Fallen Short: Foundationally and Programmatically

It would be negligent to overlook foundational challenges that CES faces. Without basic awareness and acknowledgment of these historical and systemic shortcomings, CES simply cannot advance to creating an environment of health and health equity, and certainly cannot demonstrate a commitment to health justice.

The Oppressive Past and Present of CES

Before significant advances will ever be accomplished, all CES professionals must first commit to learning more about the oppressive past and present of CES and LGUs. These systems were built upon unjust, discriminatory, and inequitable principles. To date, most CES professionals are onboarded into the organization with teachings and perception building activities that characterize the Morrill, Smith-Lever, and related Congressional Acts as life-changing, monumental movements to extend the university to all people. But looking deeper or critically, and considering consequences from history and past actions, reveals that many tragic inequities occurred as a part of this storied past and continue to exist in practices today. Without taking clear and purposeful steps to challenge our oppressive history, CES will continually lose credibility and respect among the diverse and underrepresented groups the system should be reaching. Thus, CES professionals cannot be effective community educators and changemakers by ignoring the inequities that the foundation of LGUs and CES and continued discriminatory and racist practices have caused.

Funding Disparities

LGUs and CES were founded on complex racist funding inequities that, of course, favor the predominantly white 1862 institutions. Legislative language was and continues to be plagued with ambiguities and loopholes that have caused 1890 and 1994 institutions to continually be starved of financial resources. It is well documented that Black, Indigenous, and people of color (BIPOC) face significant health disparities and inequities, yet there is a striking discrepancy between the needs of BIPOC populations and the resources allocated to the institutions that were (supposedly) established to support them. Funding disparities not only exist between institutions, but within them, as well. At state levels, Agriculture Extension is often more heavily resourced compared to human health.

Buzzwords

Diversity, inclusion, justice, and health equity. These fundamental principles contribute to social progress, innovation, and the well-being of individuals and communities. Committing to change and creating an equitable environment must serve as an integral part of the foundation of CES. Why and how systems commit to these principles must be clear; otherwise, these aspirations simply become buzzwords that are all too lightly tossed around. We need perceptions to change for greater collective action. It is frustrating to see diversity used as a check-the-box, feel-good addition to a mission statement, strategic plan, program objective, initiative focus, or evaluation report. Although there are positive intentions associated with using these terms as a demonstration of inclusivity and representation, overuse and superficial application are obvious and offensive.

In a striking example, a recently developed diversity, equity, and inclusion strategic plan by an 1862 LGU CES (institution name withheld on purpose) lists several key outcomes for creating a supportive, welcoming, inclusive, and fair working environment. Included is an instance of blatant tokenism to meet a quota: "at least one diverse representative will be appointed to [a statewide Extension advisory board]." Rather than serve their intended purpose, diversity quotas divert attention from systemic racism and clear internal structural issues, undermine authentic efforts for inclusion and equity, perpetuate the reduction of an individual's identity to their racial and ethnic background, and disregard all historical context of oppression. Statements such as these can completely erode the trust one has in their organization's willingness and capacity to pursue health equity and justice.

Misaligned Programs and Initiatives

Barn quilts. Jams and jellies. Charcuterie and butter boards. Mocktails. Air fryer and electric pressure cooker desserts. The list of misaligned programs offered by Extension is lengthy. CES must begin to seriously question what it is contributing to public health and how it is advertising and communicating its work. At a basic level, CES must be clear about the research-supported programs they offer, the demonstrated community needs being met, to whom CES is presenting or engaging, the content provided, and evidence of outcomes.

Using canning-related programming as an illustration, we can undeniably recognize the significance of food safety. Nevertheless, we must scrutinize whether this type of programming effectively reaches and addresses the needs of CES's most crucial audiences. Often, canning programs predominantly engage a relatively small demographic, consisting mainly of white, older, middle-class or even highly educated women, who typically have access to an abundance of homegrown or store-bought foods suitable for canning. In contrast, individuals with food insecurity do not enjoy the same privileges; they often lack a surplus of foods (particularly those suitable for canning) and do not have the financial means to obtain essential canning equipment and supplies.

A second example is from an August 2023 Google and Facebook search by this author for certain terms ("Instant Pot cooking class cooperative extension"; "instapot" and "extension," "Instant Pot extension") that revealed hundreds of CES educational programs and resources on this or related topics. Only 20 percent of CES program advertisements reviewed mentioned food safety, which should be a fundamental expectation for such programming. Furthermore, success stories were laden with concerning narratives such as "the most popular recipe in the class has been the New York cheesecake," and there were often questionable learning objectives such as determining whether you should buy the appliance, familiarizing oneself with "all the features and buttons," and learning how to avoid "tying up you, your oven, or stovetop."

As a system, CES must reflect: Why is there continued allocation of substantial resources to cater to small groups of predominantly white, relatively well-resourced individuals, while those most in need of CES services are missed or excluded? How are these programs meeting the emerging and devastating public health crises in the United States? How would a legislator respond to CES funds being spent to make cheesecake? CES should not compete with basic information that is readily available from other in-person, print, and online sources. Instead, CES can consider complementing contemporary interests via providing unbiased, high-impact, research- and evidence-based programming and implementing Health Extension approaches in innovative ways. A parting thought on this issue of misaligned programs: if you can find it on Pinterest, should Extension have interest?

Rigor

Compounding misaligned programming is the limited rigor of some CES programs (especially in FCS). Even when efforts may align with perceived or actual community needs (e.g., nutrition and physical inactivity), the method and execution of intervention (e.g., blender bikes) can have limited or no effectiveness. Moreover, the extent to which some of these programs are developed solely from within the limited expertise of CES rather than drawing from the vast literature is problematic. Without rigor, direct education programs can be developed and disseminated in communities with little to no oversight or accountability for utilizing research- and evidence-based materials. Although well-documented evidence-based programs exist and CES demonstrates significant impact in the utilization of those programs, the freedom of the "meeting local needs" nature of CES seems to open a loophole that sometimes allows for the avoidance of evidence-based direct education programming that requires significant investment of time, program fidelity, or evaluation. Adapting a program to meet local needs can be achieved with scientific methods, but there must be intent and purpose to do this well and with rigor. Additionally, it is not sufficient to solely rely on CES "experts" to develop, refine, deliver, and evaluate programs, particularly when the topic does not match with their educational background and expertise. LGUs and other academic communities have scholars and resources outside of CES that can and should be integrated into CES efforts, thus making it unnecessary to have a sole reliance on state-level CES specialists. CES must begin and/or continue to draw upon larger, more diverse bases of experts—not only those at LGUs—to advance its rigor, efficiency, and effectiveness.

Audience Depictions

CES has had an incredible reach to a myriad of audiences since its inception and those successes are well-recognized and valued. However, outside of SNAP-Ed and EFNEP, the system has had significant and pervasive failures in directly reaching diverse and under-resourced audiences. CES continues to disproportionately serve white, middle-class youth and older adults. This is evident in news articles, annual reports, social media, and website photographs depicting traditional FCS programming audiences, which resemble the CES professional themselves (primarily white women). Even when racial and ethnic diversity is visually depicted, the majority are stock photos that can easily be found from popular creative commons photo sites. The facts that it is so easy to see the lack of representation, and that CES programs are not always serving those with the greatest need, are concerning.

Culture

Culture is a complex, dynamic, and ever-evolving concept that influences every aspect of the human condition. Acknowledging, working to understand, and respecting cultural diversity is a moral imperative and practical necessity for building inclusive, productive, and thriving societies. There must be action-oriented, mandated expectations for cultural competence and sensitivity within CES that move beyond the minimum standard. The needs and approaches are vast, and insufficiency is expressed in some of the smallest of ways. For example, an informal review of several online program advertisements from fifteen 1862 FCS webpages reveals that direct education programs are typically offered in physical spaces where some individuals may not feel comfortable or be safe, such as places of worship (e.g., churches) or government buildings. Cultural barriers and facilitators are plentiful, yet CES has fallen short in building an environment of and expectation for cultural awareness, sensitivity, and competence (e.g., Fields & Moncloa, 2022).

Health Extension's Opportunity to Transform CES

CES is well positioned to create sustainable, meaningful community change—a true opportunity to transform Extension as a partner in community health. With more than thirty-five thousand professionals from 112 LGUs in all fifty states, its capacity is unparalleled. Although CES has foundational and programmatic challenges that must be addressed, there are vast opportunities to pursue meaningful change via educational health interventions and programs. Here, several process-focused recommendations are shared to help ignite a spark within CES professionals to continue making strides toward creating healthy, equitable communities and to serve as a way forward for Health Extension.

Expand and Build Upon (Smaller p) Programming

Whenever a CES professional is preparing to design or implement a direct-education program, they must ask themselves, "How can I take this a step further?," "How can I reach a greater number of people?," "Am I reaching the individuals that need this information the most?" There are many considerations to ensuring CES is garnering the most significant reach and impact, and constantly questioning and pushing for excellence is key. Perhaps the biggest hurdle here can be ignorance—where do I start? Following evidence-based best practices (e.g., Community Tool Box, 2023), executing multilevel interventions (e.g., Lytle, 2022), implementing evidence-based programs, and learning from leaders in the field are some key considerations for success. CES must move away from the heavy reliance on expert model and single-touch direct education (small p programming) to more purposeful community-wide efforts that strive for PSE change with multiple sectors collaborating toward achieving health equity (big P programming). This could range from coupling or stacking one-time events with additional information and larger scale PSE work with community partners rooted in addressing the SDOH and vital conditions for health and well-being.

Take Upstream Action

The popular parable of "chucking kids in the river" (Upstream, 2014) describes upstream, midstream, and downstream thinking and interventions that impact health. From a public health lens, simply put, upstream focuses on community conditions, midstream addresses individual needs, and downstream efforts include clinical interventions. All are critical to resolving public health crises and improving community and individual-level health outcomes, but taking a singular approach is ineffective. CES must transform beyond traditional direct education programming and expert knowledge (i.e., downstream education) in pursuit of upstream interventions. Ensuring that the opportunity for upstream pursuits exists within CES is paramount, with the onus falling on CES administrators and leaders to ensure value and reward for this multilevel work. This will require data-driven decision making, strong leadership, responsible use of funds, and the ability to empower local CES professionals to push their own boundaries, learn new facilitation skills, and have the courage to protect the system from naysayers, obstructionists, gatekeepers, and change-averse stakeholders.

Team Up to Dream Up

Both National Cooperative Extension health frameworks (Braun et al., 2014; Burton et al., 2021) highlight partnerships and coalitions as keys to success and reinforce that CES can play numerous roles in teaming up—convening, leading, facilitating, supporting, resourcing, hosting, and participating. There is also significant guidance on working closely with community partners to centralize efforts and capitalize on each other's knowledge and resources. Locally, CES is well known for being a great community partner and coalition member, but purpose, value, and alignment must remain a focus; just because CES is well known does not mean CES professionals have to say "yes!" to everything. Nevertheless, CES professionals must partner to make the biggest impact—that is nonnegotiable. More critical to this conversation are the partnerships CES has within the organization. The field of health is not just home economics, FCS, or Health Extension—it is all aspects of CES. But not every CES professional or administrator sees themselves fitting into health efforts. CES professionals must destroy their silos and work to complement their programming with greater health-focused efforts. Finally, CES must seek to continue building partnerships with large-scale and federal funders, health centers, researchers, public health organizations, health-oriented nonprofits, and the like. Keep in mind, though, that these organizations will need to want to work with CES, which will require (re)building systems of mutual trust, reimagining roles, and co-developing strong goals.

Demand Strong Leaders and Accountability

The progress of CES toward Health Extension is contingent upon the presence of robust and diverse leadership. Leaders with a wealth of health-related expertise, fresh perspectives, and a commitment to innovation can dismantle the status quo and create systems capable and accepting of necessary change. These ideals must be accompanied by a commitment to allocate sufficient resources to support Health Extension and, perhaps most importantly, overt demonstrations of its priority within CES. Given that members of the current cast of CES leaders are primarily male and from agriculture-focused disciplines, there is a significant barrier to meaningfully advancing Health Extension. Therefore, there exists responsibility for all levels of CES and its stakeholders to advance this mission including at the local level (CES professionals, their boards and county commissioners, and stakeholders) and among regional and state specialists, CES administrators, funders, higher education administrators, APLU, USDA NIFA, FNS, and beyond. Together, these systems must hold leaders and themselves accountable, change metrics against which the system's success is measured, set transformational priorities, and demand a level of achievement that pushes CES out of the past. Doing less is a disservice to the system and the potential it has to contribute to the health, well-being, and health equity of individuals, families, and communities.

The needs are vast. The evidence is here. The time is now. Who will act?

REFERENCES

American Association for the Advancement of Science. (2022, November). *Research by science and engineering discipline: Total by discipline, 1970—2021.* [Data set.] American Association for the Advancement of Science. https://www.aaas.org/programs/r-d-budget-and-policy/research-science-and-engineering-discipline

Ansah, J. P., & Chiu, C. T. (2023). Projecting the chronic disease burden among the adult population in the United States using a multi-state population model. *Frontiers in Public Health, 10.* https://doi.org/10.3389/fpubh.2022.1082183

Arias, E., Tejada-Vera, B., Kochanek, K., & Ahmad, F. B. (2022). *Provisional life expectancy estimates for 2021.* Report No. 23. U.S. Department of Health and Human Services National Vital Statistics Systems. https://www.cdc.gov/nchs/data/vsrr/vsrr023.pdf

Association of Public Land-Grant Universities. (n.d.). *Board on Health and Human Sciences.* https://www.aplu.org/members/ commissions/food-environment-and-renewable-resources/board-on-health-and-human-sciences

Association of SNAP Nutrition Education Administrators (ASNNA). (2023, November). *A roadmap to equity in SNAP-Ed.* https://snapedtoolkit.org/training/programs/a-roadmap-to-equity-in-snap-ed-position-paper-introduction

Baker, S. S., Cunningham-Sabo, L., Lillemor, K., Franck, K. M., & Mullins, J. (2023). Development of EFNEP and SNAP-Ed core competencies in the land-grant university system. *Journal of Nutrition Education and Behavior*, 55(1), 30–37. https://doi.org/10.1016/j.jneb.2022.10.001

Battelle. (2015, November). *Analysis and value of family & consumer sciences Extension in the north central region.* https://www.nccea.org/multistate-activities/fcs-battelle-report-2015

Bloom, J. D., Lelekacs, J., Hofing, G., Stout, R., Marshall, M., & Davis, K. (2020). Integrating food systems and local food in family and consumer sciences: Perspectives from the pilot Extension Master Food Volunteer Program. *Journal of Agriculture, Food Systems, and Community Development*, 9(2), 197–220. https://doi.org/10.5304/jafscd.2020.092.013

Brandt, R. (2022, October 26). *Our roots run deep: From home economics to human ecology.* https://norton.arizona.edu/news/our-roots-run-deep-home-economics-human-ecology

Braun, B., Bruns, K., Cronk, L., Kirk Fox, L., Koukel, S., Le Menestrel, S., Lord, L., Reeves, C., Rennekamp, R., Rice, C., Rodgers, M. Samuel, J., Vail, A., & Warren, T. (2014). *Cooperative Extension's national framework for health and wellness.* Washington, DC: Extension Committee on Organization and Policy.

Burton, D., Canton, A., Coon, T., Eschbach, C., Gunn, J., Gutter, M., Jones, M., Kennedy, L., Martin, K., Mitchell, A., O'Neal, L., Rennekamp, R., Rodgers, M., Stluka, S., Trautman, K., Yelland, E., & York, D. (2021). *Cooperative Extension's national framework for health equity and well-being.* Washington, DC: Extension Committee on Organization and Policy.

Case, A., & Deaton, A. (2017). Mortality and morbidity in the 21st century. *Brookings Papers on Economic Activity, 2017*(1), 397–443. https://doi.org/10.1353/eca.2017.0005

Clancy, K. (1999). Reclaiming the social and environmental roots of nutrition education. *Journal of Nutrition Education, 31*(4), 190–193.

Community Tool Box. (2023). *Databases of best practices.* https://ctb.ku.edu/en/databases-best-practices

Dreilinger, D. (2021). *The secret history of home economics: How trailblazing women harness the power of home and changed the way we live.* New York: W. W. Norton.

Dwyer, J. W., Contreras, D., Eschbach, C. L., Tiret, H., Newkirk, C., Carter, E., & Cronk, L. (2017). Cooperative Extension as a framework for health extension: The Michigan State University model. *Academic Medicine*, 92(10), 1416–1420.

Extension Foundation. (2023). *The EXCITE project.* https://excite.extension.org

Fields, N. I., & Moncloa, F. (2022). Culture and culturally relevant programming. In N. I. Fields & T. J. Shaffer (Eds.), *Grassroots engagement and social justice through Cooperative Extension* (pp. 51–61). East Lansing: Michigan State University Press.

Gleason, S., Pooler, J., Gutuskey, L., & Gabor, V. (2022). *SNAP-ED needs assessment toolkit.* U.S. Department of Agriculture Food and Nutrition Service. https://insightpolicyresearch.com/

wp-content/uploads/2023/02/SNAPEdNeeds-AssessmentToolkit_12162022.pdf

Gunn, V. R. (1995). "Industrialists not butterflies: Women's higher education at Kansas State Agricultural College, 1873–1882." *Kansas History, 18*, 2–17.

Hart, L., Stevens, H., Heaton, L., & Forester, D. (1996). *Kentucky home economics Extension history 1913–1996*. https://fcs-hes.ca.uky.edu/files/kentucky_home_economics_extension_history_published_1996.pdf

Heggestad, M. (2023). *About: Home economics*. HEARTH—Home economics archive: Research, tradition, history. https://digital.library.cornell.edu/collections/hearth/about

Journal of Human Sciences and Extension. (2018)., 6(2), 10. https://doi.org/10.55533/2325-5226.1177

Lindemann, J., Alter, T. R., Stagner, F., Palacios, E., Banuna, L., & Muldoon, M. (2022). Building urban community resilience through university extension: Community engagement and the politics of knowledge. *Socio-Ecological Practice Research, 4*, 325–337. https://doi.org/10.1007/s42532-022-00126-6

Lytle, L. A. (2022). *Designing interventions to promote community health: A multilevel, stepwise approach*. Washington, DC: American Psychological Association.

Meendering, J. R., McCormack, L., Moore, L., & Stluka, S. (2023). Facilitating nutrition and physical activity-focused policy, systems, and environmental change in rural areas: A methodological approach using community wellness coalitions and Cooperative Extension. *Health Promotion Practice, 24*(1). https://doi-org.er.lib.k-state.edu/10.1177/15248399221144976

Morris, F. B. (1937). Planning agricultural extension programs. In *Extension service circular* 260. Washington, DC: United States Department of Agriculture.

National Commission on Excellence in Education. (1983, April). *A nation at risk: The imperative for educational reform*. https://edreform.com/wp-content/uploads/2013/02/A_Nation_At_Risk_1983.pdf

Neary, S. (2014). Professional identity: What I call myself *defines* who I am. *Career Matters, 2*(3), 14–15.

New York State College of Home Economics. (1942). *Annual report of the New York State College of Home Economics at Cornell University*. https://hdl.handle.net/2027/uc1.b3359666

Rossiter, M. W. (1995). *Women scientists in America: Before Affirmative Action, 1940–1972*. Baltimore, MD: Johns Hopkins University Press.

Schneider, C. (2014). *Aligning and elevating university-based low-income nutrition education through the land-grant university Cooperative Extension system*. National Institute of Food and Agriculture. https://files.eric.ed.gov/fulltext/ED571846.pdf

Simerly, C. B., Ralston, P. A., Harriman, L., & Taylor, B. (2000). The Scottsdale initiative: Positioning the profession for the 21st century. *Journal of Family and Consumer Sciences, 92*(1), 75–80.

Smith, C. B., & Wilson, M. C. (1930). *The agricultural extension system of the United States*. New York: John Wiley & Sons.

Stage, S., & Vincenti, V. B. (1997). *Rethinking home economics: Women and the history of a profession.* Ithaca, NY: Cornell University Press.

Substance Abuse and Mental Health Services Administration. (2022, June 13). *Rural opioid technical assistance (ROTA).* Substance Abuse and Mental Health Services Administration. https://www.samhsa.gov/rural-opioid-technical-assistance-rota

Upstream. (2014). *Introduction to upstream* [video]. YouTube. https://www.youtube.com/watch?v=qarQXqKbmLg

U.S. Department of Agriculture. (2016, June). *USDA "one health" approach—Fact sheet.* https://www.usda.gov/sites/default/files/documents/fact-sheet-one-health-06-16-2016.pdf

U.S. Department of Agriculture. (2018, September 11). *A short history of SNAP.* Food and Nutrition Service. https://www.fns.usda.gov/snap/short-history-snap

U.S. Department of Agriculture (2022). *2022 Impacts: Expanded food and nutrition program (EFNEP).* National Institute of Food and Agriculture. https://www.nifa.usda.gov/sites/default/files/2023-03/EFNEP%202022%20Impact%20Report.pdf

U.S. States Department of Agriculture. (2023a, August). *SNAP data tables.* USDA Food and Nutrition Service. https://www.fns.usda.gov/pd/supplemental-nutrition-assistance-program-snap

U.S. Department of Agriculture. (2023b, August). *Expanded Food and Nutrition Education Program (EFNEP).* National Institute of Food and Agriculture. https://www.nifa.usda.gov/grants/programs/capacity-grants/efnep/expanded-food-nutrition-education-program

U.S. Department of Agriculture. (2023c, August). *Supplemental Nutrition Education Program—Education (SNAP-Ed).* National Institute of Food and Agriculture. https://www.nifa.usda.gov/grants/programs/capacity-grants/efnep/snap/supplemental-nutrition-education-program-education-snap-ed

U.S. Department of Agriculture. (2023d, August). *Fiscal year (FY) 2024 Supplemental Nutrition Assistance Program Nutrition Education (SNAP-Ed) estimated allocations.* https://snaped.fns.usda.gov/administration/funding-allocations

U.S. Department of Agriculture. (2023e, August). *USDA FY 2024 budget summary.* https://www.agri-pulse.com/ext/resources/2023/03/09/2024-usda-budget-summary.pdf

Vincenti, V. B. (1997). Home economics moves into the twenty-first century. In S. Stage & V. B. Vincenti (Eds.), *Rethinking home economics: Women and the history of a profession* (pp. 301–320). Ithaca, NY: Cornell University Press.

Vines, K. (2017). *Engagement through Cooperative Extension: Towards understanding meaning and practice among educators in two state Extension systems.* Doctoral dissertation, Pennsylvania State University. Proquest Dissertations Publishing.

Yetter, D., & Tripp, S. (2020). *SNAP-Ed FY2019: A retrospective review of the land-grant university SNAP-Ed programs and impacts.* TEConomy Partners, LLC. https://snaped.fns.usda.gov/sites/default/files/documents/LGU-SNAP-Ed-FY2019-Impacts-Report-12-16-2020_508.pdf

Sowing Seeds: Health Extension's Role in Supporting Agricultural Mental Health

Courtney Cuthbertson

This chapter contains mentions of mental health, mental illness, suicide, death, substance use, gun violence, racism, and colonialism.

Ginnie Peters felt awash with dread on May 12, 2011, when her husband had not answered his phone or returned home in the evening (Weingarten, 2017). After having sleepless nights earlier that week, concerned about the timing of planting crops and the potential for disruptive weather, Matt Peters left a note in his farm workshop and took his own life. Matt was one of hundreds of farmers who have died by suicide in the recent past, and the piece in *The Guardian* featuring the Peters' story sent alarm bells throughout the United States and across the world that signaled that something needed to be done to help struggling farmers (Weingarten & Mulkern, 2017). Since that time, Extension health programs about farm stress have proliferated. This chapter details some of this recent history and contextualizes it with research findings and frameworks with which to consider farm stress, suicides, and mental health, in addition to identifying new directions.

Farm Stress in Extension Context

Since 2016, many organizations have developed resources to address farm stress, although Extension's roots in dealing with farm stress stretch back to the 1980s farm crisis. The Michigan Department of Agriculture and Rural Development (MDARD) approached Michigan State University (MSU) Extension in 2016, concerned about mental well-being of Michigan's agricultural producers after having heard of several deaths by suicide in the agricultural community. MDARD requested that MSU Extension provide research-based training and workshops to support agricultural communities across the state. In 2017, MSU Extension formed the Community Behavioral Health team, and programs about farm stress were incorporated in the team's efforts, with new programs developed and offered in mere months. I led MSU Extension's Community Behavioral Health team when it was created and was one of the lead developers of the two MSU Extension farm stress programs mentioned. A large part of the Community Behavioral Health team's work was training all MSU Extension staff in Mental Health First Aid (MHFA), a research- and evidence-based mental health literacy training program including information about depression, suicide, anxiety, trauma, psychosis, and substance use.

MSU Extension professionals from different programmatic backgrounds—family and consumer science, health, mental health, agriculture, livestock management, farm finances—came together to create two training programs specific to the agricultural context (Eschbach et al., 2022). Communicating with Farmers under Stress (CFS) was intended for people who worked with agricultural producers, such as seed dealers, mechanics, veterinarians, and loan officers, and included topics such as unique agricultural stressors, signs of distress and suicide, communication skills to help a distressed producer, and how to refer someone to other resources. Weathering the Storm: Cultivating a Productive Mindset (WTS) was created for farmers and farm families directly, including many of the same topics as CFS as well as stress management strategies. In January 2019, MSU Extension held the first train-the-trainer and hosted nearly one hundred Extension educators from other states to offer CFS and WTS in their own communities (Eschbach et al., 2022). The success of the programs led to partnerships with the North Central Regional Center for Rural Development (NCRCRD), Farm Credit Council, American Farm Bureau Federation, and National Farmers Union to create an online course about farm stress tailored to specific audiences, and a version available to the public for no cost. MSU Extension also partnered with NCRCRD and the U.S. Department of Agriculture (USDA) Farm Service Agency (FSA) to create a farm stress training for FSA staff, which included example scenarios in FSA offices and an in-person pilot training in September 2019 for participants to practice their skills (Cuthbertson, Brennan, Shutske, Leatherman, et al., 2022; Cuthbertson, Brennan, Shutske, Zierl, et al., 2022). Since that time, there have been many more resources, largely mental health literacy information (e.g., knowledge of symptoms, skills in how to help, and resources to refer someone to), made available to farmers by agricultural advocacy groups, nonprofit organizations, and foundations.

While the Farm and Ranch Stress Assistance Network (FRSAN) was established in the Farm Bill in 2008 (Food, Conservation, and Energy Act of 2008), federal funding was not appropriated toward FRSAN until ten years later. FRSAN funding is distributed via the USDA National Institute of Food and Agriculture (NIFA). Four one-year projects were funded through a competitive grants process in 2019, with one award to each USDA region (Northeast, North Central, South, West). In 2020, four three-year projects were funded. In 2021 some additional funds as part of the Coronavirus Response and Relief Act were made available to state departments of agriculture for additional FRSAN activities. In 2023, due to delays in congressional approval for the Farm Bill, one year of FRSAN funding was appropriated for existing grantees to apply to continue work. Based in the legislative authority, FRSAN activities include stress assistance and stress reduction resources for farmers that may include professional counseling, helplines and websites, trainings and workshops for agricultural professionals and supporters, support groups, and outreach activities (USDA NIFA, 2023).

Many of the programs offered under FRSAN efforts focus on mental health literacy, to train participants in signs and symptoms of mental health issues, communication skills to talk with a distressed person, and referral skills to share additional resources with a distressed person (Jorm, 2012, 2015; Kutcher et al., 2016). MHFA is one example of a mental health literacy program, and there are several others. Youth Mental Health First Aid focuses on teaching adults who work with youth to identify differences between typical adolescence and emerging mental health issues, and how to talk about mental health with youth (Kelly et al., 2011). MHFA and Youth MHFA can be offered in person, online, or blended, and take around eight hours for participants to complete. MHFA and Youth MHFA have been popular among farm stress efforts because of the strong evidence base showing the program to be effective in improving knowledge, skills, and confidence to help distressed people (Jorm et al., 2019), but it is not specific to agricultural contexts. The strong focus on program fidelity has meant instructors have little room for adapting information to potential participants. Nevertheless, MHFA provides a valuable foundation of common understanding, and MSU Extension staff reported they could readily apply what they learned in both work and home environments.

There are not many agriculture-specific mental health literacy programs. MSU Extension's CFS and WTS are two examples. Some FRSAN collaborators have also used COMET (Changing Our Mental & Emotional Trajectory), a program developed by the High Plains Research Network to help distressed people in rural communities. SafeTALK is a four-hour training focused on suicide prevention skills. Question.Persuade.Refer. (QPR) focuses on teaching participants skills for suicide prevention and takes approximately one hour for participants to complete. QPR can be tailored somewhat to agricultural communities.

Aside from mental health literacy programs, FRSAN funding enabled social support programs like Bienvenido for farmworkers, connections to mental health professionals through voucher programs, and clearinghouse websites of resources for agricultural community members to find more information and assistance.

The Elephant in the Room: Dealing with Stigma

Conversations around building and offering farm stress Extension programs since 2016 have necessarily included how to deal with mental health stigma in agricultural communities. Stigma refers to "an attribute that is deeply discrediting" (Goffman, 1963, 3) or, in other words, is a difference about a person or group that is degrading (Bos et al., 2013; Goffman, 1963). Stigma is not about an inherent trait or value but about social relationships and context (Bos et al., 2013; Goffman, 1963; Hebl & Dovidio, 2005; Pescosolido & Martin, 2015). Mental illness and mental health challenges are of the second kind of stigma Goffman delineated, those socially believed to be of "individual character," indicating immorality, problematic beliefs, untrustworthy behavior or beliefs, and, ultimately, danger. Stigma creates in a stigmatized person shame about the stigmatized attribute, uncertainty regarding what others think of them, discrepancies between valuation of self by self and by others, and potentially attempts to conceal the stigmatized attribute to "pass" as nonstigmatized. Stigma leads nonstigmatized people to keep social or interpersonal distance and to be reluctant to interact, thus limiting opportunity and life chances for stigmatized people. Stigma confers loss of status within a community, as well as discrimination (Pescosolido & Martin, 2015).

Public perceptions of mental illness have evolved since the 1950s, when most people thought of mental illness as psychosis, to the 1990s, when a broader proportion of people the United States thought of mental illness as anxiety or depression (Markowitz, 2005). However, this shift in public perception has not aligned with a shift in public perceptions of mental illness that are less stigmatizing (i.e., public stigma), as surveys revealed a greater proportion of people believed mental illness symptoms involved violence in the late 1990s compared to more than forty-five years earlier (Markowitz, 2005; Pescosolido, 2013). Most such studies use vignette style questions as part of surveys, presenting survey respondents with a story about an individual and their experience before asking what, if anything, might be wrong with the person and asking the respondents how willing they would be to interact with a person like the one in the vignette, across a broad range of contexts. More people can identify clusters of experience as symptoms of different mental illnesses, but stigma and desire for social distance persist (Phelan et al., 2000; Sickel et al., 2014; Silton et al., 2011), especially for schizophrenia and substance use (Pescosolido et al., 1999). A more recent study is one of few to find a decrease in depression-related stigma from 2018 compared to 2006 and 1996 (Pescosolido et al., 2021). There is some evidence that stigma is generational, in that older generations hold more stigmatizing beliefs than do younger generations (Pescosolido et al., 2021; Stewart et al., 2015). Mental health stigma has been associated with lower self-efficacy among people experiencing mental illness (Sickel et al., 2014), which is important in the context of one study demonstrating that the only coping strategy significantly associated with farmers' suicide risk was self-blame (Bjornestad et al., 2021).

The costs of stigma are real: aside from lost interpersonal interactions and opportunity, stigma is a barrier to seeking care. Stigma has contributed to distrust of mental health services (Cheesmond et al., 2019) and avoidance of care (Clement et al., 2015; Cooper et al., 2003), perhaps due to label avoidance and not wanting to experience discrimination that one may expect because of perceived stigma (Corrigan et al., 2014). Concern about courtesy stigma (Goffman, 1963)—that stigma around mental illness experienced by one person will extend to and impact one's family and friends—may also serve as a barrier to help-seeking (Corrigan et al., 2014).

Few studies have examined mental health stigma within U.S. agricultural communities; one study found self-stigma significantly predicted farmers' mental health help-seeking behavior (Baker et al., 2022). Canadian farmers have described mental health stigma in agricultural settings as beliefs that mental illness is not a real or legitimate health issue, beliefs one must keep struggles and difficulties to oneself, and reduced willingness to reach out for help or acknowledge problems (Hagen et al., 2022). An Australian program aimed to reduce stigma among farming men, with mixed results (Kennedy et al., 2020).

While agricultural mental health stigma research is limited, in the U.S. context some have investigated urban and rural differences. For instance, some studies have found people in rural communities to hold more stigma (Schroeder et al., 2021), even if they can better recognize mental illness (Loveridge et al., 2023). One qualitative study found rural people with mental illness were told they were faking it, to rely on religion, and to simply "get over it" (Crumb et al., 2019). Stigma for rural residents has been related to stoicism (e.g., silently coping without asking for help), and both serve as barriers to seeking care (Cheesmond et al., 2019). While findings from rural communities are important and relevant, we must be cautious generalizing, as agriculture is not exclusive to or comprehensive of rural communities.

Stigma also impacts farm stress outreach, prevention efforts, and Extension programs. MSU Extension's process creating WTS and CFS included ongoing conversations about what to call the programs, with concern that a program labeled "suicide prevention" would result in few, if any, participants. Programs continue to be discussed as being about "stress" because the term is more accessible and acceptable within agricultural communities. Indeed, wording impacts individual willingness to engage in mental health-related programs and services (Corrigan et al., 2014). Even then, MSU Extension staff heard that some interested participants drove more than three hours to attend farm stress programs, not because that was the closest program offered, but because those participants were concerned about having people from their own community see them at the program. How to word programs and messages about suicide prevention, stress management, and mental health within agricultural spaces is a challenge between breaking down stigma instead of reinforcing it, while also creating space where participants feel welcomed and willing to consider new information and perspectives.

Recent Research

Farm stress research has accelerated since the original MSU Extension curricula were developed, yet concrete answers about relationships between stressors and adverse mental health continue to evade our understanding. Pooled and longitudinal data and meta-analyses confirm that people who work in farming have elevated risk of suicide (Arif et al., 2021; Klingelschmidt et al., 2018; Peterson et al., 2020; Ringgenberg et al., 2018). In alignment with general literature around suicide and suicide prevention (Skegg et al., 2010), access to lethal means increases risk for people in farming, and those in farming may have more ready access to lethal means than other workers (Booth et al., 2000; Browning et al., 2008; Klingelschmidt et al., 2018). Most suicide deaths in farming in the United States were completed using firearms (Browning et al., 2008; Gunderson et al., 1993; Kennedy et al., 2021; Miller & Rudolphi, 2022; Stallones, 1990).

Many have attempted to understand what impacts and could predict suicidality for people in agriculture. Studies using data from death records have found the largest proportion of suicide decedents who were farmers to be older, white, male, and with a high school education or less, with nearly half being married (Bower & Emerson, 2021; Kennedy et al., 2021; Miller & Rudolphi, 2022; Scheyett et al., 2019). For more than a century, suicide rates have been higher among white people than people of color (Malat et al., 2018). Suicide deaths among farmers have been associated with physical health problems and relationship conflict, strain, or loss (Miller & Rudolphi, 2022; Scheyett et al., 2019), although these associations were significantly related to age, where relationship problems were related to suicide among younger farmers, while physical health problems were associated with suicide among older farmers (Bower & Emerson, 2021; Miller & Rudolphi, 2022). One study found that the only coping strategy that significantly predicted farmer suicide risk was coping through self-blame (Bjornestad et al., 2019). Results are mixed and largely lean toward farmer suicide deaths and suicide risk not being related to history of mental illness (Bower & Emerson, 2021; Scheyett et al., 2019). Farmers who have died by suicide are less likely to have a history of mental illness compared to nonfarming suicide decedents (Kennedy et al., 2021). For those farmers who died by suicide and did have a history of mental illness, the vast majority had depression or dysthymia (Bower & Emerson, 2021).

Studies have shown mixed results but tend to show farmers either are significantly less likely to have depression or are not significantly different from the general population (Reed & Claunch, 2020; Roche et al., 2016); however, several studies have demonstrated linkages between pesticide exposure and depression (Kori et al., 2020; Reed & Claunch, 2020). One Wisconsin study found more than half of young farmers experienced major depressive disorder, which was associated with stress from finances, time pressure, relationships with employees, and economic conditions (Rudolphi et al., 2020). In a study of farmers in Hawaii, more than a third experienced at least mild depression, and depression was associated with younger age (Le et al., 2023).

Anxiety disorders and adjustment disorder have also been the focus of studies related to farmer stress and suicide. Nearly three-quarters of young Wisconsin farmers experienced anxiety disorder in one study (Rudolphi et al., 2020), and in other studies, about one-third of farmers were found to experience generalized anxiety disorder (Bjornestad et al., 2019; Jones-Bitton et al., 2020). Heaberlin and Shattuck (2023) argue that given strong linkages between adjustment disorder and suicide more broadly, adjustment disorder ought to be the focus of research about farmer suicides; they found that the most frequent mental health issue of callers to a Nebraska farm hotline was adjustment disorder.

Frameworks

The way we think about any issue shapes what possibilities we can envision for solutions; as such, it is important to acknowledge the theoretical models that have been used to understand farm stress and related issues. There are at least five theoretical models used for farm stress research, though much of the existing research is atheoretical. The first model is one that often is assumed or implied rather than explicitly elaborated within research articles, and that is the medical model of disease that frames mental health issues as health problems that can be treated with guidance of medical professionals. U.S. society has managed mental health within a medical framing starting in the 1950s but accelerating in the 1970s and 1980s with the emergence of the community mental health movement, in a shift away from institutionalization as primary "treatment" for people experiencing mental illness (Clarke et al., 2010; Conrad, 2007; Conrad & Schneider, 1980). Prior to the medical model, mental health had been socially managed as an issue of deviance, and before that, as an issue of poor morality or religiosity (Conrad & Schneider, 1980). There have been challenges to the medical model as well: that it is individualistic and at times devoid of attention to social context. The antipsychiatry movement in the 1970s included an attempt to demonstrate that instead of considering individuals as mentally ill or "insane," we should consider that behavior indicating "insanity" is a "sane reaction to insane circumstances" (Laing, 1965; Scheff, 1999; Szasz, 1961, 1987). This perspective from social constructionism points out that medical labels can be stigmatizing and can treat people as though their reaction, rather than the originating circumstance, is the problem to be treated.

Most epidemiological studies about farm stress and suicides come from a medical model and attempt to show connections between problematic mental health and suicide deaths. Many of the studies previously mentioned fall within this approach, showing demographic characteristics of being older, white, male, and less educated being most consistently associated with suicide among farmers (Bower & Emerson, 2021; Kennedy et al., 2021; Miller & Rudolphi, 2022; Scheyett et al., 2019).

The diseases and deaths of despair framing that is popular in public health (Case & Deaton, 2015, 2020, 2021) has also been relied upon in farm stress research. Rooted in a medical model, the diseases and deaths of despair framework sets suicidality, drug use, and alcohol use as coping mechanisms for intolerable and seemingly unchangeable social environments. It is a fitting framework for farm stress research because the majority of stressors named by farmers are outside the control of any single person. One study using the deaths of despair framework found farming, fishing, and forestry to be the occupational group with highest increases in annual mortality rates related to deaths of despair in Massachusetts from 2000 to 2015 (Hawkins et al., 2020). While such studies help to demonstrate that deaths of despair is a meaningful framework, this framework should point toward upstream factors that can be influenced to reduce despair and, hopefully, reduce related deaths. Working upstream from deaths of despair has not been fully realized; qualitative research could help in identifying what people who work in agriculture think would be meaningful change in upstream causes of farm stress. Additionally, the deaths of despair framework has been critiqued for centering white Americans around health disparity issues that have impacted people of color for substantially longer; the notion of stress from gaps between one's social or economic goals and systems creating challenges achieving goals is not new, but the creation of a framework around the concept when it is demonstrated to impact white Americans has been critiqued as dismissive of people of color (Brown & Tucker-Seeley, 2018).

Building on deaths of despair framing for farm stress, one recent study used the theoretical framing of rural sacrifice zones (Heaberlin & Shattuck, 2023). Mainly an economic argument, the rural sacrifice zone framework posits that farmers' primary stressors are financial in nature and that we must understand the context of decades of financial disinvestment that rural communities have experienced, that in turn create and exacerbate stress at personal and social levels. Notably, Heaberlin and Shattuck (2023) critique MSU Extension farm stress programs and FRSAN efforts as pathologizing individual farmers by not focusing on macrolevel economic restructuring, while offering few recommendations of their own that would alleviate suffering for people in agricultural industries. The critique also ignores several states' FRSAN efforts to provide farm financial and business programs to farmers to reduce farm stress.

The stress process model was developed in social psychology and sociology in the 1980s onward as a way to understand how exposure to a stressor may or may not lead to adverse mental health outcomes (Pearlin et al., 1981). The stress process model posits that individuals experience a stressor that may be acute or chronic, and their subsequent mental health is a result of what resources the individual engages. Resources, in this model, refer to three types: psychological, social, and coping. Psychological resources include things like a sense of mastery or efficacy, such that the individual has a sense of being able to control aspects of their lives. Social resources are things like social support and can come from a variety of sources, such as family, friends, significant others, and beyond. Coping resources may include different strategies or mechanisms, like use of humor or positive comparisons. Over time, the stress process model has been built upon and expanded to include chronic and traumatic stressors, and values and meanings of stress (Aneshensel & Avison, 2015; Aneshensel & Mitchell, 2014; McLeod, 2012; Pearlin, 2010; Pearlin et al., 2005). The stress process model has been used in agricultural context to understand the impact of the 1980s farm crisis on Texas farmers (Luedke, 1993), and more recently to investigate relationships between musculoskeletal symptoms, stress, sleep, and exhaustion (Chengane et al., 2021). This framework seems underutilized in farm stress research, although that could be because it focuses highly on individuals and not within context; even updated versions of the stress process model include "society and culture" in large print to the side with an arrow toward the typical stress process model diagram, without being sufficiently operationalized for research purposes.

The social ecological model is yet another theoretical framework used within farm stress research. Originally from Bronfenbrenner (1979), the social ecological model situates individuals within social context to demonstrate how various factors at multiple levels impact an individual's lived experience. One person does not exist in isolation, but rather nested in relationship to family, within a work environment, in a community, and within broader society. Things that happen at any level can have ripple effects toward the individual to impact their experience. The social ecological model has been reworked for agricultural contexts, considering unique safety and health concerns and that children often work on farms with parents (Lee et al., 2017). The social ecological model is useful for considering the many complex and intertwined relationships a person has and social forces impacting lived experiences. The model tends to focus on who or what impacts an individual, rather than on how that impact happens.

Although several theoretical frameworks inform farm stress research, there are gaps that have gone unaddressed. Agriculture as an industry is predominantly white, older, male, cisgender, straight, and multigenerational family farmers. This is not accidental; histories of land dispossession (Horst & Marion, 2019) and discrimination in farm loans (Buechler, 2022; Carpenter, 2012; Cowan & Feder, 2013; Grant et al., 2012; Tyler & Moore, 2013) are evidence of structural forces shaping who "counts" as a farmer and who gets to engage in agriculture as an occupation. Even so, there is some diversity among people who work in agriculture. Farm stress research and programs have not fully accounted for this diversity. While programs often have an implied "one size fits all" approach, tailored programs would better meet public health promotion goals (Kahan & Goodstadt, 2001), for example, by creating programs that address racial discrimination and disparities for Black farmers (Hinson & Robinson, 2008), acculturative stress of migrant Spanish-speaking farmworkers (Ramos et al., 2015), and cis-sexism and heterosexism faced by LGBTQ+ farmers (Hoffelmeyer, 2021).

Conversations We're Not Having: A Move Upstream

Despite being the norm and stereotype of who constitutes a farmer in the United States, suicide rates are higher among older white men in farming. Taking a social determinants of mental health approach to farm stress and farmer suicide would mean seriously grappling with such findings by interrogating associated social structures of masculinity, whiteness, and capitalism to understand why this group is at elevated risk.

The social structure of gender includes hegemonic masculinity, meaning socially idealized norms of how to be a man that influence behavior and actions (Connell, 2020; Connell & Messerschmidt, 2005). Hegemonic masculinity operates to maintain hierarchical power of heterosexual men over women, and varies across cultures, making use of other systems of power such as racism to maintain dominance of men over women (Connell, 2020). Hegemonic masculinity includes ideals of stoicism, pushing through, and figuring things out on one's own (Oliffe & Phillips, 2008; Seidler et al., 2016). Masculine ideals such as being tough, independent, strong, and self-reliant are hypothesized to work against men's health (Courtenay, 2000), and greater adherence to them has had negative impacts on men's health, including higher conformity to masculine norms being associated with risk of depression (Herreen et al., 2021; Mahalik et al., 2007; Ragonese & Barker, 2019 ; Seidler et al., 2016).

Depression tends to be diagnosed at higher rates among women compared to men, although some attribute this to measurement tools and standards being insufficiently attentive to externalizing symptoms that men display more frequently, such as substance use or focusing more time on work (Oliffe et al., 2019). Alignment with masculine toughness has been associated with greater substance use among depressed men (Sileo & Kershaw, 2020). In some instances, men consider hegemonic masculinity as contributing to depression, whether they have achieved hegemonic masculine ideals or not (Valkonen & Hänninen, 2013).

Men tend to avoid seeking mental health care because of masculine ideals of strong emotional control and self-reliance, where asking for help is associated with vulnerability and loss of power (Emslie et al., 2006; Mahalik & Di Bianca, 2021). Because help-seeking challenges masculine ideals, avoiding help-seeking is part of an active construction of masculinity, while seeking help may be seem as diminishing one's own masculinity (Courtenay, 2000). Internalized hegemonic masculinity is a barrier to men's help-seeking (McCusker & Galupo, 2011; Oliffe et al., 2019; Staiger et al., 2020), and for some men, suicide is in alignment with masculine ideals (Apesoa-Varano et al., 2018). Some have suggested and tested the use of masculine ideals within mental health care, such as emphasizing strength, responsibility, courage, altruism, and social connection, to entice men to seek care (Ragonese & Barker, 2019; Rochlen et al., 2005; Seidler et al., 2016, 2018). To encourage men to seek care, a somewhat reductive billboard campaign by the Agency for Healthcare Research and Quality and the Ad Council declared, "This year thousands of men will die from stubbornness" of not going for needed health screenings (Agency for Healthcare Research, 2010). Yet suggestions of using hegemonic masculinity to entice men into seeking care do not reduce the weight or force of the social structure itself; rather, they encourage people to develop skills to live within a structure compelling men and masculine people to believe their own identities and worth are reduced by caring for themselves. A more powerful solution would be to challenge systems of gender themselves, to create environments where such coping strategies are unnecessary.

Hegemonic masculinity takes a particular shape in agricultural contexts where masculinity is tied with dominance over land and animals (Alston & Kent, 2008), as well as technology (Barlett & Conger, 2004; Little, 2002), although there have been geographic variations in agricultural masculinity (Barlett & Conger, 2004). For example, Barlett and Conger (2004) identified at least three types of agricultural masculinity: industrial (focusing on farming as a breadwinning job allowing for certain standards of living), agrarian (focusing on continuity on the farm, partnerships, and farm life), and third wave (focusing on farming for sustainability, as spiritual practice, for relationships with nature). Masculinity has been constructed as part of what it means to be a "true" or "good" farmer (Burton et al., 2020; Liepins, 2000). Being masculine helps women to be successful in agriculture while simultaneously reinforcing the hold of hegemonic masculinity within agricultural spaces (Pilgeram, 2007). Part of the construction of agricultural work as masculine was rooted in the work being physically demanding (Anderson, 2020). Even though agricultural work has shifted to include greater use of and dependence on technological innovation and machinery to do the work of farming, hegemonic masculinity too has shifted such that increased farm technology use paired with seeking knowledge from agribusiness experts defines new boundaries of agricultural masculinity (Carter & Lopez, 2019). Some have referred to this as a manipulative deskilling of farmers, working to alienate them from the land they work on (Bell et al., 2015). Alienation of workers is core to capitalist systems (Marx & Engels, 2014), and ownership of the means of production—in this case, land, animals, machinery—is aspirational to attaining status in the elite upper class.

Hegemonic masculinity within agriculture is inextricably linked to capitalism and the notion that one's worth is tied to the earnings their labor power brings to provide for their family. Under capitalism, the value of an individual person is in the labor power they bring to the market. Capitalism created a gendered division of labor including in rural areas where agriculture was more common (Osterud, 1993). Being a sole breadwinner, in addition to owning and caring for land, and then ultimately passing that land on to the next generation, are all part of what defines being a moral and good farmer (Burton et al., 2020). Ties to individual identity are strong enough that even into retirement, farming men wish to maintain their farming identity by negotiating their farm roles, in part to counteract negative messages about aging (Riley, 2016).

In the United States, the ownership of farmland cannot be detached from the land's history of dispossession from Indigenous people through projects of colonialist white supremacy (Magdoff, 2013), through which white supremacy can endure in material practice (Bonds & Inwood, 2016). Significant disparities exist by race and ethnicity in agriculture, as white people own 98 percent of farm land and operate 94 percent of it (Horst & Marion, 2019). While beyond the scope of the current chapter, a critical perspective implores us to reflect on how this reality is not accidental. The image of the white farm family—the icon of successful agriculture since the late 1800s (Harris, 2015; Ron, 2016)—solidified colonialism's "success" and served nationalism, idealized through post office murals (Wyman, 2005) and works like *American Gothic* (Harris, 2015).

Racial categories in the United States are fluid and changing, impacting people at macro levels of social structure and hegemonic ideologies as well as micro levels of interpersonal interaction and individual identity (Bonilla-Silva, 1997; Omi & Winant, 2014). The racial structure of the United States was developed as a part of capitalist enterprise that required creation of racial categories and devaluing and dehumanizing people outside of the privileged group (Nayak, 2007; Zinn, 2015). In the late 1700s, "American" was codified to mean white immigrants (Wyman, 2005). Whiteness is a socially constructed identity imbued with privilege (McIntosh, 1990). Gaining the privileged status of whiteness comes with erasure of ethnic identity ties and a socialized belief that one does not have a racial identity (Gallagher, 1997; Roediger, 2007). Racially minoritized people have to take on white perspectives and consciousness for survival (Fanon, 2008). As a result of racialized capitalism in the United States, many values seen as "American"—of hard work, individual responsibility, and meritocracy—are also built in to capitalist and white ideologies.

White ideology and white culture are invisibilized by being treated as normative and used to define appropriate or good behavior, achievement, or way of being (Gillborn, 2015; Nayak, 2007). White culture involves not seeing whiteness and related privileges, allowing white people to believe we do not have a culture and enabling us to see ourselves merely as individuals (Mahoney, 1997). (Note that I use first person pronouns here [we] to position myself as a white person relative to the topic and do not intend to alienate readers of color.) Importantly, among white cultural values are avoiding conflict, avoiding intense emotions, and limiting acceptable emotions (Gulati-Partee & Potapchuk, 2014); as such, whiteness conspires with hegemonic masculinity to perpetuate norms of stoicism as cultural barriers to white farming men reaching out for help or discussing difficulties with others. Simultaneously, ideologies of whiteness and capitalism collude to render white people's sense of value hollow unless actively working toward and achieving economic success. Financial issues—a top cited stressor among farmers (Furey et al., 2016; Grocke-Dewey et al., 2023; Heaberlin & Shattuck, 2023)—transform from an external problem to be solved to an indictment of one's identity and worth.

Whiteness as a structure has resulted in a multigenerational cultural lack of resilience among white people; privilege comes with an expectation not to face adversity and thus not building skills to overcome it (Malat et al., 2018). In the current historical moment, white men hold both entitlement and a sense of victimization (Kimmel, 2017), in part because white Americans on average have come to see racial equity as inherently detrimental to white people (Norton & Sommers, 2011).

In agriculture, whiteness operates at structural, interpersonal, and individual levels as well. Whiteness has become synonymous with land ownership in farming (Wald, 2016). One study revealed that white agricultural education students learned toxic masculinity, heteronormativity, and white-centric ideas from their farming families (M. J. Martin & Hartmann, 2022). Agricultural organizations rely on white cultural values to socialize the next generation of farmers (M. Martin et al., 2023; Rosenberg, 2016). Some white LGBTQIA+ farmers have used whiteness as an appeal to sameness in farming communities where fitting in and being the same are highly valued, to navigate sexual or gender marginalization (Hoffelmeyer, 2021).

Conclusion

Mental health, well-being, and stress in agriculture are complex topics to understand and to address through Extension health programs. Most farm stress programs have approached people in agriculture with interventionist or preventionist approaches, to learn how to help distressed people or to learn coping techniques to use in times of stress. Largely, such programs have not addressed more upstream social structural and cultural issues that shape how people define, experience, and respond to stress and challenging situations. Extension can do both.

With the Cooperative Extension Sytem's history and mission to provide research-based information to communities across the country, it is worth noting that the research base around farm stress has also largely sidestepped investigations of macro-level structures impacting well-being and, in particular, has avoided in-depth studies of how whiteness shapes agricultural mental health. To guide future research in this area, related questions include

- What upstream causes of farm stress do farmers identify? What do farmers think solutions should be?
- What is the relationship between agricultural masculinity and mental health?
- How does geography influence relationships between agricultural mental health, masculinity, capitalist ideology, and white cultural values?
- How can hegemonic masculinity, white cultural values, and/or capitalist ideology be operationalized in farm stress research?
- How could the notion of a "good farmer" be used in Extension programs to break down mental health stigma in agricultural communities?
- How do farmers' agricultural practices and ideology impact mental well-being?

Additionally, finding that the largest proportion of farm suicides is due to firearms, researchers must investigate gun control and related policy as a matter of suicide prevention. For Extension to grow in approaches, the research base informing Extension must grow as well. This is not to say that Extension lacks programs that may address structural issues; programs about racial healing offered in several states may help agricultural communities and strengthen mental health (Walcott et al., 2020, 2023).

Extension health programs about farm stress have also primarily focused on individual knowledge and skill. Such knowledge and skills are important, and Extension health programs could benefit by adopting a policy, systems, and environment (PSE) approach that has already been adopted within Extension's nutrition and physical activity programs (Naja-Riese et al., 2019). A PSE approach to agricultural mental health would mean looking into existing policies at community and broader levels, as well as agricultural systems and the environments farmers work, in to be able to identify actionable steps and strategies to improve agricultural mental health. Developing a PSE framework for agricultural mental health (and mental health more broadly) should be a top priority for Extension, as the topic is relevant across core program areas of agriculture, agribusiness, community and economic development, family and consumer sciences, and youth development.

REFERENCES

Agency for Healthcare Research and Quality. (2010, June 15). *AHRQ and Ad Council encourage men to take preventive steps in their health care.* Press release. https://www.ahrq.gov/news/press/pr2010/menshealthpr.htm

Alston, M., & Kent, J. (2008). The big dry: The link between rural masculinities and poor health outcomes for farming men. *Journal of Sociology, 44*(2), 133–147. https://doi.

org/10.1177/1440783308089166
Anderson, J. L. (2020). "You're a bigger man": Technology and agrarian masculinity in postwar America. *Agricultural History, 94*(1), 1–23. https://doi.org/10.3098/ah.2020.094.1.004
Aneshensel, C. S., & Avison, W. R. (2015). The stress process: An appreciation of Leonard I. Pearlin. *Society and Mental Health, 5*(2), 67–85. https://doi.org/10.1177/2156869315585388
Aneshensel, C. S., & Mitchell, U. A. (2014). The stress process: Its origins, evolution, and future. In *Sociology of mental health: Selected topics from forty years, 1970s–2010s* (pp. 53–74). New York: Springer Science + Business Media.
Apesoa-Varano, E. C., Barker, J. C., & Hinton, L. (2018). "If you were like me, you would consider it too": Suicide, older men, and masculinity. *Society and Mental Health, 8*(2), 157–173. https://doi.org/10.1177/2156869317725890
Arif, A. A., Adeyemi, O., Laditka, S. B., Laditka, J. N., & Borders, T. (2021). Suicide mortality rates in farm-related occupations and the agriculture industry in the United States. *American Journal of Industrial Medicine, 64*(11), 960–968. https://doi.org/10.1002/ajim.23287
Baker, C. N., Strong, R., McCord, C., & Redwine, T. (2022). Evaluating the effects of social capital, self-stigma, and social identity in predicting behavioral intentions of agricultural producers to seek mental health assistance. *International Journal of Environmental Research and Public Health, 19*(19), article 19. https://doi.org/10.3390/ijerph191912110
Barlett, P. F., & Conger, K. J. (2004). Three visions of masculine success on American farms. *Men and Masculinities, 7*(2), 205–227. https://doi.org/10.1177/1097184X03257409
Bell, S. E., Hullinger, A., & Brislen, L. (2015). Manipulated masculinities: Agribusiness, deskilling, and the rise of the businessman-farmer in the United States. *Rural Sociology, 80*(3), 285–313. https://doi.org/10.1111/ruso.12066
Bjornestad, A., Brown, L., & Weidauer, L. (2019). The relationship between social support and depressive symptoms in Midwestern farmers. *Journal of Rural Mental Health, 43*(4), 109–117. https://doi.org/10.1037/rmh0000121
Bjornestad, A., Cuthbertson, C., & Hendricks, J. (2021). An analysis of suicide risk factors among farmers in the midwestern United States. *International Journal of Environmental Research and Public Health, 18*(7), article 7. https://doi.org/10.3390/ijerph18073563
Bonds, A., & Inwood, J. (2016). Beyond white privilege: Geographies of white supremacy and settler colonialism. *Progress in Human Geography, 40*(6), 715–733. https://doi.org/10.1177/0309132515613166
Bonilla-Silva, E. (1997). Rethinking racism: Toward a structural interpretation. *American Sociological Review, 62*(3), 465–480. https://doi.org/10.2307/2657316
Booth, N., Briscoe, M., & Powell, R. (2000). Suicide in the farming community: Methods used and contact with health services. *Occupational and Environmental Medicine, 57*(9), 642–644. https://doi.org/10.1136/oem.57.9.642
Bos, A. E. R., Pryor, J. B., Reeder, G. D., & Stutterheim, S. E. (2013). Stigma: Advances in theory and research. *Basic and Applied Social Psychology, 35*(1), 1–9. https://doi.org/10.1080/01973533.2012.746147
Bower, K. L., & Emerson, K. G. (2021). Exploring contextual factors associated with suicide

among older male farmers: Results from the CDC NVDRS dataset. *Clinical Gerontologist, 44*(5), 528–535. https://doi.org/10.1080/07317115.2021.1893885

Bronfenbrenner, U. (1979). *The ecology of human development: Experiments by nature and design.* Cambridge, MA: Harvard University Press.

Brown, L., & Tucker-Seeley, R. (2018). Commentary: Will 'deaths of despair' among whites change how we talk about racial/ethnic health disparities? *Ethnicity & Disease, 28*(2), 123–128. https://doi.org/10.18865/ed.28.2.123

Browning, S. R., Westneat, S. C., & McKnight, R. H. (2008). Suicides among farmers in three southeastern states, 1990–1998. *Journal of Agricultural Safety and Health, 14*(4), 461–472.

Buechler, M. (2022). The never-ending drought for black farmers: The lasting effects of Pigford and the continuance of USDA discrimination notes. *University of Louisville Law Review, 61*(1), i–252.

Burton, R. J. F., Forney, J., Stock, P., & Sutherland, L.-A. (2020). *The good farmer: Culture and identity in food and agriculture.* New York: Routledge. https://doi.org/10.4324/9781315190655

Carpenter, S. (2012). The USDA discrimination cases: Pigford, In re Black Farmers, Keepseagle, Garcia, and Love. *Drake Journal of Agricultural Law, 17*(1), 1–36.

Carter, A., & Lopez, A. L. (2019). Rebranding the farmer: Formula story revision and masculine symbolic boundaries in U.S. agriculture. *Feminist Formations, 31*(3), 25–50. https://doi.org/10.1353/ff.2019.0029

Case, A., & Deaton, A. (2015). Rising morbidity and mortality in midlife among white non-Hispanic Americans in the 21st century. *Proceedings of the National Academy of Sciences, 112*(49), 15078–15083. https://doi.org/10.1073/pnas.1518393112

Case, A., & Deaton, A. (2020). *Deaths of despair and the future of capitalism.* Princeton University Press. https://press.princeton.edu/books/hardcover/9780691190785/deaths-of-despair-and-the-future-of-capitalism

Case, A., & Deaton, A. (2021). Life expectancy in adulthood is falling for those without a BA degree, but as educational gaps have widened, racial gaps have narrowed. *Proceedings of the National Academy of Sciences, 118*(11), e2024777118. https://doi.org/10.1073/pnas.2024777118

Cheesmond, N. E., Davies, K., & Inder, K. J. (2019). Exploring the role of rurality and rural identity in mental health help-seeking behavior: A systematic qualitative review. *Journal of Rural Mental Health, 43*(1), 45–59. https://doi.org/10.1037/rmh0000109

Chengane, S., Beseler, C. L., Duysen, E. G., & Rautiainen, R. H. (2021). Occupational stress among farm and ranch operators in the midwestern United States. *BMC Public Health, 21*(1), 2076. https://doi.org/10.1186/s12889-021-12053-4

Clarke, A. E., Mamo, L., Fosket, J. R., Fishman, J. R., & Shim, J. K. (Eds.). (2010). *Biomedicalization: Technoscience, health, and illness in the U.S.* Durham, NC: Duke University Press.

Clement, S., Schauman, O., Graham, T., Maggioni, F., Evans-Lacko, S., Bezborodovs, N., Morgan, C., Rüsch, N., Brown, J. S. L., & Thornicroft, G. (2015). What is the impact of mental health-related stigma on help-seeking? A systematic review of quantitative and qualitative studies. *Psychological Medicine, 45*(1), 11–27. https://doi.org/10.1017/S0033291714000129

Connell, R. W. (2020). *Masculinities* (2nd ed.). New York: Routledge. https://doi.org/10.4324/9781003116479

Connell, R. W., & Messerschmidt, J. W. (2005). Hegemonic masculinity: Rethinking the concept. *Gender & Society, 19*(6), 829–859. https://doi.org/10.1177/0891243205278639

Conrad, P. (2007). *The medicalization of society*. Baltimore, MD: Johns Hopkins University Press. https://doi.org/10.56021/9780801885846

Conrad, P., & Schneider, J. W. (1980). *Deviance and medicalization: From badness to sickness*. St. Louis, MO: C. V. Mosby Company.

Cooper, A., Corrigan, P. W., & Watson, A. C. (2003). Mental illness stigma and care seeking. *Journal of Nervous & Mental Disease, 191*(5), 339–341. https://doi.org/10.1097/01.NMD.0000066157.47101.22

Corrigan, P. W., Druss, B. G., & Perlick, D. A. (2014). The impact of mental illness stigma on seeking and participating in mental health care. *Psychological Science in the Public Interest, 15*(2), 37–70. https://doi.org/10.1177/1529100614531398

Courtenay, W. H. (2000). Constructions of masculinity and their influence on men's well-being: A theory of gender and health. *Social Science & Medicine, 50*(10), 1385–1401. https://doi.org/10.1016/S0277-9536(99)00390-1

Cowan, T., & Feder, J. (2013). *The Pigford cases: USDA settlement of discrimination suits by Black farmers*. Washington, DC: Congressional Research Service.

Crumb, L., Mingo, T. M., & Crowe, A. (2019). "Get over it and move on": The impact of mental illness stigma in rural, low-income United States populations. *Mental Health & Prevention, 13*, 143–148. https://doi.org/10.1016/j.mhp.2019.01.010

Cuthbertson, C., Brennan, A., Shutske, J., Leatherman, J., Bjornestad, A., Zierl, L., Macy, K., Skidmore, M., Schallhorn, P., Dellifield, J., & Lin, E. (2022). An effective mental health literacy program for farm financial service providers. *Journal of Agromedicine, 28*(2), 127–135. https://doi.org/10.1080/1059924X.2022.2058666

Cuthbertson, C., Brennan, A., Shutske, J., Zierl, L., Bjornestad, A., Macy, K., Schallhorn, P., Shelle, G., Dellifield, J., Leatherman, J., Lin, E., & Skidmore, M. (2022). Developing and implementing farm stress training to address agricultural producer mental health. *Health Promotion Practice, 23*(1), 8–10. https://doi.org/10.1177/1524839920931849

Emslie, C., Ridge, D., Ziebland, S., & Hunt, K. (2006). Men's accounts of depression: Reconstructing or resisting hegemonic masculinity? *Social Science & Medicine, 62*(9), 2246–2257. https://doi.org/10.1016/j.socscimed.2005.10.017

Eschbach, C., Cuthbertson, C., Shelle, G., & Bates, R. (2022). Expanding effective behavioral health literacy programs to address farm stress. *Journal of Extension, 60*(2). https://doi.org/10.34068/joe.60.02.19

Fanon, F. (2008) *Black skin, white masks*. New York: Grove Paperback. https://groveatlantic.com/book/black-skin-white-masks

Food, Conservation, and Energy Act of 2008. (2008). H.R. 2419, 110th Congress. http://www.

congress.gov/bill/110th-congress/house-bill/2419/text

Furey, E. M., O'Hora, D., McNamara, J., Kinsella, S., & Noone, C. (2016). The roles of financial threat, social support, work stress, and mental distress in dairy farmers' expectations of injury. *Frontiers in Public Health, 4*. https://doi.org/10.3389/fpubh.2016.00126

Gallagher, C. A. (1997). White racial formation: Into the twenty-first century. In R. Delgado & J. Stefancic (Eds.), *Critical white studies* (pp. 6–11). Philadelphia: Temple University Press.

Gillborn, D. (2015). Intersectionality, critical race theory, and the primacy of racism: Race, class, gender, and disability in education. *Qualitative Inquiry, 21*(3), 277–287. https://doi.org/10.1177/1077800414557827

Goffman, E. (1963). *Stigma: Notes on the management of spoiled identity*. New York: Simon & Schuster. https://www.simonandschuster.com/books/Stigma/Erving-Goffman/9780671622442

Grant, G. R., Wood, S. D., & Wright, W. J. (2012). Black farmers united: The struggle against power and principalities. *Journal of Pan African Studies, 5*(1), 1–22.

Grocke-Dewey, M., Brennan, A., Freeman, B., Weas, H., Gutheil, J., Stallones, L., & McMoran, D. (2023). Perceived stress, stressors, and preferred stress management strategies among western agricultural producers. *Journal of Rural Mental Health, 47*(3), 152–162. https://doi.org/10.1037/rmh0000233

Gulati-Partee, G., & Potapchuk, M. (2014). Paying attention to white culture and privilege: A missing link to advancing racial equity. *Foundation Review, 6*(1). https://doi.org/10.9707/1944-5660.1189

Gunderson, P., Donner, D., Nashold, R., Salkowicz, L., Sperry, S., & Wittman, B. (1993). The epidemiology of suicide among farm residents or workers in five north-central states, 1980–1988. *American Journal of Preventive Medicine, 9*(3), 26–32. https://doi.org/10.1016/S0749-3797(18)30675-5

Hagen, B. N. M., Sawatzky, A., Harper, S. L., O'Sullivan, T. L., & Jones-Bitton, A. (2022). "Farmers aren't into the emotions and things, right?": A qualitative exploration of motivations and barriers for mental health help-seeking among Canadian farmers. *Journal of Agromedicine, 27*(2), 113–123. https://doi.org/10.1080/1059924X.2021.1893884

Harris, A. P. (2015). [Re]integrating spaces: The color of farming. *Savannah Law Review, 2*(1), 157–200.

Hawkins, D., Davis, L., Punnett, L., & Kriebel, D. (2020). Disparities in the deaths of despair by occupation, Massachusetts, 2000 to 2015. *Journal of Occupational and Environmental Medicine, 62*(7), 484. https://doi.org/10.1097/JOM.0000000000001870

Heaberlin, B., & Shattuck, A. (2023). Farm stress and the production of rural sacrifice zones. *Journal of Rural Studies, 97*, 70–80. https://doi.org/10.1016/j.jrurstud.2022.11.007

Hebl, M. R., & Dovidio, J. F. (2005). Promoting the "social" in the examination of social stigmas. *Personality and Social Psychology Review, 9*(2), 156–182. https://doi.org/10.1207/s15327957pspr0902_4

Herreen, D., Rice, S., Currier, D., Schlichthorst, M., & Zajac, I. (2021). Associations between conformity to masculine norms and depression: Age effects from a population study of

Australian men. *BMC Psychology*, 9(1), 32. https://doi.org/10.1186/s40359-021-00533-6

Hinson, W. R., & Robinson, E. (2008). "We didn't get nothing": The plight of black farmers. *Journal of African American Studies*, *12*(3), 283–302. https://doi.org/10.1007/s12111-008-9046-5

Hoffelmeyer, M. (2021). "Out" on the farm: Queer farmers maneuvering heterosexism and visibility. *Rural Sociology*, *86*(4), 752–776. https://doi.org/10.1111/ruso.12378

Horst, M., & Marion, A. (2019). Racial, ethnic and gender inequities in farmland ownership and farming in the U.S. *Agriculture and Human Values*, *36*(1), 1–16. https://doi.org/10.1007/s10460-018-9883-3

Jones-Bitton, A., Best, C., MacTavish, J., Fleming, S., & Hoy, S. (2020). Stress, anxiety, depression, and resilience in Canadian farmers. *Social Psychiatry and Psychiatric Epidemiology*, *55*(2), 229–236. https://doi.org/10.1007/s00127-019-01738-2

Jorm, A. F. (2012). Mental health literacy: Empowering the community to take action for better mental health. *American Psychologist*, *67*, 231–243. https://doi.org/10.1037/a0025957

Jorm, A. F. (2015). Why we need the concept of "mental health literacy." *Health Communication*, *30*(12), 1166–1168. https://doi.org/10.1080/10410236.2015.1037423

Jorm, A. F., Kitchener, B. A., & Reavley, N. J. (2019). Mental Health First Aid training: Lessons learned from the global spread of a community education program. *World Psychiatry*, *18*(2), 142–143. https://doi.org/10.1002/wps.20621

Kahan, B., & Goodstadt, M. (2001). The interactive domain model of best practices in health promotion: Developing and implementing a best practices approach to health promotion. *Health Promotion Practice*, 2(1), 43–67. https://doi.org/10.1177/152483990100200110

Kelly, C. M., Mithen, J. M., Fischer, J. A., Kitchener, B. A., Jorm, A. F., Lowe, A., & Scanlan, C. (2011). Youth mental health first aid: A description of the program and an initial evaluation. *International Journal of Mental Health Systems*, *5*(1), 4. https://doi.org/10.1186/1752-4458-5-4

Kennedy, A., Cerel, J., Kheibari, A., Leske, S., & Watts, J. (2021). A comparison of farming- and non-farming-related suicides from the United States' National Violent Deaths Reporting System, 2003–2016. *Suicide and Life-Threatening Behavior*, *51*(3), 504–514. https://doi.org/10.1111/sltb.12725

Kennedy, A. J., Brumby, S. A., Versace, V. L., & Brumby-Rendell, T. (2020). The ripple effect: A digital intervention to reduce suicide stigma among farming men. *BMC Public Health*, *20*(1), 813. https://doi.org/10.1186/s12889-020-08954-5

Kimmel, M. (2017). *Angry White Men.* New York: Bold Type Books.

Klingelschmidt, J., Milner, A., Khireddine-Medouni, I., Witt, K., Alexopoulos, E. C., Toivanen, S., LaMontagne, A. D., Chastang, J.-F., & Niedhammer, I. (2018). Suicide among agricultural, forestry, and fishery workers: A systematic literature review and meta-analysis. *Scandinavian Journal of Work, Environment & Health*, *44*(1), 3–15.

Kori, R. K., Mandrah, K., Hasan, W., Patel, D. K., Roy, S. K., & Yadav, R. S. (2020). Identification of markers of depression and neurotoxicity in pesticide exposed agriculture workers. *Journal of Biochemical and Molecular Toxicology*, *34*(6), e22477. https://doi.org/10.1002/jbt.22477

Kutcher, S., Wei, Y., & Coniglio, C. (2016). Mental health literacy: Past, present, and future. *Canadian Journal of Psychiatry, 61*(3). https://journals.sagepub.com/doi/full/10.1177/0706743715616609

Laing, R. D. (1965). *The divided self: An existential study in sanity and madness.* New York: Penguin Books.

Le, T. N., Zhang, W., Brown, E., Crum, J., & Wong, A. (2023). Risks & protective factors for depression & suicide among Hawai'i agricultural producers. *Journal of Agromedicine, 28*(4), 734–745. https://doi.org/10.1080/1059924X.2023.2226131

Lee, B. C., Bendixsen, C., Liebman, A. K., & Gallagher, S. S. (2017). Using the socio-ecological model to frame agricultural safety and health interventions. *Journal of Agromedicine, 22*(4), 298–303. https://doi.org/10.1080/1059924X.2017.1356780

Liepins, R. (2000). Making men: The construction and representation of agriculture-based masculinities in Australia and New Zealand. *Rural Sociology, 65*(4), 605–620. https://doi.org/10.1111/j.1549-0831.2000.tb00046.x

Little, J. (2002). Rural geography: Rural gender identity and the performance of masculinity and femininity in the countryside. *Progress in Human Geography, 26*(5), 665–670. https://doi.org/10.1191/0309132502ph394pr

Loveridge, S., Skidmore, M., Shupp, R., Miller, P. K., Cuthbertson, C., & Goetz, S. (2023). Rural US residents recognize anxiety better than urbanites and suburbanites but hold similar stigma. *Journal of Rural Health*, 1–10. https://doi.org/10.1111/jrh.12757

Luedke, A. J. (1993). *Factors affecting levels of financial stress and distress among Texas farm families: The 1980s farm crisis.* Thesis, Texas A&M University. https://oaktrust.library.tamu.edu/handle/1969.1/ETD-TAMU-1993-THESIS-L948

Magdoff, F. (2013). Twenty-first-century land grabs. *Monthly Review, 65*(6), 1. https://doi.org/10.14452/MR-065-06-2013-10_1

Mahalik, J. R., Burns, S. M., & Syzdek, M. (2007). Masculinity and perceived normative health behaviors as predictors of men's health behaviors. *Social Science & Medicine, 64*(11), 2201–2209. https://doi.org/10.1016/j.socscimed.2007.02.035

Mahalik, J. R., & Di Bianca, M. (2021). Help-seeking for depression as a stigmatized threat to masculinity. *Professional Psychology: Research and Practice, 52*(2), 146–155. https://doi.org/10.1037/pro0000365

Mahoney, M. R. (1997). The social construction of whiteness. In R. Delgado & J. Stefancic (Eds.), *Critical white studies* (pp. 330–333). Philadelphia: Temple University Press. https://www.jstor.org/stable/j.ctt1bw1kc5.74

Malat, J., Mayorga-Gallo, S., & Williams, D. R. (2018). The effects of whiteness on the health of whites in the USA. *Social Science & Medicine, 199*, 148–156.

Markowitz, F. E. (2005). Sociological models of mental illness stigma: Progress and prospects. In P. W. Corrigan (Ed.), *On the stigma of mental illness: Practical strategies for research and social change* (pp. 129–144). Washington, DC: American Psychological Association. https://doi.org/10.1037/10887-005

Martin, M., Hartmann, K., & Archibeque-Engle, S. (2023). A critical whiteness exploration of the National FFA Organization. *Journal of Agricultural Education, 64*(1), Article 1. https://

doi.org/10.5032/jae.v64i1.34

Martin, M. J., & Hartmann, K. (2022). Intersectionality of whiteness, racism, and homophobia among agriculture students. *Whiteness and Education, 7*(1), 78–92. https://doi.org/10.1080/23793406.2020.1839942

Marx, K., & Engels, F. (2014). *The communist manifesto.* New York: International Publishers Co. https://www.intpubnyc.com/browse/communist-manifesto

McCusker, M. G., & Galupo, M. P. (2011). The impact of men seeking help for depression on perceptions of masculine and feminine characteristics. *Psychology of Men & Masculinity, 12*(3), 275–284. https://doi.org/10.1037/a0021071

McIntosh, P. (1990). White privilege: Unpacking the invisible knapsack. *Independent School, 49*(2), 31.

McLeod, J. D. (2012). The meanings of stress: Expanding the stress process model. *Society and Mental Health, 2*(3), 172–186. https://doi.org/10.1177/2156869312452877

Miller, C. D. M., & Rudolphi, J. M. (2022). Characteristics of suicide among farmers and ranchers: Using the CDC NVDRS 2003-2018. *American Journal of Industrial Medicine, 65*(8), 675–689. https://doi.org/10.1002/ajim.23399

Naja-Riese, A., Keller, K. J. M., Bruno, P., Foerster, S. B., Puma, J., Whetstone, L., MkNelly, B., Cullinen, K., Jacobs, L., & Sugerman, S. (2019). The SNAP-Ed Evaluation Framework: Demonstrating the impact of a national framework for obesity prevention in low-income populations. *Translational Behavioral Medicine, 9*(5), 970–979. https://doi.org/10.1093/tbm/ibz115

Nayak, A. (2007). Critical whiteness studies. *Sociology Compass, 1*(2), 737–755. https://doi.org/10.1111/j.1751-9020.2007.00045.x

Norton, M. I., & Sommers, S. R. (2011). Whites see racism as a zero-sum game that they are now losing. *Perspectives on Psychological Science, 6*(3), 215–218. https://doi.org/10.1177/1745691611406922

Oliffe, J. L., & Phillips, M. J. (2008). Men, depression and masculinities: A review and recommendations. *Journal of Men's Health, 5*(3), 194–202. https://doi.org/10.1016/j.jomh.2008.03.016

Oliffe, J. L., Rossnagel, E., Seidler, Z. E., Kealy, D., Ogrodniczuk, J. S., & Rice, S. M. (2019). Men's depression and suicide. *Current Psychiatry Reports, 21*(10), 103. https://doi.org/10.1007/s11920-019-1088-y

Omi, M., & Winant, H. (2014). *Racial formation in the United States* (3rd ed.). New York: Routledge.

Osterud, N. G. (1993). Gender and the transition to capitalism in rural America. *Agricultural History, 67*(2), 14–29.

Pearlin, L. I. (2010). Life course and the stress process: Some conceptual comparisons. *Journals of Gerontology, 65B*(2), 207–215.

Pearlin, L. I., Menaghan, E. G., Lieberman, M. A., & Mullan, J. T. (1981). The stress process. *Journal of Health and Social Behavior, 22*(4), 337–356. https://doi.org/10.2307/2136676

Pearlin, L. I., Schieman, S., Fazio, E. M., & Meersman, S. C. (2005). Stress, health, and the life course: Some conceptual perspectives. *Journal of Health and Social Behavior, 46*(2),

205–219. https://doi.org/10.1177/002214650504600206
Pescosolido, B. A. (2013). The public stigma of mental illness: What do we think; What do we know; What can we prove? *Journal of Health and Social Behavior*, *54*(1), 1–21. https://doi.org/10.1177/0022146512471197
Pescosolido, B. A., Halpern-Manners, A., Luo, L., & Perry, B. (2021). Trends in public stigma o mental illness in the US, 1996–2018. *JAMA Network Open*, *4*(12), e2140202. https://doi.org/10.1001/jamanetworkopen.2021.40202
Pescosolido, B. A., & Martin, J. K. (2015). The stigma complex. *Annual Review of Sociology*, *41*(1), 87–116. https://doi.org/10.1146/annurev-soc-071312-145702
Pescosolido, B. A., Monahan, J., Link, B. G., Stueve, A., & Kikuzawa, S. (1999). The public's view of the competence, dangerousness, and need for legal coercion of persons with mental health problems. *American Journal of Public Health*, *89*(9), 1339–1345. https://doi.org/10.2105/AJPH.89.9.1339
Peterson, C., Sussell, A., Li, J., Schumacher, P. K., Yeoman, K., & Stone, D. M. (2020). Suicide rates by industry and occupation—National Violent Death Reporting System, 32 states, 2016. *Morbidity and Mortality Weekly Report*, *69*(3), 57–62. https://doi.org/10.15585/mmwr.mm6903a1
Phelan, J. C., Link, B. G., Stueve, A., & Pescosolido, B. A. (2000). Public conceptions of mental illness in 1950 and 1996: What is mental illness and is it to be feared? *Journal of Health and Social Behavior*, *41*(2), 188–207. https://doi.org/10.2307/2676305
Pilgeram, R. (2007). 'Ass-kicking' women: Doing and undoing gender in a U.S. livestock auction. *Gender, Work & Organization*, *14*(6), 572–595. https://doi.org/10.1111/j.1468-0432.2007.00372.x
Ragonese, C., & Barker, G. (2019). Understanding masculinities to improve men's health. *The Lancet*, *394*(10194), 198–199. https://doi.org/10.1016/S0140-6736(19)31609-5
Ramos, A. K., Su, D., Lander, L., & Rivera, R. (2015). Stress factors contributing to depression among Latino migrant farmworkers in Nebraska. *Journal of Immigrant and Minority Health*, *17*(6), 1627–1634. https://doi.org/10.1007/s10903-015-0201-5
Reed, D. B., & Claunch, D. T. (2020). Risk for depressive symptoms and suicide among U.S. primary farmers and family members: A systematic literature review. *Workplace Health & Safety*, *68*(5), 236–248. https://doi.org/10.1177/2165079919888940
Riley, M. (2016). Still Being the 'Good Farmer': (Non-)retirement and the preservation of farming identities in older age. *Sociologia Ruralis*, *56*(1), 96–115. https://doi.org/10.1111/soru.12063
Ringgenberg, W., Peek-Asa, C., Donham, K., & Ramirez, M. (2018). Trends and characteristics of occupational suicide and homicide in farmers and agriculture workers, 1992–2010. *Journal of Rural Health*, *34*(3), 246–253. https://doi.org/10.1111/jrh.12245
Roche, A. M., Pidd, K., Fischer, J. A., Lee, N., Scarfe, A., & Kostadinov, V. (2016). Men, work, and mental health: A systematic review of depression in male-dominated industries and occupations. *Safety and Health at Work*, *7*(4), 268–283. https://doi.org/10.1016/j.shaw.2016.04.005
Rochlen, A. B., Whilde, M. R., & Hoyer, W. D. (2005). The real men. Real depression campaign:

Overview, theoretical implications, and research considerations. *Psychology of Men & Masculinity*, 6(3), 186–194. https://doi.org/10.1037/1524-9220.6.3.186

Roediger, D. (2007). *The wages of whiteness: Race and the making of the American working class.* Brooklyn, NY: Verso. https://www.versobooks.com/products/2966-the-wages-of-whiteness

Ron, A. (2016). Farmers, capitalism, and government in the late nineteenth century. *Journal of the Gilded Age and Progressive Era*, *15*(3), 294–309. https://doi.org/10.1017/S1537781416000165

Rosenberg, G. N. (2016). *The 4-H harvest: Sexuality and the state in rural America.* Philadelphia: University of Pennsylvania Press. https://www.jstor.org/stable/j.ctt173zm92

Rudolphi, J. M., Berg, R. L., & Parsaik, A. (2020). Depression, anxiety and stress among young farmers and ranchers: A pilot study. *Community Mental Health Journal*, *56*(1), 126–134. https://doi.org/10.1007/s10597-019-00480-y

Scheff, T. (1999). *Being mentally ill: A sociological study* (3rd ed.). New York: Routledge. https://www.routledge.com/Being-Mentally-Ill-A-Sociological-Study/Scheff/p/book/9780202305875

Scheyett, A., Bayakly, R., & Whitaker, M. (2019). Characteristics and contextual stressors in farmer and agricultural worker suicides in Georgia from 2008–2015. *Journal of Rural Mental Health*, *43*(2–3), 61–72. https://doi.org/10.1037/rmh0000114

Schroeder, S., Tan, C. M., Urlacher, B., & Heitkamp, T. (2021). The role of rural and urban geography and gender in community stigma around mental illness. *Health Education & Behavior*, *48*(1), 63–73. https://doi.org/10.1177/1090198120974963

Seidler, Z. E., Dawes, A. J., Rice, S. M., Oliffe, J. L., & Dhillon, H. M. (2016). The role of masculinity in men's help-seeking for depression: A systematic review. *Clinical Psychology Review*, *49*, 106–118. https://doi.org/10.1016/j.cpr.2016.09.002

Seidler, Z. E., Rice, S. M., Ogrodniczuk, J. S., Oliffe, J. L., & Dhillon, H. M. (2018). Engaging men in psychological treatment: A scoping review. *American Journal of Men's Health*, *12*(6), 1882–1900. https://doi.org/10.1177/1557988318792157

Sickel, A. E., Seacat, J. D., & Nabors, N. A. (2014). Mental health stigma update: A review of consequences. *Advances in Mental Health*, *12*(3), 202–215. https://doi.org/10.1080/18374905.2014.11081898

Sileo, K. M., & Kershaw, T. S. (2020). Dimensions of masculine norms, depression, and mental health service utilization: Results from a prospective cohort study among emerging adult men in the United States. *American Journal of Men's Health*, *14*(1), 1557988320906980. https://doi.org/10.1177/1557988320906980

Silton, N. R., Flannelly, K. J., Milstein, G., & Vaaler, M. L. (2011). Stigma in America: Has anything changed? Impact of perceptions of mental illness and dangerousness on the desire for social distance: 1996 and 2006. *Journal of Nervous and Mental Disease*, *199*(6), 361. https://doi.org/10.1097/NMD.0b013e31821cd112

Skegg, K., Firth, H., Gray, A., & Cox, B. (2010). Suicide by occupation: Does access to means increase the risk? *Australian & New Zealand Journal of Psychiatry*, *44*(5), 429–434.

Staiger, T., Stiawa, M., Mueller-Stierlin, A. S., Kilian, R., Beschoner, P., Gündel, H., Becker, T.,

Frasch, K., Panzirsch, M., Schmauß, M., & Krumm, S. (2020). Masculinity and help-seeking among men with depression: A qualitative study. *Frontiers in Psychiatry, 11.*

Stallones, L. (1990). Suicide mortality among Kentucky farmers, 1979–1985. *Suicide and Life-Threatening Behavior, 20*(2), 156–163. https://doi.org/10.1111/j.1943-278X.1990.tb00098.x

Stewart, H., Jameson, J. P., & Curtin, L. (2015). The relationship between stigma and self-reported willingness to use mental health services among rural and urban older adults. *Psychological Services, 12,* 141–148. https://doi.org/10.1037/a0038651

Szasz, T. (1961). *The myth of mental illness: Foundations of a theory of personal conduct.* New York: Dell Publishing Co.

Szasz, T. (1987). *Insanity: The idea and its consequences.* Hoboken, NJ: John Wiley & Sons.

Tyler, S., & Moore, E. (2013). Plight of Black farmers in the context of USDA Farm Loan Programs: A research agenda for the future. *Professional Agricultural Workers Journal, 1*(1). https://tuspubs.tuskegee.edu/pawj/vol1/iss1/6

USDA NIFA. (2023). *Farm and Ranch Stress Assistance Network (FRSAN).* http://www.nifa.usda.gov/grants/programs/farm-ranch-stress-assistance-network-frsan

Valkonen, J., & Hänninen, V. (2013). Narratives of masculinity and depression. *Men and Masculinities, 16*(2), 160–180. https://doi.org/10.1177/1097184X12464377

Walcott, E., Ostrom, M., Burton, D., & Kay, D. (2023). How facilitating dialogues on race is fostering systemic change in Cooperative Extension. *SRDC Special Topics.* Mississippi State University. https://scholarsjunction.msstate.edu/cgi/viewcontent.cgi?article=1000&context=srdctopics-racialunderstanding

Walcott, E., Raison, B., Welborn, R., Pirog, R., & Emery, M. (2020). We (all) need to talk about race: Building Extension's capacity for dialogue and action. *Journal of Extension, 58*(5).

Wald, S. D. (2016). *The nature of California: Race, citizenship, and farming since the Dust Bowl.* Seattle: University of Washington Press.

Weingarten, D. (2017). Why are America's farmers killing themselves? *The Guardian.* https://www.theguardian.com/us-news/2017/dec/06/why-are-americas-farmers-killing-themselves-in-record-numbers

Weingarten, D., & Mulkern, A. (2017, December 15). I wrote about farmers' suicides—and the reaction has been overwhelming. *The Guardian.* https://www.theguardian.com/environment/2017/dec/15/i-wrote-about-farmers-suicides-and-the-reaction-has-been-overwhelming

Wyman, M. (2005). Affirming whiteness: Visualizing California agriculture. *Steinbeck Studies, 16*(1), 32–55. https://doi.org/10.1353/stn.2007.0022

Zinn, H. (2015). *A people's history of the United States.* New York: HarperCollins.

An Overview of Disaster Education in Extension and Implications for Health Extension

Josh Gunn

Health Extension's focus on social determinants of health creates an opportunity to address numerous social issues that intersect by removing the complexities through a holistic and collaborative approach. This is especially true when looking at Health Extension's role in helping people before, during, and after disasters, where various disasters can create and exacerbate environmental conditions that further impact an individual's health. Negative physical health effects can occur directly from a disaster through bodily harm, or more indirectly through impacts on environmental variables like food, water, and air. Disaster events can result in mental health consequences due to trauma suffered (Makwana, 2019). Further, without addressing these issues, individuals have an increased risk of suffering negative health effects from future disasters (Leppold et al., 2022).

Extension has a long history helping individuals, families, businesses, and communities prepare for and recover from disasters. This chapter provides an overview of the history and current status of disaster education across the Cooperative Extension System (CES) and provides examples that demonstrate the various pre- and postdisaster efforts that occur in different state Extension programs. A discussion of challenges and opportunities facing the foundation and future of both disaster education and Health Extension follows. Recommendations are also provided for how CES is uniquely suited to expand disaster education and Health Extension so both initiatives continue to equitably support the growing need for these types of services in the United States.

Early History of Extension and Disasters

While the CES has supported disaster education and helped with response and recovery efforts in various states and counties across the United States since 1914, when Cooperative

Extension was created, the earliest coordinated effort at the national level occurred in the 1960s. As background, the Federal Civil Defense Act of 1950 was passed and signed into law and established a formal U.S. policy on disaster relief (Federal Civil Defense Act, 1950). President Truman said at the time of signing the law that the purpose was a "basic framework for preparations to minimize the effects of an attack on our civilian population, and to deal with the immediate emergency conditions such an attack would create" (Homeland Security Digital Library, 2023). Section 2 of the Act (1246) states "the policy and intent of Congress to provide a plan of civil defense for the protection of life and property in the United States from attack," "that responsibility for civil defense shall be vested primarily in the several States and their political subdivisions," and that "the Federal Government shall provide necessary coordination and guidance . . . and shall provide necessary assistance as hereinafter authorized."

The Federal Civil Defense Administration, which fell under the U.S. Department of Defense (not the U.S. Department of War, where the branches of the military were held at the time), was directed to carry out these roles and by 1962 was structurally located in the Office of Civil Defense. At this time, President Kennedy enacted Executive Order 10998, which was an effort to de-silo these responsibilities by coordinating with other agencies in different departments. Among these were specific responsibilities assigned to the Secretary of Agriculture intended to leverage the land-grant network of county agents located across the country (Purcell, 1968).

In 1963, the U.S. Secretary of Agriculture issued a memo outlining CES responsibilities to address rural civil defense (RCD), specifically the development and implementation of the Rural Civil Defense Education Program, which supported various programs, including community shelter planning and implementing an annual fallout protection survey. Each state had an RCD leader who conducted training for county defense boards. In addition to a focus on agriculture, coordination occurred in other program areas, including 4-H youth development and family and consumer sciences (home economics). Emergency preparedness week was a regular event that CES engaged in to increase awareness nationally on what steps individuals, families, communities, and businesses could take to prepare for future disasters (Purcell, 1968).

This national experiment was short-lived, because in 1968, the Office of Civil Defense discontinued funds to the CES. Rural civil defense leader positions were terminated and absorbed into other state agency budgets or by state Extension programs (Purcell, 1968). Extension's response to the termination of these funds varied by state, and while the details of how each state responded are not well documented, today's vast differences among state Extension programs in their offerings of disaster education services hint at which programs continued to provide this service after the funding ended. For example, in Michigan, there was no coordinated effort at the state level after the withdrawal of funds after 1968, but there was a continued practice for County Extension directors (CEDs) to maintain engagement with county emergency managers. When a reorganization of programmatic and administrative units occurred at the state Extension level in 2010, the CED model was replaced with a regional/district model, and without a statewide expectation of maintaining this involvement in county emergency management, this function disappeared, further separating Extension from providing this type of support locally.

Modern History (EDEN) of Extension and Disasters

For nearly 25 years following the end of RCD funding, there was a lack of a national coordinated effort to support Extension professionals who work on disaster education and technical assistance. However, the concept of a multistate coordinated disaster network reemerged after the Mississippi and Missouri River floods of 1993 significantly impacted farmland, homes, and businesses. Due to the region not being familiar with this level of extreme disaster, Extension professionals from various state programs began a regional effort known as the "North Central Region Disaster Reduction Group." After a few years of coordinating at this level, and as a result of interest from outside the region, the group initiated efforts to expand to a national organization in 1998 known as the Extension Disaster Education Network (EDEN).

Whether it was because disasters became more regular, more costly, or more prominent in the news, Extension found itself being called to assist with disasters more regularly in the early 2000's (EDEN, n.d.-a). This increase in demand for assistance has been credited to the September 11, 2001, terrorist attacks and the subsequent mandates by the U.S. government for state and local governments to have a disaster preparedness plan (Black, 2012). The 2000s and 2010s also saw major hurricanes hit the Gulf Coast (Allison [2001], Katrina [2005], Ike [2008], and Harvey [2017]) and the eastern seaboard (Superstorm Sandy [2010]), which damaged unprecedented amounts of property and caused a tragic loss of lives. More recently, the impacts of climate change are being seen on areas where population growth continues at rapid levels, infrastructure has not been maintained nor improved, and buildings are designed and located where they are at risk.

Extension Disaster Education Today

Today, EDEN serves as the primary national network for state Extension staff to connect for professional development and to access resources they can use to help people in their community when a disaster occurs. EDEN hosts regular training across program areas, including pre- and postdisaster phases, an annual conference to continue learning, and networking opportunities and an online resource called the EDEN Resource Dashboard (n.d.-b). is funded in part by a U.S. Department of Agriculture (USDA) National Institute of Food and Agriculture (NIFA) grant that supports the Food and Agriculture Defense Initiative (FADI). The FADI grant is limited in scope for what funds can cover, and Extension professionals who participate in EDEN also obtain funding through more traditional means, including time funded through their state's cooperative agreement that pools local, state, and federal funds, or through competitive funding that is targeted at a specific issue or geography. Funding outside of the FADI grant funds provide EDEN members an opportunity to address larger issues through expanded resources. Examples of how this separate funding has been successful in some states are described later in this chapter.

One way to characterize CES's involvement in disaster education across the network is to place engagement on a three-category continuum: (1) institutions that conduct little or no disaster education, (2) institutions that have statewide or targeted efforts to educate on disaster preparedness and other ways to make community more resilient from disasters, and (3) institutions that have staff in certain counties or statewide who are formally included in local or statewide emergency management plans. There are also institutions that would be somewhere between category 2 and category 3 in engagement level.

EDEN is structured in a way that institutions are members, and each member institution has a point of contact (POC) and allows for additional faculty and staff to participate as a delegate. While the majority of member institutions are 1862 land-grant universities (LGUs), there is a strong contingent of 1890 LGUs, as well as Sea Grant programs. More recently, there has been an effort to include 1994 land-grant tribal colleges, as well as other organizations that have a mission similar to EDEN's or could otherwise partner with EDEN to conduct disaster education activities. Even without this designation, EDEN makes sure that the tools and resources developed and shared by their members are open to all by placing them on the EDEN Resource Dashboard.

There are several subcommittees in EDEN that focus on programmatic aspects (Agriculture, Natural Resources, Community/Economic Development, 4-H, Family and Consumer and Sciences) and on specific initiatives identified as a priority by the EDEN Executive Committee and POCs. Chairs of each subcommittee have a seat and a voice on the EDEN Executive Committee. This ensures that EDEN efforts are relevant to as many different types of Extension professionals as possible, while also providing leadership to key efforts like the annual conference, marketing and membership, and development of standards to support disaster exercises led by Extension professionals.

There is a complexity that needs to be recognized in the current model of how disaster education is conducted by various CESs, as disaster education work is also conducted by Extension professionals nationally who have no affiliation with EDEN. This work is vital to the communities being served, but difficult to catalogue and share. As such, the next section focuses primarily on work being done by Extension professionals affiliated with EDEN but attempts to include examples regardless of this affiliation, where appropriate.

Overview and Phases of Disasters

While several models for disaster management exist that range from being more conceptual to more practical, there are generally four phases that occur before and after a disaster occurs. These include prevention/mitigation and preparation before the event, and response and recovery after the event. Conceptualized as a system, recovery should then inform the two predisaster phases to reduce or eliminate impacts from future disaster events (see the disaster management cycle figure).

Disaster management cycle from existing literature identifying four phases.

Mitigation and prevention pertain to any efforts that focus on policy, social, physical, or economic changes that will reduce or eliminate the impact of a future disaster. It may be helpful to consider these efforts occurring in ways that modify the larger systems that dictate how a disaster might affect communities, businesses, families, and individuals. Examples of mitigation activities include reinforcing or protecting infrastructure that ensures continuity of services after a disaster (e.g., power, roads), the construction of physical barriers like dams, dykes, and levees designed to protect flood-prone areas, policies that prevent new construction in disaster-prone areas like wildfire zones and floodplains, and incentive programs that provide financial support for floodproofing or protecting existing property from future disasters.

While sometimes confused with mitigation, preparation efforts are less focused on broader systems change and more focused on being prepared to implement actions when a disaster occurs. Examples of preparation include increasing awareness of risks through education and outreach, and practicing actions that should be taken when a disaster occurs. For example, a household could develop and implement an evacuation plan and have food and supplies ready. On a larger scale, a municipality or other government entity may run scenarios or "exercises" that include all organizations that are a part of the plan and walk through steps that should be taken when a particular disaster occurs.

The response phase of a disaster occurs during and immediately after a disaster event. Due to interconnectedness to the field of emergency management and policy language, there is an increased focus on immediate risks to "life and property" that is valuable to understand. Moreover, it is important to acknowledge that there are many other impacts that are more difficult to quantify but are still important to consider. If an emergency management plan is in place, then the response to a disaster typically follows that plan by coordinating with relevant actors and organizations until the risks to life and property have been eliminated.

The disaster recovery phase begins when the immediate threat to life and property has been eliminated. Activities that may occur during the recovery phase include conducting damage assessments, and efforts to help families, businesses, and communities return to a "predisaster normalcy" or "new normal" that is more resilient to impacts of future disasters.

The conceptual framework outlined in the disaster management cycle figure is intended to help readers understand the policy and management aspects of disasters, particularly as they relate to different roles of emergency managers. In addition, the figure may be helpful to researchers who apply a systems approach to conceptualizing how societies can achieve resilience. In their book *Resilience Thinking*, Walker and Salt define resilience as being "the capacity of a system to absorb disturbance and still retain its basic function and structure" (2006, xiii). While this conceptual framework clarifies the basic activities that occur before and after a disaster, in practice there are many more nuances where phases may overlap, or different terminology may be used if different fields of study or practice are involved.

Phases Through a Lens of Recovery

One additional model that is beneficial to understanding how various actors engage in post-disaster activities is the recovery continuum, which highlights that response and recovery are not distinct phases, but overlapping ones where coordination among actors involved in both needs to occur. The disaster phases figure frames preparedness as an ongoing activity in a community and visualizes not only how response and recovery can overlap, but also that different types of recovery efforts have very different time scales.

In exploring the role businesses can play in communities to assist recovery following disasters, MacDonald et al. (2015) provide great examples of activities that can occur in each of four phases. Preparedness activities are ongoing activities that can include planning of recovery strategies and actions, investing in infrastructure to mitigate impacts of disaster, educating the public to increase resilience, performing disaster exercises to test disaster preparedness, and helping businesses with continuity planning. Short-term response activities typically occur within the first days and weeks and can include helping in search and rescue operations, supporting basic human needs (food, waters, shelter) and creating support services, assessing health and safety issues, and establishing temporary health services.

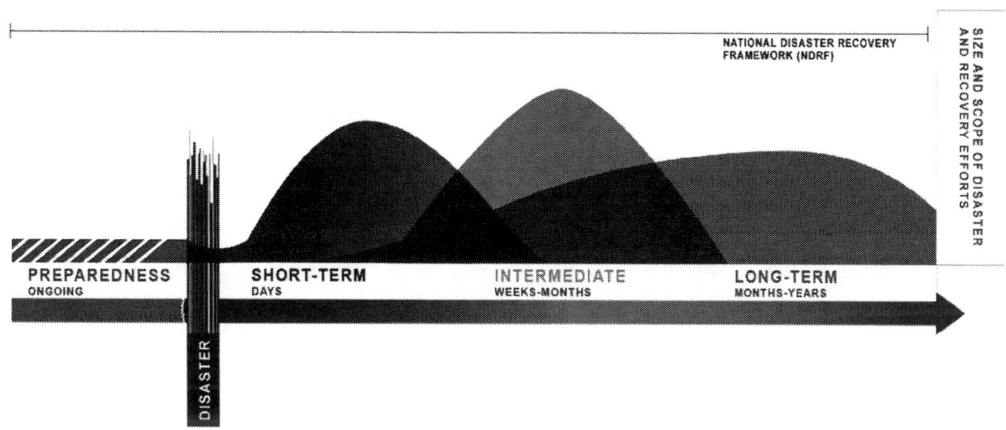

Disaster phases through a lens of response and recovery. Model adapted from U.S. Department of Homeland Security's National Disaster Recovery Framework (2016), which informs the Federal Emergency Management Agency.

Intermediate Recovery activities occur within a time frame of weeks to months and can include providing interim housing, removing debris and damaged buildings,) securing support for social, physical, and mental health, continuing to repair and rebuild buildings and infrastructure, and keeping the community updated on status of recovery. Long-term recovery activities occur on a time frame of months to years and can include establishing permanent housing solutions, rebuilding infrastructure for future needs, continuing psychosocial or mental health support, and establishing other support for businesses and the local economy.

Phases Through a Lens of Health and Human Services

Creating new Health Extension strategies to be a part of each disaster phase can support Extension Disaster Education to purposefully include health and community-based healthcare dimensions. At the mitigation and prevention phases, including local health care professionals, human service collaboratives, and multisector coalition members in disaster planning will generate community input and buy-in to those plans. During the mitigation and prevention phases, health equity concepts should also push communities to consider population inequities and health disparities in planning and responsiveness. Using health data, demographic Census data, and geospatial information to make decisions is recommended. Health Extension in the disaster response phase looks like equitable services for all, including a role for CES community-based education, research, programming, and interventions to support health care. Finally, Health Extension in the disaster recovery phase looks like fair and equal access to resources for all populations and communities. Centering health equity into EDEN priorities may lead CES to design much-needed culturally sensitive approaches for disaster planning and response across languages and ethnicities.

Other connections between health and disasters that may inspire new strategies, include the following:

- Physical conditions and mental health factors of an individual can dictate the ability or degree to which they may be able to prepare for and respond to a disaster.
- A disaster could be a slow-moving, chronic problem where there is sustained contamination and contact with individuals that causes health issues (i.e., air and water quality issues), or could be a more acute event that quickly affects individual or public health (i.e., disease outbreak).
- Trauma can occur from both an acute, single-disaster event, as well as chronic ones if disasters are repetitive.
- Like chronic disasters effecting trauma, repetitive exposure to disaster events can create a feedback loop that further impairs an individual's ability to prepare for or respond to the next disaster.

While these are just a few examples, one of the most important ways Health Extension can help communities prepare for and respond to disasters is through strengthening capacity around mental health. By addressing mental health issues before, during, and after a disaster, Health Extension can create resiliency that allows people to "return to normalcy" or otherwise prevent health impacts from future disaster events. One framework that could be helpful when building out implementation strategies for Health Extension efforts when it comes to disasters is from the *Training Manual for Mental Health and Human Service Workers in Major Disasters* (DeWolfe, 2000). A summary of critical moments during disasters identified in this Department of Health and Human Services (DeWolfe, 2000, 15–22) training manual include the following:

- Predisaster: Increased alertness of a disaster as it moves from a threat, to warning, and impact.
- Heroic: The response during and immediately after a disaster that can take tremendous physical and mental energy.
- Honeymoon: Immediate danger is no longer present, and people are happy to have survived. This phase can also create a sense of optimism that resources will be arriving to assist in short- and long-term recovery.
- Disillusionment: Grief and anger may be felt due to mentally processing any losses that occurred, family and financial stressors, and resentment due to resources not becoming available to the degree that they might have been previously perceived.
- Reconstruction: Grief continues, but people begin to move forward trying to return to a sense of normalcy. Can be impaired by trigger events. Being

impacted by additional disasters, seeing other disasters occur, or "anniversary reactions" may all cause traumatic responses well after the first disaster occurred.

The frameworks just outlined provide context for how CES currently provides disaster education and new growth areas that can support communities. The next section provides several examples of this work, but still uses the four basic phases of disaster management as a framework for when these activities occur within communities.

Predisaster Extension Work

Some of the most successful Extension programs that support disaster education receive additional funding from state and federal sources to do so. The U.S. Department of Homeland Security and Federal Emergency Management Agency (FEMA) provide support to several education programs within and outside of university systems. One of the university-funded programs is led by the Texas A&M Engineering Extension Service (TEEX), a part of the Texas A&M University System. TEEX provides several educational programs, including "Community Resilience for Senior Leaders," "Critical Infrastructure Protection," "Cybersecurity," "Disaster Recovery," "EMS/Public Health Emergency Preparedness," "Incident Management and Response," "Response-Hazardous Materials Search and Rescue," Sports and Special Events Management," and other online trainings. Many states are required to go through TEEX's homeland security training office or state office of emergency management to register (TEEX Programs, 2023).

EDEN also provides coordination and support to help communities prepare for disasters. One significant example is the training materials and technical support provided to help create community capacity through the development of local networks of individuals and organizations termed community organizations active in disaster (COADs). The terms COADs and VOADs (volunteer organizations active in disaster) are often used interchangeably, but one nuance is that COADs are typically comprised of community organizations at the local level and focus on providing otherwise unmet services during and after a disaster. VOADs can be active during all phases of a disaster, are typically statewide, and have membership designed to bring resources to local COAD efforts. COADs still operate within the state/territory VOAD system (Center for Volunteer and Nonprofit Leadership, 2023). Participating in and coordinating the development of COADs occurs regularly across CES programs. EDEN has even developed a resource for Extension professionals to help support COADs, the *Community Organizations Active in Disaster Manual* (Extension Disaster Education Network, 2023).

EDEN has a committee dedicated to developing materials that support Extension professionals conducting disaster exercises in their community. Disaster exercises require a great deal of coordination and strong relationships with applicable emergency managers and response organizations, and a state Extension's role is often to help facilitate connecting these and other groups for the purposes having them all work together as they perform a walk-through of a simulated disaster scenario. While state and federal governments often coordinate these activities for larger scale disasters, because local emergency managers typically do not have the capacity to do this themselves while also actively managing the scenario, Extension's role can be significant.

EDEN and partner members also help communities develop hazard mitigation plans (HMPs), which are essential to reducing the impact of disasters through identifying all pertinent risks and vulnerabilities and developing long-term strategies for the community to adopt that protect lives and property from such events. While 85 percent of the nation's population lives in an area already covered by a HMP, there are still many counties (particularly rural ones) that do not (FEMA, 2023). Further, HMPs need to be updated and resubmitted for approval every five years, which can be a burdensome process for communities where this responsibility is a collateral duty of an elected or appointed official who may lack technical expertise around disasters or knowledge on how to access FEMA funds that can be used to support the development of HMPs by outside consultants or other organizations.

One of the best examples of how Extension helps communities to develop HMPs is in Illinois, where the Extension program not only is active in several local HMPs being developed annually but also is involved in leading the development of the state's HMP, which provides guidance for local HMPs in the state. Additionally, funding from a USDA NIFA Special Needs grant is providing support for Michigan State University and the University of Illinois to work with EDEN and other Extension programs to develop a train-the-trainer program that helps Extension professionals learn how to assist their local communities in the development of hazard mitigation plans. This training will be offered to Extension professionals nationally in 2024.

A Look at Coastal Communities

One of the foundations of Extension education is that learning is most effective through an experiential process. Like walking through a disaster exercise, there are a few examples of tools and training that have been developed that make it easier for communities to engage in various predisaster educational opportunities. Two examples of how Extension has successfully developed tools that facilitate conversations include materials and training developed by Extension professionals from the Gulf of Mexico region designed to support preparedness activities to help communities become more resilient to hurricanes.

The Coastal Community Resilience Index (CCRI) is a tool developed by the Mississippi–Alabama Sea Grant Consortium and the National Oceanic and Atmospheric Administration (NOAA) Coastal Storms Program. CCRI is a series of questions that guide conversations among community members to identify any potential vulnerabilities the community might have and want to address before the next disaster. In addition to developing the tool, Extension's role as convener and facilitator helps community members engage in an approximately three-hour process to facilitate preparation. The benefits of such a tool are that it is inexpensive and relatively easy to use (both for the community as well as for the Extension professional). The CCRI has been modified and expanded for use in other areas, and the suite of tools now includes a Ports Resilience Index and a resilience index supporting coastal businesses, including tourism, fisheries, and oyster farming (Coastal Community Resilience Index, 2021).

A more data-intensive tool also developed in the Gulf of Mexico is the Community Health and Resource Management (CHARM) system. It facilitates conversations that support participatory planning using geographic information systems software and has a tabletop apparatus that allows participants to look at current data models (e.g., land use, soils, vegetation, impervious surface cover) and to create scenarios for modeling various community development options to see potential social and economic impacts of various disasters on new development. Getting the tool ready takes a great deal of time, as data collection and cleaning happen beforehand, but once CHARM is ready for a community there are several exercises that Extension professionals can use to facilitate different conversations around resilience and future development scenarios that can help inform community decision making (Texas Community Watershed Partners, 2023).

One exciting recent development related to providing disaster education and support for communities is being led by Dr. Gavin Smith and the Coastal Resilience and Sustainability Initiative at North Carolina State University. While the effort seeks to partner with Extension and Sea Grant programs, it is geared more broadly to leveraging several different sources of university expertise to provide "direct, coordinated, and place-based assistance and capacity building to ensure that disadvantaged communities have the opportunity to access and deliver generational resilience and infrastructure investments." This is through an effort supported by funding from FEMA's Hazard Mitigation Assistance Grants program (North Carolina State University Coastal Resilience and Sustainability Initiative, 2023). The cadre of academic professionals developed through this effort will hopefully bring needed capacity to underserved communities who need technical assistance with navigating the complexities of applying for and managing funds in pre- and postdisaster contexts.

Postdisaster Extension Work in Response and Recovery

In addition to education and technical assistance, there are still many state Extension programs that are involved in postdisaster response efforts, at least at the county level. This is likely due to both the historical tradition of Extension professionals being administratively located within a county government, and the initial focus of Extension on Disaster Rural Civil Defense Education outlined in the 1963 memo mentioned earlier in this chapter. How these structures have evolved over time varies greatly from state to state, but most commonly county Extension professionals are written into a county emergency response plan due to their presumed technical expertise around agriculture-related topics.

After Hurricane Harvey hit the Texas coast in 2017, the governor established the Commission to Rebuild Texas, which did, among other things, reorganize the state's Division of Emergency Management, moving it from the Texas Department of Public Safety to the Texas A&M University System (TAMUS). This change, in addition to establishing the division as a stand-alone agency, also allowed the division increased access to university resources, including research, laboratories, students, and the LGU Extension program (TAMUS, 2020). With the move also came funding to support the development of six regional disaster assistance response teams (DARTS), including more than 30 new Extension positions focused on providing support to communities so they can become more resilient to disasters. In addition to providing regional support to local communities pre and post disaster, they are also deployable via a strike team model, to enter a community after a disaster and in coordination with emergency management officials, conduct damage assessments and provide other critical support related to animal sheltering and supply operations (Texas A&M AgriLife Extension Service, 2022).

Opportunities and Challenges with Growing Health Extension and Disaster Education

There are several challenges and opportunities facing the growth of disaster education and Health Extension efforts in the United States. Broadly speaking, these shared challenges fall into two categories: (1) capacity, funding, and relevancy, and (2) leaning into strengths while acknowledging limitations.

Funding and Communicating Need and Relevancy

Concerns around funding are nothing new for CES programs. Federal Extension funding through the Smith–Lever Act of 1914 has been stagnant for decades, state budgets fluctuate depending on political priorities, financial crises, and budget boons, and declining populations in rural counties mean a lower tax base, which all impair an ability to be strategic and think long term about program priorities. McDowell (2004) argued that Extension's relevancy (and therefore funding) is diminished by CES's paradoxical dependence on our traditional agriculture roots while needing to also expand into more diverse program areas (like health). McDowell continued that this creates a "downward spiral" when set within a funding mechanism where state and local partners prioritize funding for agriculture-related activities over other program areas, which can, at a minimum, lead Extension programs to prioritize conducting and reporting on agriculture-related activities and, at worst, result in cutting funding for all non-agriculture-related activities.

That has not been this author's experience, however. As the Texas Sea Grant Extension Program Leader from 2014 to 2017, I was fortunate enough to be involved in a partnership with FEMA's Region Six team that provided funding to support pre-disaster planning activities to communities across the Texas coast and even inland in other disaster-prone areas, an estimated $500,000 annually in new funding that continues today. At Michigan State University, the state of Michigan regularly funds MSU Extension to address critical and emerging issues. For example, during the 2008 financial and housing crisis, the state of Michigan directed $5 million to MSU Extension to support education around finance and homeownership, including assistance on household budgeting and understanding the foreclosure process so people can work to try and keep their home, sell their home, or minimize the impact if the foreclosure process occurs. In addition to funding provided by the state to address the housing crisis, there are other initiatives that have been prioritized and funded by the state of Michigan beyond the traditional funding that is provided to MSU Extension as match for federal funds, particularly around natural resource management and community development. These projects, however, are often short term and in support of a state agency priority that recognizes MSU Extension as a valued partner in connecting with local communities to achieve desired outcomes. It's likely that Extension Directors and Program Leaders across the country have similar stories on how their program has been supported financially through these types of special projects. However, McDonnell's argument does make sense when looking at a nationally consistent funding mechanism. In addition to Smith-Lever funds not increasing significantly over the past several decades, the historical underfunding of 1890 LGUs and 1994 land-grant Tribal colleges still must be addressed. Funding and prioritization from the federal level seem to comprise an obvious solution to continuing to do the great work CES is known for, while simultaneously creating capacity around other program priorities like disaster education and Health Extension.

Another factor tied closely to funding is CES's relevance. It is often said that Extension is the best kept secret of the state's LGU, and while it is important to demonstrate that we are utilizing public funds in a wise manner, we often do not do a good enough job marketing our work on a more regular basis. DeBord (2007) argues that CES programs need to be adaptive and have an organizational structure that addresses flexibility in being responsive to emerging or different programming needs, but also have a marketing and communications strategy that engages various decision makers at the local, state, and federal levels at all phases of the program cycle, from program development to evaluation and reporting on impacts.

Another aspect of CES's relevancy is articulating need. Disasters of all types are becoming more costly and significant events occur more regularly. This is expected as populations in urban areas increase, temperatures continue to rise, rainfall occurs less regularly but individual precipitation events get more intense, and other environmental changes occur along with our changing climate. Each event is tragic, but each one is also an opportunity to demonstrate CES's ability to help families, communities, and businesses respond, recover, and prepare for the next one.

Leaning into Strengths While Recognizing Limitations

By far, CES's competitive advantage is our longstanding relationships within communities. While many state Extension programs maintained strong local relationships by continuing disaster education programming since the early 1960s when the U.S. Secretary of Agriculture outlined CES's roles in supporting communities related to rural civil defense, Extension programs that stopped disaster education programming likely lost relationships at local levels. However, there are good examples of how relationships can be reforged. In Illinois, this occurred after the Midwest floods of June 2008. While Illinois Extension had been involved with EDEN by then, it had mostly conducted disaster education work in limited communities. Through an initiative called the Illinois ResourceNet, which at the time provided financial support to nonprofits and communities for training that helped build capacity with the goal of increasing access to state and federal financial resources, Illinois Extension began helping four counties identified as needing assistance developing HMPs. This effort was so successful that the Quad Cities Community Foundation then requested Illinois Extension's assistance with modifying a previous program called "Ready Business," which helped businesses develop continuity and disaster preparedness plans for nonprofit organizations in their area. Through sustained effort and initial and continued funding from various partners, Illinois Extension now provides statewide support for HMP development in counties across the state, leads the effort in developing COADs in communities across the state, and has been designated by the state of Illinois to coordinate the effort to develop the statewide HMP (Carrie McKillip, personal communication, August 22, 2023).

One weakness that the author of this chapter and the volume co-editors recognize is the lack of peer-reviewed literature that captures the history and work of CES in the area of disaster education. There is a lack of strategy around how Extension scholarship is evaluated, published, and accessed. The lack of peer-reviewed publications has impaired disaster education efforts across CES because this history is missing. One reason for this is that the performance review criteria for many county- or district-based Extension professionals is fundamentally different than for faculty, or those Extension professionals housed in academic departments under a tenure system. Generally speaking, field staff (off-campus) Extension professionals are evaluated on products developed, attendance at events, and measurable impacts from programs, which are prioritized over journal articles and grant acquisition success. Although it is not possible to generalize across all Extension programs in CES, in some cases the minimum expectation of Extension professionals is direct education programming, and if they are able to engage with faculty on scholarship efforts, that is a bonus.

There is likely a great deal of Extension-related work documented in other peer-reviewed journals across disciplines, but many of the Extension professionals that publish in these journals do not necessarily lead with their role in Extension. As a result, it is often difficult to distinguish a publication from a regular faculty member from one with an Extension appointment. EDEN, like similar national Extension coordinating bodies, has tried to address this by collecting and housing publications within its own group (i.e., the EDEN Resource Dashboard mentioned earlier in this chapter). However, these efforts still result in siloing of Extension products, and risk products disappearing whenever the coordinating body for EDEN moves, requiring documents to be moved to new servers with different capabilities and requirements.

One of the most impressive systems for archiving Extension publications is the National Sea Grant Library, which was created early on in Sea Grant history. Established in 1970 (initially called the Sea Grant Depository), it set up standards for naming documents so the state it was created in, the year it was created, and the subject matter could all be easily identified, which helped with searching and retrieving documents, as well as facilitated the process for reviewing and revising older documents (University of Southern California Libraries, 2023). In 2021, this collection moved from a host institution (University of Rhode Island) to the NOAA Institutional Repository and Central Library Catalog (Sea Grant Collection, 2023).

Regional Differences

One argument against a national strategy to conduct disaster education work is that each state has different levels of infrastructure and funding for related activities, and different regions are susceptible to different types of disasters. The volcanoes, earthquakes, and forest fires on the West Coast do not all carry the same level of risk in other areas that may be more susceptible to hurricanes and oil spills, like the Gulf of Mexico. However, the facts that CES exists across the United States, that local relationships are already well established, and that the skill sets of facilitation and dissemination of educational materials are ubiquitous across expectations of Extension professionals allow for this regional variation of disaster type, as long as there are subject-matter experts from academia and state/federal agencies that Extension professionals can reach out to for technical expertise.

Other Organizations Potentially Better Suited to Do the Work

One of the greatest challenges facing CES programs is recognizing our own limitations. Specifically, our greatest competitive advantage of having long-standing relationships in communities across the state is not necessarily true in some areas, particularly urban areas. In these areas, there may be long-standing nongovernment organizations (NGOs), urban-serving universities, or other organizations that have a similar mission to Extension but have a stronger relationship to the community. While CES may rush to provide services in these communities that have been historically underserved, as for all work in health equity, we want to be mindful of existing relationships and come to terms with the fact that CES may not play a predominant role in providing leadership.

As mentioned, Health Extension in the recovery phase has a focus on fair, equal access to resources for all populations and communities. EDEN has supported this approach as well by building this competency across the CES. Over the past few years, led by EDEN members from 1890 LGUS, EDEN has offered trainings across the United States in different CES regions on "religious and cultural literacy and competency in disasters" that covers different topics, including how religious and cultural language is different from government culture and language, and the importance of engaging with different religious and cultural communities before and after disaster.

Existing Infrastructure and Capacity in FEMA

Another factor that CES programs must consider when planning disaster education programming is that FEMA has evolved over the past few decades and currently provides several services that overlap with how Extension operates. In fact, the foray of FEMA into community-based engagement, postdisaster deployment of resources, its massive portfolio of educational initiatives, and funding of targeted and competitive efforts are all a reason that CES programs should not reinvent the wheel or compete with FEMA, and instead should find out how to complement these programs or fill in gaps as needed. FEMA has an incredible network of funding and education already available and has expanded its recruitment and hiring of professionals with a community planning background to help understand and support community needs before and after disasters occur. Examples of FEMA resources include the following:

- The National Disaster Recovery Framework (FEMA, 2016) is a comprehensive approach to facilitate coordination of recovery assistance across different agencies and different levels of government.
- The FEMA Emergency Management Institute provides trainings for community leaders, as well as state, federal, and tribal government officials, and coordinates the Higher Education Program, which is designed to support and connect formal university-based programs (degree-granting) in areas of emergency management, homeland security, and more.
- National Fire Academy, under the U.S. Fire Administration/FEMA, provides accreditation to municipals, as well as college/universities, that provide education to first responders on fire and emergency services.
- Center for Domestic Preparedness in Anniston, Alabama, has on-campus incident management, mass casualty response, and response to terrorist attacks and natural disasters.
- Rural Domestic Preparedness Consortium consists of academic partners knowledgeable in the curriculum of educational materials at the Department of Homeland Security.
- Continuing Training Grants Program consists of cooperative agreements through a competitive process for organizations to deliver FEMA-certified trainings that are needed in their state/region. In 2023, the program provided $6 million to competitive applications, $8 million for cybersecurity preparedness

to members of the National Cybersecurity Preparedness Consortium, and $2 million to members of the Alliance for System Safety of Unmanned Aircraft Systems for the development of new trainings.

Conclusion

What does this mean for the future of CES's role in Disaster Education and Health Extension? There remain at least three major questions that need to be answered before a clear path emerges. First, what is the current national role of CES in Disaster Education and Health Extension, where are the gaps in activities, and where can Extension fit in? Fortunately, members of EDEN have already begun efforts to develop a survey internal to Extension professionals to better understand at the local and state level what disaster education programs are being offered, what phase(s) of a disaster are addressed, and whether or not the program is available statewide or only in some localities. However, this effort is only the beginning. More importantly, a national needs assessment that surveys state and federal agency personnel involved in pre- and postdisaster efforts (FEMA, U.S. Department of Health And Human Services, etc.), as well as local actors like emergency managers and representatives from COADs, would help create a clearer picture of the status of CES in disaster education nationally. Are these federal, state, and local actors aware of CES? If so, have they worked with CES? For those who are not aware, by highlighting the mission of CES, do these actors see a potential role for Extension in disaster management? If so, what might that role be? Such a survey would significantly inform the understanding of the status of CES in disaster management and education efforts nationally and help identify the direction CES should take moving forward.

A second question is, what services and functions should a national disaster education network provide? One direction the CES should take is developed from the first question—a national network like EDEN should help support CES in moving in that direction. Creating a space where faculty researchers and Extension professionals can engage with one another would be a valuable first step to facilitating collaboration, developing a common language, and building competency in both groups that allows for research results and applied efforts to be shared with one another that can advance work in both arenas.

This national network should also help support addressing the third question, which is, how are we to create and fund a national network that is integrated at the local, state, and federal levels? The simple answer is that for this to occur, it needs to become a national priority with appropriate funding. Due to the overlap of Health Extension and disaster education, this could occur simultaneously, but it would not be essential to do so. Like the calls by Grumbach and Mold (2009) for a Primary Care Cooperative Extension Service, and the Cooperative Extension's National Frameworks for Health (Braun et al., 2014; Burton et al., 2021), recognition of the need for national prioritization and funding for initiatives is a common occurrence. While not all have a mission to conduct Extension work like LGUs, universities also enjoy status as Sea Grant, Sun

Grant, and Space Grant programs designed to integrate university's teaching, research, and Extension missions. Jacob (2013) has previously called for an Urban Grant system to replicate the successes of traditional CES programs in urban areas. EDEN does seem primed to help lead this effort into the future. With a network already in place and increasing connectivity with partners and agencies at a national level, this could increase recognition so that changes occur down the road. If that does happen, it should be in close partnership with FEMA and their vast resources. Without a nationally coordinated effort, a more pragmatic approach on how CES might increase integration with disaster management efforts could be termed "muddling through," where state Extension programs figure this out on their own.

Both the top-down success that occurred in Texas, where the state formally identified and charged its Extension program with key disaster management responsibilities (and appropriate funding), and the bottom-up evolution that occurred in Illinois, where its Extension program had worked in this area for years and the state has slowly increased financial support into key areas like HMPs and the development of COADs, are examples of "mini-experiments" that demonstrate how other states can attempt such efforts successfully in their own states. Whether there is a successful national strategy, or ad hoc successes at the state level, disaster education provides a critical service that CES is uniquely structured to provide. Finally, and most importantly, advancing efforts for both disaster education and Health Extension means providing essential support to individuals, families, communities, and businesses that can work to ensure equitable services and public safety for all.

REFERENCES

Black, L. (2012). Disaster preparedness and the Cooperative Extension Service. *Journal of Extension, 50*(3), article 45. https://doi.org/10.34068/joe.50.03.45

Braun, B., Bruns, K., Cronk, L., Kirk Fox, L., Koukel, S., LeMenestrel, S., Lord, L., Reeves, C., Rennekamp, R., Rice, C., Rodgers, M., Samuel, J., Vail, A., & Warren, T. (2014). *Cooperative Extension's national framework for health and wellness.* Washington, DC: Extension Committee on Organization and Policy.

Burton, D., Canton, A., Coon, T., Eschbach, C., Gunn, J., Gutter, M., Jones, M., Kennedy, L., Martin, K., Mitchell, A., O'Neal, L., Rennekamp, R., Rodgers, M., Stluka, S., Trautman, K., Yelland, E., & York, D. (2021). *Cooperative Extension's national framework for health equity and well-being.* Washington, DC: Extension Committee on Organization and Policy.

Center for Volunteer and Nonprofit Leadership. (2023). https://blog.volunteernow.org/coad-voad

Coastal Community Resilience Index. (2021). *Sea Grant Mississippi-Alabama.* https://masgc.org/coastal-storms-program/resilience-index

DeBord, K. (2007). How integrated Extension programming helps market Cooperative Extension: The North Carolina recommendation. *Journal of Extension, 45*(5), article 2. https://tigerprints.clemson.edu/joe/vol45/iss5/2

DeWolfe, D. J. (2000). *Training manual for mental health and human service workers in major disasters* (2nd ed.). Report no. ADM-90-538. Washington, DC: Federal Emergency Management Agency.

Extension Disaster Education Network (EDEN). (n.d.-a). History. https://extensiondisaster.net/about/history

Extension Disaster Education Network (EDEN). (n.d.-b). *Resource dashboard.* https://extensiondisaster.net/resource-dashboard

Extension Disaster Education Network. (2023). *Community organizations active in disasters manual.* https://extensiondisaster.net/hazard-resources/community-economic/community-organizations-active-in-disaster

Federal Civil Defense Act. (1950). Public Law 920, 81st Congress (64 Stat. 1245). https://www.hsdl.org/c/tl/federal-civil-defense-act-1950

Federal Emergency Management Agency (FEMA). (2016). *National disaster recovery framework* (2nd ed.). U.S. Department of Homeland Security.

Federal Emergency Management Agency (FEMA). (2023). https://www.fema.gov/emergency-managers/risk-management/hazard-mitigation-planning/status

Grumbach, K., & Mold, J. W. (2009). A health care cooperative extension service: Transforming primary care and community health. *Journal of American Medical Association, 301*(24), 2589–2591.

Jacob, J. S. (2013). Experts, extension and democracy: A prospectus for a new urban grant. *Journal of Extension, 51*(5), article 11.

Homeland Security Digital Library. (2023, August). https://www.hsdl.org/c/tl/federal-civil-defense-act-1950

Leppold, C., Gibbs, L., Block, K., Reifels, L., & Quinn, P. (2022). Public health implications of multiple disaster exposures. *The Lancet,* Public Health, *7*(3), e274–e286.

MacDonald C., Davies B., Johnston D. M., Paton D., Malinen S., Näswall K., Kuntz J., & Stevenson J. R. (2015). *A framework for exploring the role of business in community recovery following disasters.* GNS Science Report 2015/62. GNS Science, Lower Hutt, New Zealand.

Makwana, N. (2019). Disaster and its impact on mental health: A narrative review. *Journal of Family Medicine and Primary Care, 8*(10), 3090–3095.

McDowell, G. (2004). Is Extension an idea whose time has come—and gone? *Journal of Extension, 42*(6), article 2.

North Carolina State University Coastal Resilience and Sustainability Initiative. (2003). https://coastalresilience.ncsu.edu/expertise/gsmith5

Purcell, G. (1968, May). *Emergency preparedness: A part of the county Extension program.* Extension memo EM 2941. Washington State University. https://hdl.handle.net/2376/10462

Sea Grant Collection (2023). *National Oceanic and Atmospheric Administration.* https://seagrant.noaa.gov/inside-sea-grant/seagrantcollection

Texas A&M AgriLife Extension. (2022). *Improving community resiliency through disaster assessment & recovery.* https://agrilifeextension.tamu.edu/wp-content/uploads/2023/03/Disaster-Assessment-Recovery_2023-03.pdf

Texas A&M Engineering Extension Service (TEEX). (2023). *Department of Homeland Security.*

FEMA-funded. https://teex.org/dhs-fema-funded
Texas A&M University System (TAMUS). (2020). *Administrator's statement.* 87th Regular Session, Agency Submission, Version 1.
Texas Community Watershed Partners. (2023). https://www.communitycharm.org
University of Southern California Libraries (2023). *National sea grant library.* https://libraries.usc.edu/databases/national-sea-grant-library
Walker, B. H., & Salt, D. (2006). *Resilience thinking: Sustaining ecosystems and people in a changing world.* Washington, DC: Island Press.

Community-Based Approaches to Address Opioid Misuse

Elizabeth H. Weybright, Courtney Cuthbertson, Dusti Linnell, and Kylie Pybus

Since the rise of prescription opioid overdose deaths in the late 1990s, the opioid crisis has been unrelenting, likely due to the complex systems that contribute to misuse, overdose, and death (Centers for Disease Control and Prevention, National Center for Injury Prevention and Control, 2023). The opioid crisis is described as having three "waves" related to dominant patterns of substance use. The first wave started in 1999 with the rise in prescription opioid overdose deaths. The second wave started around 2010 with a rise in prescription opioid and heroin overdose deaths (Cruz & Martín-del-Campo, 2022), and the third wave began around 2013 with the rise in synthetic opioid overdose deaths, largely driven by fentanyl (Jenkins, 2021). Current evidence suggests we have entered a fourth wave of the crisis characterized by stimulant and opioid use, along with more prevalent mental illness comorbidities. The compounding effect of stimulant use and mental illness alongside opioid use is hitting rural areas even harder due to the scarcity of behavioral health resources there (Jenkins, 2021).

What is apparent is that it will take health care systems and providers working alongside community-based organizations to address opioid misuse more effectively, especially among those individuals and communities most impacted. Just as Extension's role has expanded over time to incorporate behavioral health, it has also expanded in the scope of substance use efforts from general prevention to now an explicit focus on opioids. This is likely due to the inherent strengths in the Extension system, including serving as a trusted resource to disseminate research and evidence-based information, existing infrastructure of county-based offices paired with a statewide presence and federal support, and collaboration and partnership within local communities (Weybright et al., 2024).

Rural communities are disproportionately impacted by opioid use and related consequences. This is likely due, in part, to limited behavioral health services, implementation of fewer evidence-based opioid use disorder (OUD) policy and program activities, and higher distribution of opioid prescriptions as compared to urban communities (Hoffman et al., 2021; Swann et al., 2021). Predominantly located in rural areas, agricultural occupations also present some of the highest risk for injury and death (Jadhav et al., 2015) and, as a result, are at high risk for opioid misuse. As an example, we can look at the state of Oregon, where rural counties have a higher than average number of jobs in industries such as agriculture, forestry, and fishing and are also classified as economically distressed (Business Oregon, 2023). Jobs in these industries tend to be physically demanding, require long hours, have high incidences of nonfatal injuries, and have increased risk for musculoskeletal disorders and chronic pain (Dasgupta et al., 2018; Kucera et al., 2010). These conditions, made worse by risky prescribing practices, can lead to increased use of opioids for pain management and higher rates of OUD, hospitalization, and death. A recent study on opioids in agricultural occupations found just this—a negative, direct impact of OUD on individuals and families and an indirect impact on businesses and the agricultural workforce broadly (Radunovich et al., 2022). Ultimately, using the CES to address behavioral health, and opioids in particular, serves to support individual health of agricultural workers, as well as the broader economic system in which these workers operate.

History of Opioid Funding and Programming in Extension

Although substance use prevention and health promotion programming occur throughout CES, the increase in opioid-focused efforts was largely driven by availability of funds. Federal funding agencies have taken notice of the potential for Extension to address the opioid crisis. The U.S. Department of Agriculture (USDA) funded opioid efforts through the Rural Health and Safety Education mechanism to "address the needs of rural Americans by providing individual and family health education programs . . . to support the utilization of telehealth, telemedicine, and distance learning strategies for education and training in minority rural communities related to opioids" (U.S. Department of Agriculture, 2020, 3). In partnership with USDA, the Substance Abuse and Mental Health Services Administration (SAMHSA) funded land-grant institutions through the Rural Opioid Technical Assistance (ROTA) program to "develop and disseminate training and technical assistance for rural communities on addressing opioid issues affecting these communities" (Department of Health and Human Services, 2019, 4). SAMHSA funding has now shifted to a regional model in line with the ten regions Health and Human Services defines across the United States. Ultimately, this kicked off an infusion of opioid focused funding into Extension to the tune of $22.7 million dollars between 2018 and 2020 (Washburn et al., 2022).

The Extension system formally established the Extension Opioid Crisis Response Workgroup in 2017 after noting that many communities across the country were seeing increases in opioid overdose deaths (Extension Opioid Crisis Response Workgroup, 2018). The purpose of the workgroup was to identify existing frameworks and activities in the land-grant system, create a website to disseminate opioid-related resources, identify needs and potential funding sources, and start developing a framework that could be used for system-wide efforts. At the time, Extension professionals expressed concern and hesitation around working on topics related to substance use. For some, the explicit concern was that substance use was a medical issue meant for health care providers to manage, and there was implied concern that substance use was a moral issue that some did not want to get into. There was also a general discomfort among people in county-based Extension professions who felt it was a difficult topic to discuss and a new content area for them. This discomfort continues in some places today. However, Extension has a long history of working in health education and promotion and has been well situated to provide research-based information about substance use and recovery. Ultimately, the additional funding pushed Extension into places where, for some, they were less comfortable going.

The workgroup conducted a survey of people within the Extension system to understand behavioral health programs offered and capacity for opioid-related work (Extension Opioid Crisis Response Workgroup, 2018). Largely, the survey found that Extension professionals perceived a mismatch between the needs of communities and Extension's capacity to address the opioid crisis. More than two-thirds of respondents believed Extension should play a role in reducing opioid use and misuse in their state but fewer than a quarter felt their organization had capacity to do so. The workgroup report concluded with seven research-based considerations for further integrating Extension and behavioral health, specifically opioids, listed here:

1. Conduct assessments of local capacity and readiness to address behavioral health topics.
2. Provide basic behavioral health training to extension educators working in the community.
3. Prioritize existing program offerings based on level of opioid-related evidence.
4. Train state and regional leaders on models for translating science into practice.
5. Develop the "opioid response network," a training and technical assistance support system for building capacity and readiness.
6. Create a strategic plan for collaborating with federal opioid-related agencies and efforts.
7. At the federal level, increase financial investment into opioid-focused personnel and programs delivered through Extension.

In particular, the workgroup recommended that a base level of knowledge should be required for all Extension staff interacting with the public, and that coordination with federal agencies could enhance any efforts. The seven considerations provided guidance at the federal and state level for next steps in Extension.

These considerations were echoed by Washburn and colleagues (2022) in their summary of the gaps in Extension's ability to respond to the opioid crisis, where they cited a main issue of personnel capacity. Authors cite at the county level a lack of appropriate professional training in areas related to substance misuse, and at the state or national level, not enough specialists with expertise to provide such professional development. This leaves limited capacity across both program delivery and support. For states that received them, federal funds from SAMHSA and USDA did serve to increase personnel capacity for program delivery, at least in the short term. For example, a scoping review of Extension-delivered substance use programming, including in states funded by SAMHSA's ROTA mechanism, found 31 percent of records reviewed (i.e., peer-reviewed journal articles, gray literature) described delivery of opioid-related training, 29 percent described delivery of evidence-based programs or approaches, and 14 percent described research- or evidence-informed approaches (Hagaman et al., 2023). This scoping review points to how Extension is addressing opioids across the United States.

Substance use is not a new issue. It is noteworthy that it was the opioid crisis that caught the attention of the Extension system in such a large way, which was not the case with the cocaine and crack epidemic from the 1980s and early 1990s. Racial disparities in prescriptions for opioid medications have been cited as a contributing factor, as Black patients' pain is downplayed by medical professionals compared to white patients, and Black patients are often not prescribed opioid medications even when clinically indicated (Kunins, 2020; Swift et al., 2019). Some have noted as a key difference that the crisis of opioid overdose deaths starting in the 2010s primarily impacted white families and has been treated as an issue of health, compared to other substance use crises impacting communities of color that were largely criminalized and framed as issues of criminal justice (Hart & Hart, 2019; Kunins, 2020; Santoro & Santoro, 2018). Within the Extension system, we have a responsibility in our opioid and substance use-related work to acknowledge racial disparities in substance use histories and to hold ourselves accountable for racial disparities in how programs are initiated and to whom they are offered.

Across the Cooperative Extension system nationally, there are individuals and groups who are engaging communities to address opioids, with positive outcomes. This chapter focuses on existing work, framed by the Institute of Medicine's behavioral health continuum of care, and on future opportunities to expand for greater impact. These examples may serve as models for Health Extension.

Opioid-Related Efforts across the Behavioral Health Continuum

The Institute of Medicine's (IOM) (1994) behavioral health continuum of care serves as a guide to organize and understand the types of approaches implemented in Extension and related health outcomes addressed. The original continuum included prevention, treatment, and recovery but was later updated to add health promotion. The current continuum (see the figure an adapted version) views health promotion as important for the entire health continuum but also places it before prevention, treatment, and recovery. These terms are described using the IOM definitions (National Academies of Sciences, Engineering, and Medicine, 2019, 16–17):

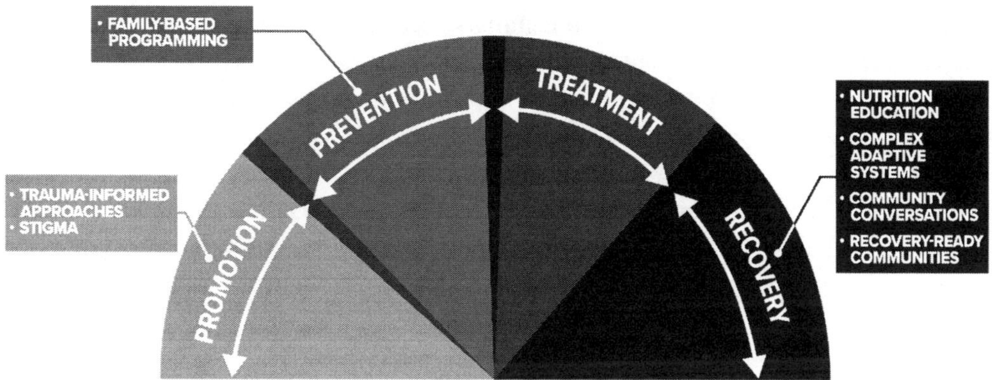

The Institute of Medicine Behavioral Health continuum with chapter examples of community-based approaches addressing opioids. Institute of Medicine (1994). Adapted and reproduced with permission from the National Academy of Sciences, courtesy of the National Academies Press, Washington, DC.

- Promotion includes "strategies to develop skills-based positive attributes such as self-regulation, self-efficacy, goal setting, and positive relationships."
- Prevention includes "strategies offered prior to the onset of a disorder that are intended to prevention reduce the risk for its development."
- Treatment refers to care given to an individual who is demonstrating [behavioral health] challenges or has been diagnosed with a behavioral health disorder" to reduce the duration, severity, and co-occurrence of behavioral health disorders.
- Recovery is called maintenance by the IOM and refers to "care given to prevent relapse, recurrence, or further deterioration of [behavioral health] status."

The IOM health continuum and definitions are useful when considering opioid-focused work within the Extension system from assessment to implementation, evaluation, and reporting. The original authors of the health continuum acknowledged that the boundaries between wedges may not be as fixed as they appear, due to overlapping outcomes and approaches serving multiple goals. We agree and have therefore illustrated these boundaries as blurred. Despite this, we feel it serves a useful frame to bridge Extension behavioral health efforts and health systems. In this chapter, we use this figure to provide examples (see callout boxes the Institute of Medicine Behavioral Health continuum figure) of how Extension programs are addressing needs within and across areas of the continuum. Our first two examples focus on health promotion.

Promotion: Using Trauma-Informed Approaches

Complex trauma is associated with opioid misuse and use disorder among adolescents (Quinn et al., 2019) and adults (Stein et al., 2017), with 70 percent of youth opioid misuse attributable to adverse childhood experiences (ACEs) (Swedo et al., 2020). Calls have been made for trauma-informed approaches to be used in addressing the opioid crisis as many trauma-related disorders occur frequently among people with substance use disorders (SUDs) and vice versa (Campaign for Trauma-Informed Policy and Practice, 2017). Incorporating trauma-informed principles into community organizations creates safe and secure environments that tend to people's physical, emotional, and mental triggers without retraumatization. Trauma-informed approaches refer to

> A program, organization, or system that . . . realizes the widespread impact of trauma and understands potential paths for recovery; recognizes the signs and symptoms of trauma in clients, families, staff, and others involved with the system; and responds by fully integrating knowledge about trauma into policies, procedures, and practices, and seeks to actively resist re-traumatization. (Substance Abuse and Mental Health Services Administration, 2014, 9)

Although such approaches could be listed under multiple wedges of the health continuum (see the Institute of Medicine Behavioral Health continuum figure), they can be used with all individuals to promote healthy emotional coping skills and prevent adverse reactions. When used by an organization, trauma-informed approaches can be an important part of developing a safe and trusting environment.

The Northwest Rural Opioid Technical Assistance Collaborative at Washington State University partnered with the Extension-based Child and Family Research Unit to develop a trauma-informed training for Extension personnel and volunteers, with the short-term goal of increasing capacity for use of trauma-informed approaches within rural communities and the long-term goal of decreasing use of opioids for mental health reasons. An abbreviated program logic model is found in table 1. Lack of professional education is a barrier to effective opioid management, and approaches to train providers in trauma-informed principles have demonstrated positive impacts on provider knowledge, attitudes, and behaviors (Haffajee et al., 2018). This example reviews components of the trauma-informed training provided and related participant outcomes. This work was funded by SAMHSA and USDA.

Efforts to build capacity for trauma-informed principles spanned two years. In year one, an eight-part, monthly, virtual webinar series provided training and professional development on principles of trauma-informed practices to Extension personnel. This training was then adapted and delivered as a five-part virtual webinar series to Extension volunteers. Table 2 describes the principles introduced in each webinar session. Participants could attend any session but attendance at the first session (live or on-demand) was required to participate in subsequent sessions. In the second year, a virtual learning community was launched to support Extension professionals who participated in the webinar series to apply the principles in their own work (e.g., programs, partnership development).

An evaluation was conducted of those who attended the trainings. Participants reported increased understanding and awareness of trauma-informed principles, with

Table 1. Abbreviated Project Logic Model

SITUATION	INPUTS	ACTIVITIES	OUTPUTS	OUTCOMES
Increasing rates of opioid-related deaths State opioid response plan not addressing unique rural needs Insufficient number of trained professionals addressing known risk and protective factors	What we invest: • Personnel • Time • Expertise	What we do: • Provide training and professional education • Provide technical assistance via small-group coaching Who we reach: • Extension personnel • Extension volunteers	• Training materials • Participants reached • Information and skills for professionals	Short-term • Increased knowledge of five key trauma-informed principles Long-term • Greater community awareness of trauma-informed principles and strategies • Decrease in use of opioids for mental health reasons

Table 2. Trauma-Informed Principles Covered in Each Session and Related Description

SESSION NUMBER AND NAME	DESCRIPTION
1. Understanding Trauma: The Role of Adverse Childhood Experiences, Toxic Stress, and Biology on Development*	Learn about the different parts of the brain and how trauma and toxic stress can impact on not only development, but future behavior, relationships, emotions, and mental health.
2. Attachment/Attunement	Learn about the attachment relationship and the attunement connection using a trauma-informed lens. Discover intentional and natural strategies to implement in everyday practices.
3. Routines, Rituals, and Validation*	Understand the importance of routines, rituals, and validation in everyday practices. Recognize the routines, rituals, and ways to validate that can be triggering versus promoting regulation and building connection.
4. Triggers	Learn how triggers can lead to survival responses and are personal and unique to each individual. Becoming aware and sensitive to an individual's environment can lead to help overcoming the impact of the experience.
5. Regulation and Coregulation*	Discover the skills needed to build self-regulation and co-regulation and how trauma can impact these learned skills. These concepts can form the foundation for future learning and behavior and the building of healthy relationships.
6. Diversity, Equity, and Inclusion	Trauma can occur in systems we live in, beyond the individual experience. Learn about systemic trauma and the prevalence, where it comes from, and the impact it can have on other and ourselves.
7. Accountability, Grace, and Resilience*	Differentiate between accountability, discipline, and punishment and how to shift the narrative to accountability with grace to increase accountability and reduce punishment. Utilizing such strategies can foster the building of resilience.
8. Well-Being, Self-Care, and Mindfulness	Identify warning signs of secondary traumatic stress and burnout. Learn how an individual can work to prevent and mitigate the impacts in a trauma-informed way that can lead to overall well-being.

* This topic was presented to volunteers in the session.

the greatest increase in knowledge among domains of attunement, routines and rituals, triggers, regulation and dysregulation, and implementation strategies to promote regulation. Participants identified connections between knowledge gained and use in their own work. For some, trauma and ACEs were new, as illustrated by one participant who stated, "This is my first training regarding ACEs. I had not heard about them until today. I feel everyone should have a common understanding of what they are and how applicable this topic is in the Extension work we do." Others felt this was especially important for individuals working in and with communities. One participant shared, "I see trauma response as being exceptionally important in interacting with colleagues, volunteers, children, and the community. I think everyone should take this type of training if at all possible." Another participant shared how they used the information learned, saying, "I help manage 350 volunteers, and directly supervise them in some of our clinics, as well as deal primarily with the public, out of most of our staff. Trauma informed response helps me address needs, resolve issues including inter/intrapersonal problems, and provide appropriate resources."

Promotion: Reducing Opioid-Related Stigma

Stigma around opioid use, especially nonprescription use, has remained a near-constant factor in the opioid crisis (Tsai et al., 2019). Stereotypes about individuals with OUD can lead to negative attitudes and discriminatory behavior. Stigma can occur at multiple levels, with negative impacts on a given individual, the community as a whole, and policies guiding treatment. Addressing stigma within the community, such as with individuals and organizations, can alter social or cultural perceptions of use. Key to this is emphasizing that OUD is a treatable condition, humanizing individuals with OUD, and illustrating barriers to seeking and obtaining treatment (Cheetham et al., 2022). We share two examples of approaches that seek to reduce opioid-related stigma at the community level. The first is an Addiction 101 program offered by the University of Kentucky to adult community members (https://psd.ca.uky.edu/addiction-101), and the second is a youth participatory action research program facilitated by Washington State University (https://hd.wsu.edu/adolescent-health-promotion-lab/substance-use).

Multiple land-grant universities (LGUs) have used funding from SAMHSA's ROTA program to provide training on substance use and opioids. At the University of Kentucky, these funds were used for programming by Alex Elswick, Ph.D., a faculty specialist with a focus in substance use prevention and recovery and a person with lived experience. As in other states, Elswick had experienced resistance to substance use programming by community members and CES professionals. In response, he led the development and delivery of an Addiction 101 professional development training for health care personnel, Extension professionals, and community leaders (such as judges; Elswick, 2022; Elswick & Jury, n.d.). The training aimed to increase capacity of community professionals to engage with clients or community members with SUD. It also served to reduce stigma related to substance use while sharing risk factors and prevention strategies. Evaluation of the training indicated increased participant knowledge of addiction as a disorder and understanding of how to interact with individuals with addiction.

In addition to professional development training, other LGUs used community-engaged programming to address opioid stigma. At Washington State University, CES professionals and specialists used a youth participatory action research (YPAR) approach to engage adolescents in researching the impact of opioids within their own communities and advocating for change. Community-based approaches, like YPAR, have the potential to directly impact social norms, attitudes, awareness, and stigma of opioid use in positive ways (Ozer, 2017). Adopting a YPAR approach is especially crucial for marginalized youth, who have been disproportionately and negatively impacted by substance misuse and whose voices need to be amplified. CES professionals in three communities across the state used the 4-H Youth Advocates for Health (YA4-H!) curriculum for YPAR (Arnold & Gifford, 2015) but varied its implementation (e.g., number of and cadence of meetings, meeting format). Groups supplemented the curriculum with educational videos on opioid topics (e.g., addiction, neurobiology) and invited guest lectures from community speakers (e.g., paramedic, physician) to discuss opioids. A pre- and post-program evaluation indicated significant, positive changes in both knowledge (i.e., opioid familiarity, harm of opioid misuse, opioid safe handling and storage, perceived impact of the opioid crisis on teens) and behavioral intentions (i.e., likelihood of engaging in opioid safety behaviors, sharing opioid safety information) (Watters et al., 2023). These findings align with other YPAR evaluations that indicated increases in alcohol and tobacco health knowledge following YPAR participation (Helm et al., 2015; Valdez et al., 2020) and expand this body of research to opioids. A key finding was that YPAR participants appeared to be learning how, and becoming empowered, to address opioid and related issues where they live.

Prevention: Delivering Strengthening Families Program for Parents and Youth 10–14

We now shift to focusing on the prevention wedge of the continuum. Extension has a long history of delivering research-informed and/or evidence-based substance use prevention programs. Community prevention systems have been implemented through and with the Extension network such as PROSPER (Promoting School-Community-University Partnerships to Enhance Resilience, https://helpingkidsprosper.org/) and Communities that Care (https://www.communitiesthatcare.net/). Within, and also separate from, these systems, evidence-based substance use prevention programs are also implemented, including Strengthening Families Program for Parents and Youth 10–14 years old, (SFP 10–14). SFP 10–14 is a multisession universal prevention program delivered in community settings to caregivers and their youth aged ten to fourteen years. For a logic model of SFP 10–14, see the program profile on the Blueprints for Healthy Youth Development site (https://www.blueprintsprograms.org/programs/189999999/strengthening-families-10-14). SFP 10–14 has a robust evidence-base with demonstrated positive outcomes on short-term shared risk and protective factors, as well as on long-term substance use behaviors. Specifically, SFP 10–14 demonstrates impacts on opioid-related outcomes, including opioid and prescription drug misuse (Spoth et al., 2013).

In Washington State, CES has provided facilitation, training and technical assistance, and evaluation and research on SFP 10–14 since 2002. In 1999, CES professionals at Washington State University (WSU) identified early adolescence as a priority area for new programming. They adopted SFP 10–14 because it was an evidence-based program, developed by CES in Iowa, and considered a model or exemplary program by several federal agencies. WSU then sought to train program facilitators across the state and collect program evaluation data to demonstrate efficacy. At the same time, WSU identified state partners to facilitate long-term program sustainability. In 2004 the culturally adapted Spanish-language version, Fortaleciendo Familias para Padres y Jóvenes de 10–14 años (FF 10–14), was incorporated into the dissemination effort. The capacity-building efforts and relationships forged in the early 2000s were instrumental to where SFP 10–14 is today in Washington State. WSU currently offers training and technical assistance in partnership with the state Division of Behavioral Health and Recovery, which funds community substance use prevention programming through local prevention coalitions. Training and technical assistance involves initial and recertification facilitator trainings, training in program fidelity monitoring, and targeted coaching and support for both English- and Spanish-language versions. WSU also partners with local prevention coalitions in delivery of programming which facilitates research and evaluation. In addition to providing evaluation support in the form of site-level program reports, this relationship between CES and state and local prevention partners allows for community-driven research on SFP 10–14.

The capacity for SFP 10–14 within WSU and collaboration between Extension and state partners mean they can be responsive to local needs. For example, at the onset of the COVID-19 pandemic, community sites delivering SFP 10–14 in-person found themselves unable to finish or continue programming as a result of restrictions to in-person programming. Conversations between states with SFP 10–14 national trainers and the developers of SFP 10–14 showed the need pivot from in-person to virtual delivery. WSU, in partnership with the developers of SFP 10–14, identified adaptations needed for delivery in a virtual environment. WSU then created supplemental resources to guide the virtual delivery process (e.g., toolkit, Zoom functions for virtual delivery, training to support sites pivoting from in-person to virtual delivery).

Adapting SFP 10–14 for virtual delivery was not the only way WSU was able to meet community need. Community leaders and state partners were receiving requests from parents for information specific to opioids to share with their youth. In response, the WSU team used funding from USDA and guidance from adaptation literature (Kirk et al., 2020; Stirman et al., 2019) to systematically adapt SFP 10–14 to incorporate opioid content, or SFP 10–14 + Opioids. Evaluation of the SFP 10–14 + Opioid pilot indicates promising results for both standard and opioid program outcomes.

Recovery: Delivering Nutrition Education in Recovery Settings

Within the recovery wedge of the continuum, we have four examples. The first focuses on the role of nutrition education to support individuals in recovery from OUD. Individuals with OUD often experience other comorbidities impacting related health outcomes, one of which relates to nutrition. Specifically, opioid use and related disorders influence nutrition in a variety of ways, such as metabolic changes, constipation, and weight loss, that may often be overlooked (Chavez & Rigg, 2020). In addition to these changes, individuals living with SUD may also experience food insecurity. Delivery of nutrition education in residential SUD settings has shown improvements in dietary behavior among residents (Cowan & Devine, 2012; Wiss, 2019). The Expanded Food and Nutrition Education Program (EFNEP) delivers nutrition education to families with low incomes that contributes to their health and well-being. EFNEP is facilitated by peer educators who belong to the communities in which they serve. In Washington State, EFNEP educators teach in residential SUD programs, as well as in health care sites such as methadone clinics. These treatment services provide an ideal interface for Extension to engage with community providers to serve those with OUD in a more holistic manner.

EFNEP participants learn about healthy eating, being physically active, keeping food safe, and planning meals. Many adults with SUD need more nutrition resources due to reliance on convenience foods and sporadic eating patterns. EFNEP educators focus on healthy eating patterns and set behavioral health goals with participants in their recovery. In addition to learning about healthy eating and being physically active, EFNEP classes create a sense of community among participants that can aid in their recovery by increasing social connections and community support.

Recovery: Using a Complex Adaptive Systems Approach for Recovery-Oriented Systems of Care

Through a grant from the North Central Cooperative Extension Association, a multistate group from North Central Regional Center for Rural Development, Purdue University, University of Illinois, and Ohio State University Extensions created and piloted a complex adaptive systems approach for recovery-oriented systems of care (https://cdextlibrary.org/resource-library/tasc; Adams et al., 2023). Navigating community resources can be a challenge for people in recovery from substance use, and the purpose of the program was to enhance community capacity to support people in recovery by enabling collaborators to more readily share information. Recovery-oriented systems of care models work to facilitate resource availability and accessibility for people in recovery from substance use and are often run by hospitals or medical providers through a hub-and-spoke model that centralizes the medical system as the conduit for information between parties. A complex adaptive system differs from a hub-and-spoke model by encouraging communication across all partners without a centralized gatekeeping organization or individual, and by equalizing power across participating community agencies.

The framework and model built by the multistate group draws from strengths in Extension community and economic development to recruit a wide and diverse variety of community organizations and entities, facilitate conversations with one another, identify pathways in the community for people who are in recovery, and identify gaps in the pathways that the community partners can work together to resolve. Extension professionals play a facilitative role in this model, helping to direct conversation and break down existing hierarchies within communities to ensure equitable participation in the effort. Topics and resources the group identifies are not limited to medical care, but rather consider a person's needs holistically and include things like employment, housing, transportation, and other resources that enable recovery journeys to continue smoothly.

Extension professionals from Purdue University successfully piloted the program in two Indiana communities, and the multistate group offered train-the-trainers for Extension professionals from other states to learn how to offer the program within their own communities.

Recovery: Legislation Designating Recovery-Ready Communities

The recovery capital framework has emerged over time as a way to view and organize the internal and external resources available to an individual to support the recovery process (Best & Hennessy, 2022). The University of Minnesota's Community-based Opioid Prevention Education project (C.O.P.E.; https://opioid.umn.edu) is driven by a recovery capital framework and outlines five types of capital, or support, important for individuals in recovery. These include the following:

1. Social: others who support an individual's recovery such as friends, family, co-workers, providers, and peers who are also in recovery
2. Physical: fulfillment of basic needs related to housing, food, transportation, and so on
3. Cultural: provision of culturally relevant care
4. Community: services available within the community for treatment (e.g., prescribers of medication-assisted treatment) and recovery (e.g., drug- and alcohol-free community events)
5. Human: an individual's experience and knowledge to support recovery

In a recovery capital framework or model, abstinence is not the goal—rather, the purpose is to understand and enhance the interrelated systems supporting recovery. One key feature is that "individuals have different amounts of recovery capital and this influences how their recovery process progresses" (Best & Hennessy, 2022, 1140). This means the more we can bolster recovery capital, the greater is the likelihood of a positive outcome.

In the state of Kentucky, legislators saw value in the recovery capital framework and in 2021 signed House Bill 7, which establishes criteria for counties or communities to become certified as "Recovery Ready." (https://rrcky.org/). House Bill 7 was the culmination of advocacy from community-based leaders, including CES professional Alex Elswick, Ph.D. Elswick describes his role in this effort:

> In August of 2020, I was invited to the BRIGHT Eastern Kentucky Leadership Academy by my friend and colleague, Karen Butcher. The Academy brings together emerging leaders from across Eastern Kentucky to identify solutions to problems that affect local communities. The focus of this summit was to identify ways to mitigate the impact of the opioid epidemic in Eastern Kentucky. I delivered a presentation entitled "Building Recovery Ready Communities" which focused on helping community leaders identify key resources (e.g., recovery capital) to mobilize recovery and remove barriers to reentry. The presentation was well-received by numerous community leaders, including state legislators.
>
> Three months later, in March of 2021, Governor Andy Beshear signed into legislation House Bill 7 which establishes an Advisory Council for Recovery Ready Communities. The legislation was first introduced and co-sponsored by Rep. Adam Bowling, an attendee at the BRIGHT Eastern Kentucky Leadership Academy. (Elswick, 2021)

The Recovery Ready Communities certification program scores communities on prevention, treatment, and recovery supports and resources. Resources include activities such as implementation of evidence-based prevention programming in schools, harm reduction program offering fentanyl test strips, pharmacies stocking and dispensing medications for OUD, family recovery or drug court system, availability of recovery housing in the community, and local employers employing individuals in treatment or recovery. A community that meets or exceeds a given score in each category and overall (score differs based on community population size) can be certified as a Recovery Ready Community. The formalization of this certificate provides clear guidance on the role communities play in building recovery capital and holistically supporting individuals in recovery.

Promotion to Recovery: Facilitating Community Conversations to Address Behavioral Health

Our final example addresses not only recovery, but really the entire behavioral health continuum. Oregon has one of the highest rates of prescription opioid misuse in the nation. Approximately five Oregonians die every day from overdose of prescription and illicit opioids (Oregon Health Authority, 2022). Oregon voters passed the Drug Addiction Treatment and Recovery Act (State of Oregon Senate Bill 755, 2021) in 2020, providing funds to establish Behavioral Health Resource Networks, coordinated systems for comprehensive, community-based services for SUDs. In addition, the state of Oregon was awarded a settlement of approximately $325 million dollars over eighteen years for OUD prevention, treatment, and recovery services (Distributor Settlement Agreement, 2021). Both Behavioral Health Resource Networks and opioid settlement funding are available to regional and local networks through an application process.

The new funding mechanisms elicited a need for government agencies and community-based organizations to coordinate to identify priorities and create action plans to apply for funding. Oregon State University's "Coast to Forest" team is supporting counties in Oregon by facilitating Community Conversations about Behavioral Health, adapted from SAMHSA's Community Conversations about Mental Health (Substance Abuse and Mental Health Services Administration, 2013). The Coast to Forest team is also providing training to facilitators to implement Community Conversations About Behavioral Health across SAMHSA Region 10 in Alaska, Idaho, Oregon, and Washington. The Coast to Forest project is a collaboration between the Oregon State University Center for Health Innovation and Extension Family & Community Health and is funded by USDA Rural Health and Safety Education and SAMHSA ROTA grants, as well as funding from CareOregon.

The purpose of the community conversations is to engage leaders and community members in assessment and action planning related to SUDs and mental health across the health continuum, including promotion, prevention, harm reduction, treatment, and recovery. The products of the conversations include priorities and action plans so that counties are prepared to apply for the Behavioral Health Resource Network, opioid settlement funds, and other funding opportunities.

Since 2021, Coast to Forest has facilitated three Community Conversations about Behavioral Health in three rural counties in Oregon. The conversations used a community-engaged approach by convening a local planning team of community leaders and behavioral health professionals to define the goals, identify participants, provide input on the sessions, and create the final report. Participants varied in each community, but all had representation from government, healthcare, behavioral health, law enforcement, judicial system, social services, education, and people affected by SUD and mental health disorders. Participants represented sectors across the health continuum. The conversations comprised four parts: developing a shared understanding of the issues by exploring public health data; creating an inventory of current services and resources in the current behavioral health system including promotion, prevention, harm reduction, treatment, and recovery; identifying current strengths and challenges; and prioritizing issues for action.

Each of the three community conversations in Oregon yielded different priorities due to local contexts, but there were common themes. All counties were concerned about the high prevalence of SUDs but were unable to meet the demands for services due to limitations of funding, staffing, and other resources. Concerns about a stressed and depleted behavioral health workforce was a key outcome consistent across conversations. Participants expressed the need for workforce development and interventions to reduce distress and burnout. Counties used the priorities and action plans to inform Behavioral Health Resource Network and opioid settlement funds, guide decision making about programs and services, and increase collaboration among service providers and community partners.

The Role of Health Extension in Addressing Opioids across the Behavioral Health Continuum

CES has come a long way over the past decades in advancing behavioral health as an important focus. Many CES professionals and community members are "running toward" this topic since they see the immediate impact of opioid use on the communities they serve. However, others are "running away" from the topic, or at least are hesitant about addressing behavioral health within their CES work. Both rural and urban communities are well into the fourth wave of the opioid crisis (Post et al., 2022) and struggling to keep up with current trends. For example, at the time of writing this chapter, youth overdose deaths are spiking, and communities are scrambling to respond. High schools in California are stocking naloxone, a medication used to reverse opioid overdose (Mays, 2022), while other communities are engaging in overdose prevention campaigns for youth and young adults (Prince William County Government, 2023).

This chapter provides examples of work within the CES for health promotion, opioid prevention, and recovery support. Although CES does not play a direct health care role in crisis response, treatment, or recovery, it can support the behavioral health system across the health continuum through community engagement to connect, create, and implement collaborative action plans. Here we want to acknowledge the lack of approaches within the treatment wedge of the behavioral health continuum. Despite CES serving as a partner with primary care providers as part of a broader community system of care and programming, there is little direct treatment provided within CES. Engaging a Health Extension approach in the realm of treatment presents challenges to integrating within healthcare systems. Given the complexity and variety of healthcare systems and avenues (or lack of) for reimbursement, among other issues, this likely is not the highest priority focus for Health Extension.

Looking back to the Institute of Medicine Behavioral Health continuum figure 1, we see evidence CES across the health continuum—from supporting use of trauma-informed approaches and efforts to reduce stigma, to facilitating community conversations and creating recovery-ready communities. In addition to these examples, CES has existing strengths in health promotion and prevention through many programs including nutrition education, physical activity, and 4-H youth development that build knowledge and skills that are protective from substance use and mental health disorders. To further support communities in promoting health and reducing the harms of opioid use, a Health Extension approach in partnership with schools, nonprofits, and social services can increase adoption, adaptation, and dissemination of evidence-based approaches to promote protective factors. Effective solutions to addressing opioids will require community-driven solutions. To guide Health Extension as it relates to behavioral health and opioids, we next outline three key strategies.

Going Where We Are Least Comfortable

To continue addressing opioids through CES efforts, Health Extension will need to "go to the places where it is least comfortable going" (A. Elswick, personal communication, August 21, 2023). Due to the hesitancy and resistance of communities, many opioid-focused CES efforts start with broader approaches to increase opioid-related and addiction knowledge and decrease stigma, often with positive outcomes. At Montana State University, this includes an informational website (https://www.montana.edu/extension/health/opioids.html) with materials for a grab-and-go toolkit (https://www.montana.edu/extension/health/opioidtoolkit/modules.html) that can be used by Extension and other community-based professionals across the state, with the option of collaboration on tailoring for dissemination to other states. South Dakota State University's Strengthening the Heartland program (https://www.sdstate.edu/strengthening-heartland) supports delivery of a program called This is (Not) About Drugs, a youth-focused opioid education program on the risks of prescription and illicit opioids.

Delivery of opioid-related educational programming is an important component of Health Extension to reach those at low-risk. However, this should be balanced with efforts to reach individuals with complex needs, such as those in detention centers, recovery housing, shelters, specialty courts, and so on. Ultimately, this requires going to the people who would benefit the most and who have been most marginalized. Doing so will allow CES professionals to lean into one of their assets, which is to foster relationships with organizations and systems, including those new to working with CES. This also will mean moving into or increasing efforts in areas such as harm reduction, which supports individuals who use substances to live healthy lives and prevent overdose and other related negative consequences of use (Substance Abuse and Mental Health Services Administration, 2023). To best support individuals with OUD means hearing from those with lived experience. This can be in an advisory capacity, as a community partner, or through intentionally hiring someone with lived experience to work in Health Extension within a state's CES.

Doing What We Know Works

As CES professionals become more comfortable incorporating an opioid focus into their state, regional, or local work and Health Extension efforts more common, it can be overwhelming to figure out where to start. Fortunately, existing frameworks and resources can serve as a foundation. At a national or state level, Spoth and colleagues' (2021) guidance on building capacity for behavioral health provides useful targets and is discussed further as a next strategy.

At a state or local level, prior research suggests that efforts targeting shared risk and protective factors (e.g., factors impacting multiple behaviors) at multiple contextual levels (e.g., family, community) that are tailored to the context in which they are implemented (i.e., fit to local context) are likely to be most effective. This means engaging in partnership with community members and organizations to provide holistic services to support individuals across the behavioral health continuum. The chapter example using and adapting SAMHSA's Community Conversations to address substance use provides a clear way forward to engage community members in understanding the issues and prioritizing existing needs. Layering Community Conversations with a menu of evidence- or research-based approaches is one way to blend community expressed needs with what works.

One direct approach to ensuring delivery of what we know works is to enact policies (e.g., statues, regulations, guidance) requiring use of evidence-based approaches (Fagan et al., 2019). Accountability can come from funders (e.g., SAMHSA, USDA) requiring use of evidence-based approaches and stringent community-based evaluation of such approaches among state and local grantees. Within CES administration and Health Extension, this could look like prioritizing training, implementation, and support of evidence-based programs, such as the example of delivering SFP 10–14 for substance use prevention. Health Extension professionals with expertise in dissemination and implementation science can provide guidance to do what we know works at a state level.

Building Capacity to Address Behavioral Health across the Continuum

One clear strategy presented in the research and recommendations of the Extension Opioid Crisis Response Workgroup (2018) and Washburn et al. (2022) is to build capacity to address opioids across all program areas in the CES. Supporting and leading such capacity building efforts is an avenue for Health Extension. Spoth et al. (2021) identified four main capacity-building goals for CES to address behavioral health, which also apply to addressing opioids:

1. leveraging CES's organizational structure for science- and evidence-based behavioral health efforts;
2. increasing behavioral-health-focused professional development for CES professionals;
3. strengthening the culture of behavioral health within CES; and
4. shifting funds or identifying new funding streams for behavioral health work.

At a system and organizational level, these capacity-building recommendations should be adopted to use the CES for its intended purpose—to disseminate research and evidence to individuals and communities. We highlight specific opportunities within each of these goals. In Goal 1, leveraging the organizational structure will require first understanding the capacity of the existing system. Not all CES professionals are prepared to address behavioral health and opioids. Conducting a readiness assessment at an organizational level can identify existing programs related to opioids and levels of support, knowledge, skill, and so on from administration and other CES personnel to inform feasibility of future efforts. In Goal 2, increasing professional development was a main outcome of the Extension Opioid Crisis Response Workgroup, who recommended that "all Extension staff who interact with the general public should have a basic level of behavioral health knowledge and skills" (Extension Opioid Crisis Response Workgroup, 2018, 11). This means that opioid efforts do not fall within one area of CES, but rather across all areas including agriculture, community development, youth development, etc. For Goal 3, strengthening the culture will require developing a shared foundation of knowledge of what "counts" as evidence-based. Prioritizing programs and approaches will require us to make judgments about the rigor of supporting evidence and a process for assessing such evidence in tandem with community needs or contextual fit. Finally, Goal 4 includes finding ways to fund this work. Many states have been successful in receiving federal (e.g., USDA, SAMHSA) and state (e.g., state opioid response, opioid settlement dollars) funds to support opioid programs. However, these may not be sustainable funding sources over the long term. We will need to be prepared to proactively advocate both within our state and as a collective at the federal level for longer term investments.

Conclusion

Opioids are not the first, nor the last, behavioral health issue to emerge that requires a community-driven, tailored response. The role of CES in addressing opioids can serve as a model for future emergent issues impacting communities across the United States. The CES is unique in its ability to identify and pivot to implementing evidence-based approaches to address future emergent health issues—a significant contribution to public health. This chapter used the Institute of Medicine's Behavioral Health Continuum to provide examples of how Extension is currently engaging with communities in opioid-related work. Within the area of behavioral health, opioids have received increased funding and programmatic focus in the CES, especially over the past five years. This infusion of funding has no doubt pushed CES to engage in opioid-related work while also highlighting the important work remaining. Health Extension has an important role to play in behavioral health and opioid prevention, recovery, and harm reduction from both a programmatic and a research perspective. This chapter provides examples of Extension professionals who are already doing this work. With increased capacity at national, state, and community levels, we have the potential to support community systems, programs, and approaches that promote use of evidence-based approaches to addressing opioid use and use community-engaged research approaches to demonstrate their effectiveness.

Acknowledgments

Programs and activities described in this chapter were supported by the SAMHSA of the U.S. Department of Health and Human Services (HHS) and the intramural research program of the U.S. Department of Agriculture, National Institute of Food and Agriculture, Rural Health and Safety Education. This information or content and conclusions are those of the author and should not be construed as the official position or policy of, nor should any endorsements be inferred by, SAMHSA, HHS, or the U.S. government. The findings and conclusions in this publication have not been formally disseminated by the U.S. Department of Agriculture and should not be construed to represent any agency determination or policy.

APPENDIX: RESOURCES CITED IN THIS CHAPTER

Extension Opioid Crisis Response Workgroup: https://extension.org/portfolio-item/opioid-response

Northwest Rural Opioid Technical Assistance Collaborative: https://www.nwrotac.org

Washington State University, Child and Family Research Unit: https://extension.wsu.edu/cafru

University of Kentucky, Addiction 101: https://psd.ca.uky.edu/addiction-101

Washington State University, Youth Participatory Action Research: https://hd.wsu.edu/adolescent-health-promotion-lab/substance-use

PROSPER: https://helpingkidsprosper.org

Communities That Care: https://www.communitiesthatcare.net

Strengthening Families Program for 10–14 year olds: https://www.blueprintsprograms.org/programs/189999999/strengthening-families-10-14; https://sfp.wsu.edu

Taking Action to Address Substance Use in Communities: A Protocol for Communities: https://cdextlibrary.org/resource-library/tasc

Substance Use and Mental Health Service Administration, Community Conversations about Mental Health: https://store.samhsa.gov/product/Community-Conversations-About-Mental-Health-Information-Brief/SMA13-4763

University of Minnesota, Community-based Opioid Prevention Education project: https://opioid.umn.edu

Kentucky House Bill 7 Recovery Ready Communities: https://rrcky.org

Montana State University, opioid informational website: https://www.montana.edu/extension/health/opioids.html

Montana State University, grab-and-go opioid education toolkit: https://www.montana.edu/extension/health/opioidtoolkit/modules.html

South Dakota State University, Strengthening the Heartland: https://www.sdstate.edu/strengthening-heartland

REFERENCES

Adams, N., Wilcox, M., Worland, E., Erich, C., Espinosa, A., Silvis, A. H., Berg, A., Cuthbertson, C. A., & Martin, K. (2023). *Taking action to address substance use in communities (TASC): A protocol for communities* [Extension handbook]. https://cdextlibrary.org/resource-library/

tasc
Arnold, M. E., & Gifford, L. (2015). *YA4-H! Youth advocates for health—Youth participatory action research.* Corvallis: Oregon State University Public Health Extension.
Best, D., & Hennessy, E. A. (2022). The science of recovery capital: Where do we go from here? *Addiction, 117*(4), 1139–1145. https://doi.org/10.1111/add.15732
Business Oregon. (2023). *Distressed areas in Oregon.* https://www.oregon.gov/biz/reports/pages/distressedareas.aspx
Campaign for Trauma-Informed Policy and Practice. (2017). *Trauma-informed approaches need to be part of a comprehensive strategy for addressing the opioid epidemic. Policy Brief 1. Campaign for Trauma-Informed Policy and Practice.* https://www.opioidlibrary.org/wp-content/uploads/2019/08/Strategy-four-Final-CTIPP_OPB.pdf
Centers for Disease Control and Prevention, National Center for Injury Prevention and Control. (2023). *Understanding the opioid overdose epidemic.* https://www.cdc.gov/opioids/basics/epidemic.html
Chavez, M. N., & Rigg, K. K. (2020). Nutritional implications of opioid use disorder: A guide for drug treatment providers. *Psychology of Addictive Behaviors, 34*(6), 699–707. https://doi.org/10.1037/adb0000575
Cheetham, A., Picco, L., Barnett, A., Lubman, D. I., & Nielsen, S. (2022). The impact of stigma on people with opioid use disorder, opioid treatment, and policy. *Substance Abuse and Rehabilitation, 13*, 1–12. https://doi.org/10.2147/SAR.S304566
National Academies of Sciences, Engineering, and Medicine; Committee on Fostering Healthy Mental, Emotional, and Behavioral Development Among Children and Youth; Board on Children, Youth, and Families; & Division of Behavioral and Social Sciences and Education. (2019). *Fostering healthy mental, emotional, and behavioral development in children and Youth: A national agenda* (25201). Washington, DC: National Academies Press. https://doi.org/10.17226/25201
Cowan, J. A., & Devine, C. M. (2012). Process evaluation of an environmental and educational nutrition intervention in residential drug-treatment facilities. *Public Health Nutrition, 15*(7), 1159–1167. https://doi.org/10.1017/S1368980012000572
Cruz, S. L., & Martín-del-Campo, R. (2022). The opioid crises. In S. L. Cruz (Ed.), *Opioids* (pp. 87–104). New York: Springer International Publishing. https://doi.org/10.1007/978-3-031-09936-6_5
Dasgupta, N., Beletsky, L., & Ciccarone, D. (2018). Opioid crisis: No easy fix to its social and economic determinants. *American Journal of Public Health, 108*(2), 182–186. https://doi.org/10.2105/AJPH.2017.304187
Department of Health and Human Services. (2019). *Rural opioids technical assistance grants (ROTA): Initial announcement.* Rockville, MD: Substance Abuse and Mental Health Services Administration, Department of Health and Human Services.
Distributor Settlement Agreement. (2021). *National opioids settlement.* https://nationalopioidsettlement.com/wp-content/uploads/2022/03/Final_Distributor_Settlement_Agreement_3.25.22_Final.pdf
Elswick, A. (2021). *Recovery ready community legislation.* https://kers.ca.uky.edu/core/

reports/Story/s/9275/2021

Elswick, A. (2022). *Addiction 101* (FCS8-125). University of Kentucky Cooperative Extension Service. https://www2.ca.uky.edu/agcomm/pubs/FCS8/FCS8125/FCS8125.pdf

Elswick, A., & Jury, K. (n.d.). *Addiction 101*. https://psd.ca.uky.edu/addiction-101

Fagan, A. A., Bumbarger, B. K., Barth, R. P., Bradshaw, C. P., Cooper, B. R., Supplee, L. H., & Walker, D. K. (2019). Scaling up evidence-based interventions in US public systems to prevent behavioral health problems: Challenges and opportunities. *Prevention Science, 20*(8), 1147–1168. https://doi.org/10.1007/s11121-019-01048-8

Haffajee, R. L., Bohnert, A. S. B., & Lagisetty, P. A. (2018). Policy pathways to address provider workforce barriers to buprenorphine treatment. *American Journal of Preventive Medicine, 54*(6), S230–S242. https://doi.org/10.1016/j.amepre.2017.12.022

Hagaman, A., Roark, K., & Washburn, L. T. (2023). U.S. Cooperative Extension's response to substance misuse: A scoping review. *Frontiers in Public Health, 11*, 1127813. https://doi.org/10.3389/fpubh.2023.1127813

Hart, C. L., & Hart, M. Z. (2019). Opioid crisis: Another mechanism used to perpetuate American racism. *Cultural Diversity & Ethnic Minority Psychology, 25*(1), 6–11. https://doi.org/10.1037/cdp0000260

Helm, S., Lee, W., Hanakahi, V., Gleason, K., & McCarthy, K. (2015). Using photovoice with youth to develop a drug prevention program in a rural Hawaiian community. *American Indian and Alaska Native Mental Health Research, 22*(1). https://doi.org/10.5820/aian.2201.2015.1

Hoffman, M. S., Ramsay-Seaner, K., Letcher, A., & Heckmann, C. (2021). Collaboration is key: Implications for successful rural opioid misuse prevention programming. *Journal of Rural Mental Health, 45*(3), 198–206. https://doi.org/10.1037/rmh0000184

Institute of Medicine. (1994). *Reducing risks for mental disorders: Frontiers for preventive intervention research* (p. 2139). Washington, DC: National Academies Press. https://doi.org/10.17226/2139

Jadhav, R., Achutan, C., Haynatzki, G., Rajaram, S., & Rautiainen, R. (2015). Risk factors for agricultural injury: A systematic review and meta-analysis. *Journal of Agromedicine, 20*(4), 434–449. https://doi.org/10.1080/1059924X.2015.1075450

Jenkins, R. A. (2021). The fourth wave of the US opioid epidemic and its implications for the rural US: A federal perspective. *Preventive Medicine, 152*, 106541. https://doi.org/10.1016/j.ypmed.2021.106541

Kirk, M. A., Moore, J. E., Wiltsey Stirman, S., & Birken, S. A. (2020). Towards a comprehensive model for understanding adaptations' impact: The model for adaptation design and impact (MADI). *Implementation Science, 15*(1), 56. https://doi.org/10.1186/s13012-020-01021-y

Kucera, K. L., Loomis, D., Lipscomb, H., & Marshall, S. W. (2010). Prospective study of incident injuries among southeastern United States commercial fishermen. *Occupational and Environmental Medicine, 67*(12), 829–836. https://doi.org/10.1136/oem.2009.053140

Kunins, H. V. (2020). Structural racism and the opioid overdose epidemic: The need for antiracist public health practice. *Journal of Public Health Management and Practice, 26*(3), 201–205. https://doi.org/10.1097/PHH.0000000000001168

Mays, M. (2022, December 8). Narcan could be required at California schools after youth fentanyl overdoses. *Los Angeles Times*. https://www.latimes.com/california/story/2022-12-08/narcan-could-be-required-at-california-schools-after-spate-of-youth-fentanyl-overdoses

Oregon Health Authority. (2022). *Opioids and the ongoing drug overdose crisis in Oregon: Report to the Legislature*. https://sharedsystems.dhsoha.state.or.us/dhsforms/served/le2479_22.pdf

Ozer, E. J. (2017). Youth-led participatory action research: Overview and potential for enhancing adolescent development. *Society for Research in Child Development, 11*(3), 173–177. https://doi.org/10.1111/cdep.12228

Post, L. A., Lundberg, A., Moss, C. B., Brandt, C. A., Quan, I., Han, L., & Mason, M. (2022). Geographic trends in opioid overdoses in the US from 1999 to 2020. *JAMA Network Open, 5*(7), e2223631. https://doi.org/10.1001/jamanetworkopen.2022.23631

Prince William County Government. (2023, July). *Prince William County launches youth fentanyl overdose prevention campaign*. https://www.pwcva.gov/news/prince-william-county-launches-youth-fentanyl-overdose-prevention-campaign

Quinn, K., Frueh, B. C., Scheidell, J., Schatz, D., Scanlon, F., & Khan, M. R. (2019). Internalizing and externalizing factors on the pathway from adverse experiences in childhood to non-medical prescription opioid use in adulthood. *Drug and Alcohol Dependence, 197*, 212–219. https://doi.org/10.1016/j.drugalcdep.2018.12.029

Radunovich, H. L., Younker, T., Rung, J. M., & Berry, M. S. (2022). The effects of the opioid crisis on agricultural industries. *International Journal of Environmental Research and Public Health, 19*(9), 5343. https://doi.org/10.3390/ijerph19095343

Santoro, T. N., & Santoro, J. D. (2018). Racial bias in the us opioid epidemic: A review of the history of systemic bias and implications for care. *Cureus*. https://doi.org/10.7759/cureus.3733

Skidmore, M., Brennan, A., Brown, R., Cuthbertson, C., Dellifield, J., Elswick, A., Johnson Ruffin, N., Klemme, R., Kowalkowski, B., Lindsay, A., Perkins, D., Rennekamp, R., Shipley, A., Sulzer, S., Chilote, A., Guin, A., Gabel, C., Hockaday, C., Perkins, D., Young, D., Crist, G. Spears, L., Wright, M. E., & Spoth, R. (2018). *Report to the Extension Committee on Organization and Policy from the Extension Opioid Crisis Response Workgroup*. Extension Publication. https://extension.org/portfolio-item/opioid-response/

Spoth, R., Franz, N., & Brennan, A. (2021). Strengthening the power of evidence-based prevention in Cooperative Extension: A capacity-building framework for translation science-driven behavioral health. *Child & Youth Care Forum, 50*(1), 121–145. https://doi.org/10.1007/s10566-020-09559-0

Spoth, R., Trudeau, L., Shin, C., Ralston, E., Redmond, C., Greenberg, M., & Feinberg, M. (2013). Longitudinal effects of universal preventive intervention on prescription drug misuse: Three randomized controlled trials with late adolescents and young adults. *American Journal of Public Health, 103*(4), 665–672. https://doi.org/10.2105/AJPH.2012.301209

State of Oregon Senate Bill 755. (2021). https://olis.oregonlegislature.gov/liz/2021R1/Measures/

Overview/SB755

Stein, M. D., Conti, M. T., Kenney, S., Anderson, B. J., Flori, J. N., Risi, M. M., & Bailey, G. L. (2017). Adverse childhood experience effects on opioid use initiation, injection drug use, and overdose among persons with opioid use disorder. *Drug and Alcohol Dependence, 179*, 325–329. https://doi.org/10.1016/j.drugalcdep.2017.07.007

Stirman, S. W., Baumann, A. A., & Miller, C. J. (2019). The FRAME: An expanded framework for reporting adaptations and modifications to evidence-based interventions. *Implementation Science, 14*(1), 58. https://doi.org/10.1186/s13012-019-0898-y

Substance Abuse and Mental Health Services Administration. (2013). *Community conversations about mental health: Discussion guide*. Substance Abuse and Mental Health Services Administration. https://store.samhsa.gov/product/Community-Conversations-About-Mental-Health-Discussion-Guide/SMA13-4764

Substance Abuse and Mental Health Services Administration. (2014). *SAMHSA's concept of trauma and guidance for a trauma-informed approach* (HHS Publication No. (SMA) 14-4884). Rockville, MD: Substance Abuse and Mental Health Services Administration.

Substance Abuse and Mental Health Services Administration. (2023). *Harm reduction*. https://www.samhsa.gov/find-help/harm-reduction

Swann, W. L., Kim, S., Kim, S. Y., & Schreiber, T. L. (2021). Urban–rural disparities in opioid use disorder prevention and response activities: A cross-sectional analysis. *Journal of Rural Health, 37*(1), 16–22. https://doi.org/10.1111/jrh.12491

Swedo, E. A., Sumner, S. A., De Fijter, S., Werhan, L., Norris, K., Beauregard, J. L., Montgomery, M. P., Rose, E. B., Hillis, S. D., & Massetti, G. M. (2020). Adolescent opioid misuse attributable to adverse childhood experiences. *Journal of Pediatrics, 224*, 102–109.e3. https://doi.org/10.1016/j.jpeds.2020.05.001

Swift, S. L., Glymour, M. M., Elfassy, T., Lewis, C., Kiefe, C. I., Sidney, S., Calonico, S., Feaster, D., Bailey, Z., & Zeki Al Hazzouri, A. (2019). Racial discrimination in medical care settings and opioid pain reliever misuse in a U.S. cohort: 1992 to 2015. *PLoS ONE, 14*(12), e0226490. https://doi.org/10.1371/journal.pone.0226490

Tsai, A. C., Kiang, M. V., Barnett, M. L., Beletsky, L., Keyes, K. M., McGinty, E. E., Smith, L. R., Strathdee, S. A., Wakeman, S. E., & Venkataramani, A. S. (2019). Stigma as a fundamental hindrance to the United States opioid overdose crisis response. *PLoS Medicine, 16*(11), e1002969. https://doi.org/10.1371/journal.pmed.1002969

U.S. Department of Agriculture. (2020). *Request for application: Rural health and safety education competitive grants program (RHSE)*. Washington, DC: National Institute of Food and Agriculture, U.S. Department of Agriculture.

Valdez, E. S., Skobic, I., Valdez, L., Garcia, D. O., Korchmaros, J., Stevens, S., Sabo, S., & Carvajal, S. (2020). Youth participatory action research for youth substance use prevention: A systematic review. *Substance Use & Misuse, 55*(2), 314–328. https://doi.org/10.1080/10826084.2019.1668014

Washburn, L. T., Franck, K. L., Upendram, S., & Yenerall, J. N. (2022). Cooperative Extension professionals' knowledge and attitudes toward the opioid epidemic: Implications for capacity development and outreach. *Frontiers in Psychiatry, 13*, 958335. https://doi.

org/10.3389/fpsyt.2022.958335

Watters, C., Weybright, E. W., Hampilos, K., Purser, E., Doering, E., White, A., Greer, M., Fees, J., & Varrella, G. (2023, April). *"I never realized how hard recovery is." Evaluation of a youth participatory action research project for opioid misuse prevention.* Annual meeting of the Society for Research on Adolescence, San Diego, CA.

Weybright, E., Doering, E. L., Hampilos, K., Roll, J. M., Barbosa-Leiker, C., & McDonell, M. (2024). Cooperative Extension as a key partner to behavioral health in rural communities [Special issue]. *Journal of Rural Mental Health.* Advance online publication. https://doi.org/10.1037/rmh0000256

Wiss, D. A. (2019). The role of nutrition in addiction recovery. In I. Danovitch & L. J. Mooney (Eds.), *The assessment and treatment of addiction* (pp. 21–42). New York: Elsevier. https://doi.org/10.1016/B978-0-323-54856-4.00002-X

The Future of Health Extension

Cheryl L. Eschbach and Jeffrey W. Dwyer

The chapters in this volume advocate for Health Extension as integral to the land-grant university (LGU) system and a significant partner in providing community-based healthcare in the United States and worldwide. The contributions of a diverse array of scholars challenge the status quo in the Cooperative Extension System (CES) by characterizing the introspection, understanding, creativity, partnerships, and leadership that will be required to improve lives and communities in the twenty-first century through an enhanced focus on health and public health. This perspective underscores the role of CES as foundational to the future of Health Extension and offers an alternative to approaches that utilize the CES as a model without the accompanying advantages of history, community embeddedness, and sustainability. This volume advances awareness and knowledge by exploring innovation in Extension health programs, engaged scholarship promoting research-based information in communities, and the evaluation and documentation of community programs and their impacts. Authors provide LGUs and university-based colleagues with information on using Cooperative Extension for community engagement in healthcare while also familiarizing those outside CES and the Academy with a roadmap for improving community-based healthcare by enhancing the role of Cooperative Extension in community-engaged research, programming, and health interventions.

We are grateful for the twenty intellectual leaders who have shared their experience, knowledge, and expertise in this volume to challenge the status quo and chart an authentic path for the future. In addition to the content of each chapter, contributions of the volume include a robust literature review intended to provide readers with foundational and provocative resources for fostering future dialogue and research; conceptual, theoretical, and methodological contributions from multiple disciplines; insight from scholars at varying career stages and with different personal and professional histories; and challenges designed for readers to initiate new thinking and research that will undoubtedly enhance our understanding of Health Extension, its role in national Extension efforts, and the opportunity to partner in community-based healthcare in the coming decades.

Reflections on System Change

The CES and its affiliation with the research and education provided by LGUs have had a fundamentally important impact on residents of the United States, particularly on farmers and people living in rural areas. CES has proven to be a sustainable, adaptable, and community-based resource, yet much has changed over the last hundred years with respect to where people live, what they do for a living, and what they need to live happy, healthy, and productive lives. Hence, significant system changes are needed if CES is to be the resource for the next hundred years that it has been in the past. We believe that Health Extension is synonymous with the ability of CES to have the kind of impact on millions of lives and generations of families in the twenty-first century that it had in the twentieth century. This chapter provides a summary of ideas and transformations needed in LGUs, within CES, among present and future leaders, and in policy, derived from the extraordinary insight of scholars developing new strategies, methodologies, and perspectives in the preceding chapters. Their calls to action are critical contributions to the literature and have profound implications for future directions in Extension research, education, and interventions. Readers interested in modernizing the national CES, especially the family and consumer science (FCS) program area, directing LGU resources to address complex issues such as human health equity, and expanding partnerships to enhance CES's role in community-based healthcare, can look to the foundation of Health Extension and these emergent strategies for evidence and ideas. If the CES is to serve traditional audiences in new ways, reach new audiences, and contribute to the nation's community-based healthcare challenges, then fundamental changes are necessary.

Health Extension includes health-focused research, education, programming, and interventions delivered by CES as the outreach and community engagement partner of LGUs to enhance community-based healthcare, academic health centers, public health, and prevention outcomes. As outlined in this volume, Health Extension is a movement that can assist community-based healthcare and public health interventions with support from higher education institutions on a variety of topics such as mental health, substance use prevention and recovery, disaster planning or management, and health promotion that have measurable impacts on human health. We continue to advocate for Health Extension as an integral part of CES and the LGU system and as a significant partner in providing community-based health research, interventions, and healthcare support (Dwyer et al., 2017). The extended history on the origins of Health Extension, included in many chapters of this volume, is important to preserve as the national CES evolves and invests in a comprehensive health initiative portfolio.

Part of thinking about the future of Health Extension is reflecting on the opportunity structure for health-related programming in CES, while considering the nation's history, laws, and social norms that challenge healthy equity for all. The 1862 LGUs have work to do to tear down systems that replicate or reproduce racist practices and discrimination. We do not believe all individuals who work at predominantly white institutions (PWIs) are guilty of exhibiting behaviors or reproducing practices that mediate intentionally against health equity. Rather, we assert that there is additional responsibility on Extension professionals working within 1862 LGUs to be cognizant of the past, fully aware of how the history is presented to new staff, partners, and clients, and open to seeing how thoughtful engagement is necessary for impactful Extension work now and into the future. Nevertheless, gatekeepers and oppressors are employed within CES and LGUs today, and their impact is both dangerous and subtle. Whether intentional or not, efforts to silence and exclude individuals and institutions from important regional and national conversations, and from other opportunities to provide intellectual leadership, persist today and are detrimental to necessary system change. By learning about the past and acknowledging racism as a public health issue, we believe people can see the present in a new light. Individual learning and organizational self-awareness are necessary for the future of CES and the advancement of health and Health Extension as a coalescing emphasis in all CES program areas.

Health Extension strategies can revitalize higher education community engagement and position CES as a dynamic partner in community-based healthcare. Reviews of history, including the shortcomings of CES, are essential for understanding the future and opportunities for higher education transformation. We want readers to understand the social context that continues to shape today's CES capabilities and connections that are predicated on infrastructure, funding, and mission. Many authors in this volume challenge CES to evolve rapidly as a system to meet emergent needs and offer approaches and methodology in prevention science and dissemination and implementation science to increase rigor and spur CES to engage intentionally in the peer-reviewed academic literature. In general, academic disciplines have an object of research, a body of accumulated knowledge, organizing theories and concepts, specific terminology, common research methods, and institutional manifestation (Krishnan, 2009). Cooperative Extension as an academic partner working on interdisciplinary research and educational activities must embrace these qualities and build capacity in Health Extension for health to be operationalized into all Extension priorities.

In realizing the potential for Health Extension in the twenty-first century, specific steps must be taken to ensure that CES can establish itself as an intellectual leader in community-based healthcare and public health and as a full partner in the scientific process. Intellectual leadership, especially in emerging disciplines, challenges existing power and leadership structures, emphasizes the importance of publication-based authority in the domain of ideas, and "can establish roots when women and minority scholars utilize opportunities for dissent and public engagement" (Oleksiyenko & Ruan, 2019, 8). To maximize the potential for CES to lead in health-related fields, Extension professionals must be trained in health behavior change theory and frameworks and principles of community organizing and community building for health. Professionals also need training in human subjects' protocol (e.g., institutional review boards [IRBs]), research design, and dissemination and implementation science. Extension professionals need to know fundamentals of program development and evaluation to bridge the gap between research and community need (Hetherington et al., 2019). In addition, administrative and institutional leaders must provide support, mentoring, and encouragement to junior and mid-career intellectual leaders, acquire new talent where needed, and commit to developing a more diverse workforce and new collaborations with university and community-based health professionals. Increasing capacity in grant writing, peer-reviewed publication, and partnership-building skills must also be prioritized to formalize the intellectual leadership of CES in Health Extension and broaden the scope of potential scholarship, funding, and partnerships beyond traditional domains.

CES needs to adopt approaches to health equity and health justice that will require enhanced commitments to diversity efforts and intentional inclusion to achieve the representation required to address the complex challenges of the world we live in. Connecting larger civic movements and concepts such as oppression, abolition, health justice, and liberation further advances the efforts of Health Extension and health equity into the future. The CES may find a renewed purpose in serving state residents as they acknowledge history and recognize the need for changing strategies and intentionally finding audiences that are currently underrepresented and marginalized in CES outreach and community engagement efforts.

The authors of this volume provide rationales for and critiques of existing literature and frameworks, as well as personal and professional observations from lived experience working in LGU and CES settings. This chapter concludes the volume by addressing future directions for Health Extension and, by association, for the CES and LGUs. Specifically, we advocate for innovations necessary to position Health Extension within CES to advance Extension and LGUs as intellectual leaders in supporting community-based healthcare. We summarize our reflections by recommending ten system changes for advancing the future of Health Extension:

1. Investing in health across all extension program areas.
2. Adopting health equity as a systemwide value.
3. Increasing diversity to advance equity and inclusion in the workforce.
4. Avoiding only performative DEI committees and policies.
5. Accelerating innovation and diversifying leadership.
6. Facilitating scholarship and funding in CES.
7. Seeking transparency in youth participation in Extension programs.
8. Improving needs assessments and priority setting.
9. Building relationships outside of traditional boundaries.
10. Promoting policy, systems, and environmental changes as Health Extension.

Investing in Health Across All Extension Program Areas

A focus on health and Health Extension can transform CES and U.S. community-based healthcare in the twenty-first century. Yet, as with the influence on agriculture in the early to mid-twentieth century, this will not have the greatest impact possible if viewed as the domain of one program area (i.e., FCS) rather than as a shared responsibility of all program areas. If CES is to address population health in the purposeful way it transformed agriculture, homes, and communities in the twentieth century (Rodgers & Braun, 2015), there is need for reflection, modernization in infrastructure and leadership, greater appreciation for nutrition education professionals already within the Extension system, and enhanced collaboration across program areas within CES and with external partners.

The social determinants of health (SDOH) have received greater attention from researchers and practitioners in the last twenty years, with a particular focus on identifying, defining, and measuring the role of SDOH in educational interventions and health disparities. The SDOH model connects to every program area in CES, and several available health-related frameworks contain comprehensive lists of data-driven recommendations to plan and do community-based work. In August 2020, the U.S. Department of Health and Human Services released one of the best collections of national priorities for health—Healthy People 2030 (Office of Disease Prevention and Health Promotion, n.d.). This guiding document is in its fifth iteration, building upon four decades of health research, interventions, and policies to outline the most pressing issues related to human health. Specific examples of SDOH include education, housing, wealth, air pollution, transportation, economic stability, access to natural environments, and many others. The intersection of health with all other CES program areas holds significant promise for the future of Health Extension. Examples of these programmatic intersections include health and climate change; health and clean water access; health and disaster planning, response, and recovery; health and safe/secure food systems; and health and youth development.

To advance the future of CES as a system, it is recommended that human health priorities be placed strategically in all Extension program areas supported by joint funding of staff. This approach is especially relevant as we contemplate challenges related to climate change, safe food and water, and employment or workforce development issues, and the approach encourages collaboration that can impact both scholarship and funding. At all universities (not just LGUs) it is common, for example, to find medical and basic science faculty unable to reach target populations of interest when conducting research, and partnering with Extension professionals is a proven strategy for overcoming this challenge (Dwyer et al., 2017). Campus-based scholars may also miss opportunities to conduct community-based needs assessments or create localized interventions that would be important in validating subsequent research and justifying new work in grant proposals. As more funding agencies add requirements for research dissemination plans and community engagement efforts, Extension professionals will increasingly be in high demand, and integrating health throughout CES by emphasizing SDOH will maximize the opportunities.

CES is an attractive partner for research and community projects with its wide range of expertise (e.g., agriculture, community and economic development, natural resources management, food systems, volunteer management, nutrition) and university staff based in communities off campus. Further, as U.S. universities deal with declining college enrollments and stagnant federal, state, and county funding in traditional budgets, LGUs and CES will need to band together across program areas and state lines to compete for regional and multistate opportunities. To meet this demand and challenge, Extension professionals will require training in research design, science dissemination, grant writing, and healthcare partnership building.

Adopting Health Equity as a Systemwide Value

LGUs and CES must adopt health equity as a systemwide core value and priority to be viable, competitive, and impactful in improving health for all, partnering in the community-based healthcare system, and effectively utilizing the CES's vast resources, infrastructure, and community-engaged history to change lives and maximize impact in the twenty-first century. Adoption of health equity by all Extension program areas is needed, as are explicit efforts to enhance collaboration among 1890, 1994, and 1862 LGU institutions. Crossing program boundaries and silos within CES (e.g., FCS and 4-H youth development) and building partnerships outside traditional collaborations are important for the future of Health Extension and the ability to implement effective healthcare solutions and public health interventions.

As a starting point in this transformation, CES must formally address historical and present-day oppressive practices such as discrimination and funding inequities among 1862, 1890, and 1994 LGUs. Working together, this means advocating by all LGUs and CES in all states and U.S. territories, calling for all institutions to receive sustained and equitable funding. Extension programs can provide leadership by initiating intentional collaboration among LGUs, including formal leadership roles for 1890 and 1994 colleagues, in multistate and external funding opportunities, providing education, programming, and interventions to underserved populations together, and considering joint academic faculty and staff hires whenever possible.

Cooperative Extension's most recent National Framework for Health Equity and Well-Being (Burton et al., 2021) includes recommendations to combat racism, xenophobia, ableism, ageism, homophobia, classism, sexism, and all other forms of intolerance that are root causes of structural inequities. CES must commit to working collectively to end and dismantle the effects of systematic racism within CES and land-grant institutions. Higher education needs to remain a safe place for the pursuit of knowledge and technical skill advancement that encourages participation by students and intellectual leaders representing all aspects of the U.S. population. The United States needs community-based educational supports as part of a quality healthcare environment designed to improve population health and to achieve equity in health for all. Investing university resources in Health Extension strategies through CES will help to catalyze health equity as a core and shared value.

Increasing Diversity to Advance Equity and Inclusion in the Workforce

Workforce diversity is important because it facilitates access to a greater range of talent, fosters creativity, and provides insight into the history, needs, and aspirations of the populations we hope to serve. The future of Health Extension depends on developing and fostering a diverse workforce representative and reflective of the American people and the nation's residents (including refugees and immigrants). Achieving diversity in hiring requires an intentional focus on altering embedded practices that subtly (or not so subtly) support the status quo. We believe there are several strategies for recruiting and developing a diverse workforce, including those that specifically take advantage of the resources available to employees of LGUs and, therefore, represent a competitive advantage.

First, the Health Extension of the twenty-first century will need content experts in a wide array of health-related fields. This includes bringing in public health and health disparity researchers and interventionists, as well as practitioners from community-based organizations that have experience reaching diverse clientele. The statewide responsibilities and infrastructure of Extension, coupled with the postpandemic capacity for enhanced remote work, mean that expertise can be recruited statewide in most cases and that candidates from other states can have the flexibility to choose their location in many instances. This flexibility increases the likelihood that new hires can live and work where they feel most aligned with the community. CES can also hire professionals from outside of traditional FCS fields and introduce them to Extension expertise in training, community engagement, and facilitation. Community health workers (CHWs) represent a plausible strategy to increase the capacity of the local healthcare workforce and to provide employment in rural and medical professional shortage areas. The CES as the LGU and academic partner in communities can be the train-the-trainer resource for CHWs and others in similar fields who are seeking certificate-issuing professional development or trainings for a fee. This advantages CES with revenue and provides a context for thoughtful examination of when an expert model or intervention is needed, or when a facilitated or coordinated process might yield greater learning, system change, or community action.

Second, because Extension staff are university employees, the positions available are often attractive to those living in less populated areas where professionally aligned opportunities may be limited. Moreover, university jobs typically have excellent benefits and incentives. Capacity-building strategies for CES should include hiring individuals who have interests, skills, and experience in public health and human services fields and who would like to work for a university and possibly earn a graduate degree. Valuable degree programs are available online and in hybrid formats, thus enhancing the likelihood that Extension professionals, once employed, can use university tuition benefits to advance their personal goals and expand community-based health professions in their community. Intentional coaching, mentoring, and support of staff who represent the communities served will revitalize CES and establish a Health Extension workforce capable of meeting the needs of a complex world.

Third, the CES can create capacity within the organization by increasing training programs for the entire Extension workforce. One example is the increased sophistication and rigor expected in the U.S. Department of Agriculture (USDA)–funded Supplemental Nutrition Assistance Program—Education (SNAP-Ed) projects. SNAP-Ed positions demand new skill sets of the workforce, moving duties away from expert or peer instruction and direct education to site-specific needs assessments, utilization of existing data, and partnership facilitation. These essential skills have altered hiring practices and the statewide plan of work, and have required Extension to support the workforce in new ways both to teach nutrition education and to promote policy, system, and environmental (PSE) changes alongside our multisector community partners. Extension already reaches low-income audiences (i.e., via SNAP-Ed eligibility) and this is a good start in connecting with audiences based on demographics, data, and partnerships.

Finally, sometimes the talent for new initiatives does not require new hiring. "The L6, [or] Level 6, is the person six levels down from the top [of an organization] . . . who knows what you badly need to know (but whose expertise) is buried under a big organization or system, [and] has no status. [They] might have a voice, but no one hears it" (Lewis, 2022). Because of the size and distribution of employees in a statewide network like Extension, expertise is often already present in existing staff hired for other roles. For example, a behavioral health expert may be working as a program evaluator, or an experienced SNAP-Ed instructor or supervisor may have an advanced public health degree and be the next best programmatic leader. CES should look "six levels down" in filling any role, to consider current staff who may not be challenged in their current position based on their experiences and knowledge. Leaders are encouraged to know the breadth and depth of Extension professionals' training, cultural backgrounds, and lived experiences, regardless of their current job responsibilities, so that they know who can be called upon when emergent needs and opportunities arise.

Avoiding Only Performative DEI Committees and Policies

There is a responsibility working at LGUs to be collectively committed to promoting a culturally inclusive, safe, and supportive environment that is free from all forms of bias, discrimination, harassment, and stereotyping. However, implementation details on how to create these environments are less often shared or supported. This means some university diversity, equity, and inclusion (DEI) committees and policies get established quickly in a department or unit and end up being only performative in nature, rather than having a measurable impact on recruiting, retention, and hiring practices and outcomes. Without exception, CES leaders need to support creative and comprehensive efforts to enhance diversity in applicant pools and challenge recruitment committees to insure the inclusion of diverse candidates among finalists. To avoid other potential shortcomings, new strategies are needed.

Rather than hire new staff for separate DEI efforts, at Michigan State University (MSU) two Extension task forces focused on health equity were formed to empower existing staff to mobilize new programming and outreach efforts to serve historically marginalized audiences. In MSU Extension's Health and Nutrition Institute, the Refugee and Immigrant Health Task Force is a team of bicultural and bilingual staff who implement nutrition, health, and food safety education. They share a professional passion and personal connection to refugee and immigrant communities. Michigan received the fourth most refugees of any state in the last decade, and there are about 678,000 immigrants residing in Michigan today. These individuals and families represent new audiences for CES and underscore the need for Health Extension. The task force started in 2021 and created a website for refugee resettlement agency partners so they can find Extension's multilingual and multicultural resources to support these communities. In addition, this internal group looks at health across SDOH and CES program areas to help refugees and immigrants to navigate new food systems and lead healthier lives, while respecting and celebrating cultures. MSU Extension offers educational resources translated to other languages, as well as specialized bundled programs adapted for refugee and immigrant communities.

The MSU Extension Health Justice and Equity Task Force (H-JET) is a collection of Extension professionals from different programming teams who are using the 2021 National Framework for Health Equity and Well-Being as a grounding document to guide implementation of various framework recommendations. Although the process of writing and rolling out the framework was flawed in several ways, the document is significant in advancing the call for addressing health equity across all LGUs and CES. H-JET is pursuing research questions and data collection efforts to address questions such as "What is the current staff/organizational capacity to do equity work?," "What is the perception of Extension for someone who has been historically excluded from programs?," and "When, why, and where are program adaptations happening to make programs culturally relevant/informed?" Finally, H-JET is helping MSU Extension look internally, more deeply and more intentionally, by auditing existing programs, developing new materials, and findings ways to co-create materials with culturally, linguistically, and ethnically diverse communities. The future of Health Extension depends upon supporting internal efforts like these Task Force examples that are driving change from within the organization and challenging the status quo for the greater good.

Accelerating Innovation and Diversifying Leadership

Change can be expedited if the CES promotes innovation, supports new leaders from underrepresented groups (e.g., Black, Indigenous, people of color, LGBTQIA+), hires new staff from atypical disciplinary backgrounds (e.g., public health), and embraces leadership from younger generations. This too will require a fundamental change in historical patterns of mentorship and leadership development throughout CES. The administrative leadership ecosystem in CES (1862 LGUs) is predominately white, mostly male, trends older, and, except for a very few recent examples, has very little experience outside of CES. This is so because the pool for Extension director and other top leadership roles is almost exclusively drawn from within CES, in part because many inside the organization believe that Extension is so unique that outside leaders would not be successful. Of course, this perspective only serves to perpetuate the leadership change dilemma. To address this problem, committees and consultants must reach beyond CES to recruit leaders from large nonprofits, community-based medical schools, governmental organizations, and nongovernmental organizations (NGOs) who can bring innovative thinking and new experiences, insight, and training to the organization. In addition, 1862 institutions should be compelled to consider colleagues from 1890 and 1994 institutions who are prepared for new challenges. Once new leaders are engaged, those in existing CES leadership roles need to be open to their input and respond accordingly. By looking outside the organization to attract new leaders, the short lists for leadership roles will naturally become more diverse. As a result, CES leadership will become less white, less male, younger, and more representative of varying identities. Greater diversity in leadership roles will undoubtedly hasten acceptance of the need to emphasize and pursue health equity and health justice.

For too long, retired Extension directors and/or very senior administrators have filled virtually all higher level national positions in organizations such as the Association of Public and Land-Grant Universities, the Extension Committee on Organization and Policy (ECOP), and new initiatives under the Extension Foundation's growing umbrella, thus limiting the potential for new (and diverse) talent and leadership to forge the future. Many of these national roles are appointed from within the organization (rather than elected or hired via committee or due process) and often without broad input. The result is that leadership for new initiatives like Health Extension is dominated by senior people with little or no specific expertise in the focus area. Open and transparent searches for key national leadership should be normative. Under current practices, the CES is missing opportunities for diverse voices (e.g., women, LGBTQIA+, new professionals, scholars of color, 1890 historically Black colleges and universities and 1994 tribal colleges and universities faculty) who could guide the acceleration of innovation and the development of Health Extension research, education, and programming more aligned with communities in need.

One recent example resulting from current leadership practices is the 2021 Cooperative Extension National Framework for Health Equity and Well-Being (Burton et al., 2021) that was written by a national group of scholars under the auspices of ECOP, not originally published in the academic literature, and subsequently published by a sole author in a national leadership position (Rennekamp, 2022). In early 2024, the Rennekamp 2022 publication was retracted by the *Journal of Community Engagement and Scholarship*. (The Retraction Statement now associated with this article provides additional explanation.)

The principal writers of the framework document include early and mid-career scholars whose advancement depends in part on publishing in the peer-reviewed literature and recognition of their intellectual contributions to assert influence within CES, compete for external funding, and advocate for CES with potential partners. Hence, gatekeeping through misguided scholarship and improper attribution is harmful to Extension professionals, the CES, and, ultimately, the populations we serve.

Facilitating Scholarship and Funding in CES

The CES (particularly FCS) needs to adopt a more standardized approach to scholarship and publication in the peer-reviewed literature. We urge LGU and CES leaders to implement structural and cultural system changes so that ideas are vetted, expert scholarship and experience are identified, rewarded, and utilized, and credit redounds to intellectual rather than administrative leaders. Some state Extension organizations have moved in this direction by implementing commonly accepted professional authorship guidelines for Extension publications. Plagiarism, especially the act of not properly sourcing the work of others, is common in Extension publications, as Rollins (2011) argued more than a decade ago. It is the responsibility of Cooperative Extension to generate credible and actionable evidence showing the quality and impacts of its programs and to demonstrate that effectiveness, to ensure resources are positively benefiting people and communities (Hetherington et al., 2019).

Another organizational and cultural aspect of CES that is perpetuated by current leaders and impedes scholarship is reliance on a regional approach when it comes to funding new and emergent programs, simply because there is a history of providing each region with comparable funding. Examples of forced regional partnerships and shared funding models include the Regional Rural Development Centers created from the Rural Development Act of 1972 and the Farm and Ranch Stress Assistance Network established in the 2008 Farm Bill with competitive regional funding made available in 2018. While this geographically based approach may have been useful in the past, it is no longer conducive to supporting the best work nationally, which could then be disseminated throughout CES as a condition of scholarship and funding. Therefore, the CES should stop practices and normative expectations that educational materials and data/research on Extension programs are shared regionally and nationally without emphasizing publication in the peer-reviewed literature. Presently, individual scholars in state systems often do not receive the attribution that they deserve if materials are produced regionally. Alternatively, when Extension work is not published in peer-reviewed literature, important intellectual and programmatic products are not readily available for citation by others, which also reduces science-building, scholarship impacts, and the ability for individuals and teams to build competitive research and publication records that make them viable potential recipients of external funding from a broad range of state and federal agencies and foundations.

Although the Extension Foundation (formerly eXtension) was established in 2006 to provide support as "an electronic publishing service for Cooperative Extension" (Extension Foundation, 2023). Its mission changed in 2014 to focus on "increas[ing] system capacity while providing programmatic services." More recently, however, the Extension Foundation has emerged as a competitor rather than a supporter of state Extension programs and scholars for external funding opportunities in some instances. Specifically, we have personally observed and experienced the exclusion of colleagues from important discussions and committees setting national agendas because their state Extension does not pay dues to the Extension Foundation and/or others believe that the region they are from "is already represented." In this context, the increasing accrual of funding under the Extension Foundation umbrella that would otherwise be led directly by scholars located at 1862, 1890, and 1994 land-grant institutions is alarming. The failure to identify and support the best experts, programming, and scholarship from within CES always is antithetical to the scientific process, diminishes the contributions of experts within the system, and ultimately reduces the competitiveness of CES professionals in obtaining new resources to support those we serve. Furthermore, the failure to solicit the best intellectual capacity from within CES, the misappropriation of the work of junior scholars to address other interests, and the frequent exclusion of needed expertise from both inside (i.e., 1890 and 1994 LGUs) and outside the system fosters disaffection, limits impact and effectiveness, and lessens the likelihood of success in obtaining competitive external funding.

A scholarly approach to authorship and establishing the credentials for success as a principal investigator on externally funded grants and contracts would expect publication in peer-reviewed journals before (or simultaneously with) widespread adoption in CES; encourage publication in venues outside of the LGU/CES context to share with others the value and outcomes of CES; and provide support to diverse early and mid-career scholars by recognizing their intellectual contributions to impactful systemwide or regional products. It is acknowledged that some state systems do better at facilitating scholarship among Extension professionals. For example, Washington State University developed successful writing groups among volunteers who applied to be part of a scholarship mentoring support group to increase their personal accountability and confidence in the writing process (Smith et al., 2018). However, increased rigor and intentional action to support academic scholarship are needed across the national, regional, and state Extension systems. It is also important to note that universities have the research infrastructure (e.g., IRBs, research integrity officers, pre- and post-award grant accounting) to support scholars not typically present in organizations like the Extension Foundation.

Seeking Transparency in Youth Participation in Extension Programs

In 2016, the 4-H Foundation launched the Grow True Leaders Campaign with a goal of "empowering 10 million true leaders over the next decade, up from nearly 6 million young people today" (National 4-H Council, 2016). A similar 4-H campaign from the national strategic plan includes a "1 in 5 by 2025" youth recruitment goal for urban, suburban, and rural communities (National Institute of Food and Agriculture, 2017). Part of the future for Health Extension is seeking transparency of youth participation in Extension programs and encouraging the alignment of 4-H and Health Extension interests. Annually, CES reports youth participation numbers across all program areas and educational initiatives on the Extension Services Form (ES-237), a report to the USDA that consists of enrollment statistics for youth ages five to eighteen years participating in Extension youth programs. LGUs produce impact reports for sharing with funding partners, stakeholders, and the public based on these numbers. In most states, Extension counts youth numbers from involvement in grants such as the SNAP-Ed and Expanded Food and Nutrition Education Program (EFNEP) nutrition and physical activity programs as 4-H youth participants, especially the school-based education outreach and afterschool group program enrollments. Without these SNAP-Ed/EFNEP youth participant numbers and the CES staffing investments focused on physical activity and community nutrition, our best estimate is that the 4-H youth participant numbers would be less than two-thirds of what is presently reported.

As a case study, in Michigan, the following four trends appeared in reviewing past es-237 reports on 4-H enrollment: First, SNAP-Ed/EFNEP programming numbers comprise about one-third of what is counted as 4-H youth participation in the state. Second, SNAP-Ed/EFNEP clientele often represent the greatest source of racial and ethnic diversity across CES and 4-H. Third, the evolving requirements of SNAP-Ed/EFNEP portend the need for better trained staff members who mirror the communities served. Fourth, the SNAP-Ed/EFNEP clientele represents a substantial opportunity for accessing additional funding and forging partnerships across LGUs and communities. In light of the substantial impact of SNAP-Ed/EFNEP in contributing to 4-H participation number counts, we suggest that all of the CES, including the 4-H Foundation, become an ally in addressing the needs of those served by SNAP-Ed/EFNEP. Presently, the contributions of community nutrition and physical activity programming, especially with youth, are undervalued and underappreciated as CES health outreach.

This issue may seem trivial to some, but it is not. The stated goal in 2016 of increasing enrollment from six million to ten million, given that SNAP-Ed/EFNEP comprise at least one-third of this number, is an outcome that CES/4-H has neither the staffing nor volunteer capability to achieve by relying solely on 4-H. Rather, to substantially increase youth participation in 4-H, increasing resources available to traditional 4-H delivery models and to SNAP-Ed and EFNEP is essential. Moreover, because SNAP-Ed and EFNEP typically serve more diverse audiences than 4-H, a greater emphasis on reaching SNAP-Ed/EFNEP eligible participants and efforts to recruit those youth into other 4-H programming would increase both numbers and impact more quickly and sustainably than other avenues of growth. Although system changes in 4-H must be implemented (i.e., improved organization, communication, belonging culture), an immediate reorientation of target populations and resources is needed to address declining 4-H youth enrollment and high first-year dropout rates (Lewis et al., 2022) that mediate against reaching growth aspirations for the traditional youth development organization.

Improving Needs Assessments and Priority Setting

Needs assessments are an important part of priority setting that allow CES professionals to engage in continuous data gathering and improvement processes to stay relevant and visible. Traditionally in Michigan, MSU Extension and our sister organization AgBioResearch (ABR) engage together in a statewide issues-identification process that involves collecting survey and focus-group data from existing clientele and partners coordinated and facilitated by staff. The problem with this approach is threefold: relying only on past participants and current stakeholders insures validation for existing efforts; no new voices or information were intentionally sought despite the fact that MSU Extension (and Extension in all states) actually serves a very small portion of the statewide population at present; and university facilitators occasionally shaped focus-group responses by indicating that "Extension does not do that" in response to some community comments or failing to record responses deemed outside "what Extension does."

In Michigan, a statewide survey was initiated in fall 2015. Jeffrey W. Dwyer started as director of MSU Extension in early 2016 and challenged the information collected up to that point because of the emphasis on existing clientele. He requested additional survey data collection from residents not already familiar with MSU Extension and that additional focus groups be held in parts of the state that would be accessible to residents identifying as Hispanic/Latinx, Middle Eastern Arab Americans, veterans, and those living in urban centers and representing Black, Indigenous, and people of color communities. Not surprisingly, responses from Michigan residents not already familiar with MSU Extension and ABR were different from those of current stakeholders and clients, with the former overwhelmingly ranking a wide range of social determinants of health and other needs not mentioned by the latter.

During the data collection period (on January 5, 2016) the governor of Michigan declared a state of emergency, which was followed by a federal state of emergency authorized by then President Obama, due to the Flint water crisis. Because of this timing, Michigan residents who completed the survey following this announcement reacted to this emergent public health issue by identifying safe food and water as the number one state priority. This expressed need for an Extension response to the Flint water crisis (a human-made public health crisis) resulted in a much different set of priorities than in the previous two statewide Extension needs assessments (2003 and 2008) that highlighted youth development, jobs creation, and the economy. The lesson learned is that it is simply not enough to only survey existing clients or other partners doing similar work, or to continue prioritizing traditional stakeholders. Moreover, emergent public health events draw attention to new priorities and the role of Extension professionals in communities as sentinels who can respond with urgency when leaders support their efforts. Bold leadership is needed by Extension leaders in state systems to stay nimble and responsive to the changing demographics and resident concerns. CES leaders must use assessments and priority setting strategies that are collaborative, data driven, and responsive to new concerns while utilizing participatory and science-building methodologies for collecting organizational information from needs assessments and identifying program priorities.

Building Relationships Outside of Traditional Boundaries

Because we typically cannot predict the next emergency, natural disaster, or public health crisis, building relationships with key individuals and organizations is critical to achieving a successful Extension or higher education response. As Stajura (2020) has argued, "When relationships are established before emergencies, everyone involved has a better sense of each other's capabilities and can increase their individual and collective capacities" (1). Historically, CES relationships have focused on rural residents, farmers and agriculture, and 4-H youth and families. Today, less than 20 percent of people in the United States live in rural America (Dobis et al., 2021); roughly 2 percent of the population is engaged in active farming; and only 4 percent of eligible youth participate in 4-H activities. Hence, it is easy to see why so few people are aware of CES or the broad range of programs that it offers.

As it relates to Health Extension, moreover, these facts require emphasis on establishing relationships with people and organizations that have not been traditional CES partners. Health providers and payors (e.g., insurance, Medicare, Medicaid), public health units, hospitals, disaster planning professionals, and many other experts should know about CES and the associated LGU, should have a relationship with key CES experts and leaders, and should know who to contact when an emergent situation arises. Healthcare payors can especially benefit from increased awareness and familiarity with CES programs and staff. As communities seek options for community-based care and support, CES can be there with education and program interventions. Carefully curating healthcare partnerships to establish Extension health program referral pathways continues to be a promising approach for CES to increase awareness and familiarity of Extension's community-based education programs (Khan et al., 2020; Tiret et al., 2019). The future of Health Extension means processing all we learned during the recent COVID-19 global pandemic, including how to get people information and provide healthcare to populations that are hard to reach and sometimes invisible to the system, and getting the word out to others about CES, including networking with academic health centers, primary care, allied health professions, and pharmacies.

The CES must make intentional efforts to reach and provide resources and educational support to underrepresented and marginalized people and communities so that the voices and needs of all individuals are represented. Pruitt and Hicks (2022) remind us that reporting the potential, eligible, and actual participants of our Extension programs helps each state establish a baseline in strategic plans. Understanding a state's demographic composition (i.e., ethnicity, language, age, disability rates, veteran status) is the first and most basic step to see how diversity, equity, and inclusion efforts can drive opportunities for new partners and audience reach. In addition, communicating a culture of inclusiveness and belonging for Extension programs means seeking all types of input (not just current clientele or past participants), looking at workforce and community development needs, revising strategic plans for higher education outreach, and aligning with emerging population trends that relate to health and the social determinants of health.

Promoting Policy, Systems, and Environmental Changes as Health Extension

Looking at history and understanding how SNAP-Ed and EFNEP funding (e.g., annual investments in program and dedicated staffing) contributed to the development of today's CES health and nutrition program areas show great potential for future growth opportunities. First, multipurpose programming or the "bundling" of nutrition topics with other health programming (e.g., nutrition and mindfulness; food shopping and diabetes prevention and self-management) alongside funder-approved curricula will lead to greater transformational change in participant and system outcomes. Second, the potential for building research projects around the SNAP-Ed and EFNEP audiences to address health inequities is still largely untapped. States interested in research projects can pursue USDA's Agriculture and Food Research Initiative grants that address Farm Bill priority areas like food safety, nutrition, and health, or states can seek the High Obesity Programs grants of the Centers for Disease Control and Prevention Division of Nutrition, Physical Activity and Obesity, funding that can support new research activities. CES research and programming in this area is also well positioned to compete for funding from foundations, the National Institutes of Health, and other agencies that support community health and prevention research and have a special interest in targeting underserved populations. The third area with growth potential is using current resources to push CES beyond minimum standards for civil rights compliance (Pruitt & Hicks, 2022). In the last fifty years, the U.S. Congress has had to pass laws to protect voting access and equal pay, and to remove policies that allowed housing, lending, and hiring discrimination. The fight for human and civil rights in this country is far from over. The CES and higher education institutions can assist democracy by upholding laws and operating within the spirit of these laws that protect civil rights.

Over the last decade, USDA's Food and Nutrition Service (FNS) has been intensifying its focus on PSE changes and calling for more efforts that combine traditional direct education and indirect education with PSE work. The FY24 guidance for SNAP-Ed funding and the national reporting system for SNAP-Ed (N-PEARS, the National Program and Evaluation Reporting System) are driving expectations for increased multisector and multilevel community nutrition and physical activity education for youth and adults. Multiple sectors identified for SNAP-Ed currently include agriculture, child care, commercial marketing, community design, education, food industry, food retailers, government, media, public health and healthcare, public safety, and transportation. A multisector focus in SNAP-Ed fits with the CES mission to cooperate with common purpose in communities. The current charge is to work with five or more sectors through coalitions and partnerships to reach sites and settings together. Setting national priorities like these tied to the funding sources creates real change in systems. Our SNAP-Ed colleagues are leading important changes in the CES.

A shift to multilevel interventions aligns with USDA's efforts to improve food and nutrition security. This shift also supports the White House Conference on Hunger, Nutrition, and Health's five strategy pillars: (1) improve food access and affordability, (2) integrate nutrition and health, (3) empower all consumers to make and have access to healthier choices, (4) support physical activity for all, and (5) enhance nutrition and food security research (The White House, 2023). States are in various stages of planning and coordinating changes in their SNAP-Ed efforts that will yield new policies and practices for CES nutrition, physical activity, food security, and obesity prevention. In 2023, conversations among SNAP-Ed implementing agencies were about testing strategies to bring racial and health equity into nutrition education and food system transformation, advocating for data disaggregation by race and ethnicity (Robert Wood Johnson Foundation, 2021), calling for a deemphasis on individual behavior change, and demanding more inclusive partnerships, even from traditional partners. It is expected these trends will continue toward more PSE work in all health program areas for CES, and we will need our community-based healthcare and public health partners engaged in similar goals. In Michigan, SNAP-Ed added academic positions for work that can be multilevel and multisector, catalyzing PSE changes to occur. In 2023, this looks like a cohort of PSE educators hired in four project areas: food access, older adults, maternal and infant health, and early childhood school-based education. This focus on settings and audiences (aligned with PSE change, plan of work goals, and funding) allows for the reimagining of recurring resources and growth in organizational capacity to do more Health Extension.

Conclusions

Health Extension is a collection of strategies offering solutions to community-based healthcare gaps and needs, yet the CES must move with greater urgency to accelerate system change. Even though Extension professionals serve as change agents in their CES positions and are often sentinels in local communities, the academic institutions they are connected to are complex and slow to change. Recommendations for system change cited in this chapter and throughout the volume are important for envisioning the future of Health Extension, but also have resonance for many parts of CES. The CES must continue to seek innovative funding, staffing, scholarly activities, and leadership changes to implement community-based healthcare solutions. Health equity and justice work in our states and communities can keep us on a path toward the goal of liberation.

An overall goal of the Health Extension movement is to uphold CES as the first-choice professional partner of university and community partners in research, education, training, and interventions. This volume highlights recent successes in CES health programs, such as efforts training CHWs, responding to farm stress/suicide awareness, mental health promotion, opioid misuse prevention and recovery, disaster planning and response, vaccine education, and more. Health Extension is dedicated to core principles such as upholding science and research-based educational materials, and employing trained staff members who are experts with degrees and credentials in a variety of health professions. A mandate that CES programs are open to all ensures fair treatment of participants and supports the calls for CES and Health Extension to reach diverse, underrepresented groups in inclusive and equitable ways, including with community partners who share similar interests in health justice pursuits. Responding to emergent needs will keep CES nimble and relevant as another century is underway. By building upon the past, CES can assist government agencies with prevention and health education beyond USDA National Institute of Food and Agriculture priorities.

This evolution of CES depends on addressing past inequities and owning our shared history. The CES infrastructure and traditional funding sources allow higher education institutions to be engaged in community-focused work emphasizing the social determinants of health, dissemination and implementation science, and community-based participatory research approaches. CES and Health Extension strategies bring together the research, education, and interventions needed in communities to advance health equity. Strategic plans can keep ever-expanding CES priorities focused enough to pursue multiple lines of funding that concurrently address a specific public health topic (Eschbach et al., 2022).

The future of Health Extension involves broadening the conversation. This movement is about Health Extension in all CES program areas and with traditional and new partners. CES needs to keep creating interdisciplinary teams to address complex societal issues, as it has in the past, to bring the vast array of CES resources together to address community health in real time. The intersection of important health needs with traditional CES program areas creates the most fertile spaces for future Health Extension innovation. Let us find ways to use Health Extension and its evolving collection of strategies together in higher education and in CES to facilitate community-based healthcare solutions. Working together, by combining expertise and sharing resources, may be our chance to preserve the best parts of the LGU history and to build a new future where CES plays an important role serving our nation to advance democracy, civil rights, justice, and health equity for all.

REFERENCES

Burton, D., Canton, A., Coon, T., Eschbach, C., Gunn, J., Gutter, M., Jones, M., Kennedy, L., Martin, K., Mitchell, A., O'Neal, L., Rennekamp, R., Rodgers, M., Stluka, S., Trautman, K., Yelland, E., & York, D. (2021). *Cooperative Extension's National Framework for Health Equity and Well-Being.* Washington, DC: Extension Committee on Organization and Policy.

Dobis, E. A., Krumel, T., Cromartie, J., Conley, K. L., Sanders, A., & Ortiz, R. (2021). *Rural*

America at a glance: 2021 Edition (*Tech. Rep.*) (pp. 1–18). U.S. Department of Agriculture, Economic Research Service, *Economic Information Bulletin No. 230*. https://www.ers.usda.gov/webdocs/publications/102576/eib-230.pdf

Dwyer, J., Contreras, D., Eschbach, C., Tiret, H, Newkirk, C, Carter, E., & Cronk, L. (2017). Cooperative Extension as a framework for health extension: The Michigan State University model. *Academic Medicine*, 92, 1416–1420. https://doi.org/10.1097/ACM.0000000000001640

Eschbach, C. L., Contreras, D. A., & Kennedy, L. E. (2022). Three Cooperative Extension initiatives funded to address Michigan's opioid crisis. *Frontiers in Public Health, 10*, 921919. https://www.frontiersin.org/articles/10.3389/fpubh.2022.921919/full

Extension Foundation (2023). Frequently Asked Questions. https://pages.extension.org/knowledge/extension-foundation-faq

Hetherington, C., Eschbach, C., & Cuthbertson, C. (2019). How evaluation capacity building grows credible and actionable evidence for Cooperative Extension programs. *Journal of Human Sciences and Extension, 7*(2), 10. https://doi.org/10.54718/GLDP7457

Khan, T., Eschbach, C., Cuthbertson, C. Newkirk, C., Contreras, D., & Kirley, K. (2020). Connecting primary care to community-based education: Michigan physicians' familiarity with Extension programs. *Health Promotion Practice, 21*(2), 175–180.

Krishnan, A. (2009, January). *What are academic disciplines? Some observations on the disciplinarity vs interdisciplinarity debate*. University of Southampton National Centre for Research Methods. Report. https://eprints.ncrm.ac.uk/id/eprint/783/1/what_are_academic_disciplines.pdf

Lewis, K. M., Hensley, S., Bird, M., Rea-Keywood, J., Miller, J., Kok, C., & Shelstad, Ń. (2022). Why youth leave 4-H after the first year: A multistate study. *Journal of Human Sciences and Extension, 10*(3), article 5.

Lewis, Michael. (2022, April 5). Against the Rules with Michael Lewis. *Episode 1: Six Levels Down*. Podcast. https://podcasts.apple.com/us/podcast/episode-1-six-levels-down/id1455379351?i=1000555532510

National 4-H Council. (2016). *Grow true leaders National 4-H Council 2016 annual report*. https://4-h.org/wp-content/uploads/2022/09/26143431/2016-Annual-Report.pdf

National Institute of Food and Agriculture. (2017). *National 4-H strategic plan*. https://www.nifa.usda.gov/sites/default/files/resources/National%204-H%20Strategic%20Plan%202017.pdf

Office of Disease Prevention and Health Promotion. (n.d.). *Healthy People 2023*. U.S. Department of Health and Human Services. https://health.gov/healthypeople

Oleksiyenko, A., & Ruan, N. (2019). Intellectual leadership and academic communities: Issues for discussion and research. *Higher Education Quarterly, 73*(4), 1–13.

Pruitt, N. E., & Hicks, L. M. (2022). Moving beyond the minimum standard: Nondiscrimination regulations, policies, and procedures. In N. I. Fields & T. Shaffer (Eds.), *Grassroots engagement and social justice through Cooperative Extension* (pp. 31–50). Transformations in Higher Education Series. East Lansing: Michigan State University Press.

Rennekamp, R. (2022). Improving the health of the nation through transdisciplinary community engagement. *Journal of Community Engagement & Scholarship, 14*(3).

Rollins, D. (2011). Plagiarism within Extension: Origin and current effects. *Journal of Extension, 49*(5), article 5Com1.

Robert Wood Johnson Foundation. (2021, May). *Advocating for data disaggregation by race and ethnicity.* In partnership with the Arab Community Center for Economic and Social Services (ACCESS), the Asian & Pacific Islander American Health Forum, the National Congress of American Indians (NCAI), the National Urban League, and UnidosUS. https://www.apiahf.org/wp-content/uploads/2021/05/FINAL-REL-DataDisaggregationMessage-Guide-December-2020.pdf

Rodgers, M., & Braun, B. (2015). Strategic directions for Extension health and wellness programs. *Journal of Extension, 53*(3), article 11.

Smith, D. K., Diaz Martinez, A., Lanigan, J., Wells-Moyes, K., & Kohler, C. (2018). Scholarly mentor program: Supporting faculty in the writing and publication process. *Journal of Faculty Development, 32*(1), 45–50.

Stajura, M. (2020, October). *Relationship building: The power of partnerships in preparing shelters.* Natural Hazards Center\, University of Colorado Boulder.

The White House. (2023, March 23). *White House challenge to end hunger and build healthy communities, announces new public & private sector actions to continue momentum from historic hunger, nutrition, and health conference.* https://health.gov/our-work/nutrition-physical-activity/white-house-conference-hunger-nutrition-and-health/make-commitment

Tiret, H., Eschbach, C. L., & Newkirk, C. (2019). Rx for Health referral tool kit techniques to promote Extension programs. *Journal of Human Sciences and Extension, 7*(3), 173–185.

About the Contributors

Laura E. Balis, Ph.D., is a research scientist at Gretchen Swanson Center for Nutrition. She earned her Ph.D. at Virginia Tech in human nutrition, foods, and exercise with an emphasis on behavioral and implementation science. Her work focuses on implementation strategies to support the uptake of physical activity environment and policy interventions in community settings. She combines her scientific training with years of real-world public health experience, including previous positions in the Cooperative Extension system as an Extension educator and an assistant professor/health specialist. Her research philosophy is grounded in participatory methods, and her investigations seek solutions to simultaneously solve real-world problems and advance implementation science.

Camaya Wallace Bechard, Ph.D. (she/her), is the assistant director for diversity, equity, inclusion, and access at University of Illinois Extension. She has a doctorate in human development and family studies from Michigan State University, a master's in social responsibility from St. Cloud State University, and a bachelor's in sociology from the University of Wisconsin–River Falls.

Kathryn E. Bruzios, Ph.D., is affiliated with the Department of Human Development Prevention Science program at Washington State University. She is the graduate research assistant for the Northwest Prevention Technology Transfer Center and a clinical research coordinator at the University of Massachusetts Chan Medical School and VA Bedford Healthcare System. Her research focuses on the implementation of evidence-based programs and the use of implementation strategies to achieve positive behavioral health outcomes for youth, families, and communities in school and clinical settings.

Brittany Rhoades Cooper, Ph.D., is an associate professor of human development, youth and family Extension specialist, and graduate faculty member in the prevention science Ph.D. program at Washington State University. She was also recently elected the president of the Society for Prevention Research and helps to co-lead the Northwest Prevention Technology Transfer Center. Cooper's research, teaching, and outreach center around the translation of prevention science for public health impact. For more than a decade, she has collaborated with federal, state, and other community stakeholders to improve the field's understanding of how best to support evidence-based prevention programs in diverse community settings.

Courtney Cuthbertson, Ph.D. (they/them), is an assistant professor and Extension specialist in human development & family studies at the University of Illinois. As a sociologist, Cuthbertson conducts research and outreach about social structural impacts on mental health and substance use, with attention to social ecological factors and intersectionality. Cuthbertson has researched farm stress and mental health, associations between mental health and COVID-19 protective practices among farmers, behavioral health impacts of the Flint water crisis, and social meanings of mental illness diagnoses in the United States and abroad using quantitative and qualitative approaches. Their current research centers on farm stress, including among LGBTQIA+ people. As part of their Extension work, Cuthbertson has developed and offered mental health literacy trainings to improve knowledge of signs and symptoms of distress and skills to assist distressed people. Cuthbertson co-directs the North Central Farm and Ranch Stress Assistance Center.

Jeffrey W. Dwyer, Ph.D., is a professor emeritus at Michigan State University (MSU) and a director emeritus of Michigan State University Extension. He has held faculty and administrative positions in nursing, gerontology/sociology, medicine, and agriculture, been the principal investigator (PI) or co-PI of many state and federally funded research and training grants, including the Geriatric Center of Michigan (Health Resources and Services Administration) from 2008 to 2015, and contributed to interdisciplinary scholarship as an author and as editor of *Family Relations: Interdisciplinary Journal of Applied Family Studies* (1997–2000). He was the senior associate dean for research and community engagement in the College of Human Medicine at MSU, a community-based medical school (2006–2016), and director of MSU Extension, a $90 million organization with more than seven hundred employees across the state of Michigan (2016–2021). In 2017, he coauthored a seminal article in *Academic Medicine*, "Cooperative Extension as a Framework for Health Extension: The Michigan State University Model."

Cheryl L. Eschbach, Ph.D., is director of Michigan State University Extension's Health and Nutrition Institute, where she provides leadership for community-based health, food safety, and nutrition education. She oversees the institute's budgets, staffing plans and performance management, strategic planning, partnerships, research, content development, and programmatic direction. She is an experienced grant writer, program implementer, and evaluator. Between 2019 and 2023, she secured more than $12 million in funding for community behavioral health education. She served as the principal investigator (PI) or co-PI on six grants that support farm stress outreach and she was PI/project director of the 2019–2022 Substance Abuse and Mental Health Services Administration–funded MiSUPER effort. In 2021, she co-developed the Michigan Vaccine Project. She is a graduate of Oakland University (B.A., psychology and sociology/anthropology) and Oregon State University (M.S. and Ph.D., human development and family sciences; gerontology). She coauthored the *Academic Medicine* innovation report, "Cooperative Extension as a Framework for Health Extension: The Michigan State University Model."

Ana Lucia Fonseca is a dedicated advocate for social change and authenticity in organizations. With a diverse background, including a B.S. in social psychology, an M.S. in forest engineering, and a Ph.D. in education, she has worked in various community engagement programs and implemented innovative rural development initiatives. As director of diversity, equity, and inclusion, she leads the Civil Rights compliance program and serves on the Oregon State Credit Union and Achievement Rewards for College Scientists (ARCS) Foundation Board of Directors. Her interests span social justice, innovation, diversity, and economic equity, reflecting her commitment to positive impact. Beyond her professional pursuits, Ana Lucia enjoys outdoor activities and spending time with her daughter.

Josh Gunn, Ph.D., serves as the associate director of the Community, Food, and Environment Institute at Michigan State University (MSU) Extension. In this capacity, he provides leadership and support to educators and specialists who conduct community, economic, and natural resources programming. He coordinates disaster education activities with MSU Extension, and maintains a research and project portfolio, particularly as it relates to hazard mitigation, flooding, and water-related issues. Josh has worked with various Extension programs since 2010 and held leadership and management roles in both a university setting and as a supervisor in the U.S. Coast Guard (2002–2010). Josh holds a B.A. in public affairs (Washington State University), and an M.S. in marine resources management and a Ph.D. in urban and regional science (both from Texas A&M University). He obtained the American Institute of Certified Planners credential in 2022.

Danielle Y. Hairston Green is the director of the Human Development and Relationships Institute (HDRI) at the University of Wisconsin–Madison (UW Madison) Division of Extension. Leading HDRI, she envisions fostering the well-being of children, youth, and adults in resilient communities across Wisconsin. Formerly, she spent seven impactful years as the Extension state specialist for nutrition and childhood obesity at Prairie View A&M University in Texas. Hairston Green is an advocate and leader, serving as chairperson of UW Madison's Division of Extension African American Employees Resource Group, second vice president of the Madison Alumnae Chapter of Delta Sigma Theta Sorority, Inc., and founder of Black and Brown Wisconsin. Her extensive action research portfolio encompasses topics such as mentoring relationships among doctoral students of color, microaggressions at a historically Black university, and the impact of food insecurity and homelessness among college students. An award-winning researcher, her recent co-authored work delves into culturally responsive pedagogical practices in urban settings. Hairston Green holds a Ph.D. in educational leadership higher education administration, a master's in community psychology and social change, and a bachelor's in criminal justice from Penn State University.

Samantha M. Harden, Ph.D., is a behavioral psychologist and five hundred–hour registered yoga teacher. She serves Virginia Cooperative Extension as the exercise specialist (25 percent) and is a dissemination and implementation science researcher (75 percent). She founded and directs the Physical Activity Research and Community Implementation (PARCI) Laboratory within the Department of Human Nutrition, Foods, and Exercise at Virginia Tech. The vision of the PARCI Lab is to use members' talents, expertise, and passion to serve others. Harden's expertise in the RE-AIM framework (reach, effectiveness, adoption, implementation, maintenance) is the foundation for her research–practice partnerships that promote healthy lifestyle interventions across various populations for chronic disease prevention and management at the individual and systems levels. She has contributed to projects resulting in $29 million in research funding and produced more than one hundred peer-reviewed journal articles.

Carmen V. Harris is a professor of history at University of South Carolina Upstate and an Michigan State University alumna. Her essay "'The Extension Service Is Not an Integration Agency': The Idea of Race in the Cooperative Extension Service," received the Agricultural History Society's 2008 Vernon Carstenen Award for best article published in the journal that year and is frequently cited on race and agricultural policy. Her research focus is race, extension policy, and civil rights, especially in South Carolina. Her work also includes "'You're Just Like Mules, You Don't Know Your Own Strength': Rural South Carolina Blacks and the Emergence of the Civil Rights Struggle" in *Beyond Forty Acres and a Mule: African American Landowning Families since Reconstruction*, "States' Rights, Federal Bureaucrats, and Segregated 4-H Camps in the United States, 1927–1969" in the *Journal of African American History* (2008), and "The South Carolina Home in Black and White: Race, Gender, and Power in Home Demonstration Work" in *Agricultural History* (2019).

Lauren E. Kennedy, Ph.D., is an Extension Specialist in community behavioral health with the Health and Nutrition Institute at Michigan State University (MSU) Extension. She has a range of content expertise in public health, including mental health and suicide prevention, chronic stress management, substance use, and community nutrition. Her role at MSU includes building Extension's capacity, at multiple levels, to improve health equity in our communities by contextualizing individual health behaviors and outcomes within broader socioecological systems and structures. She studies and develops ways that traditional Cooperative Extension delivery models and practices can be enhanced through use of implementation science frameworks, critical race theory, and authentic community engagement.

Dusti Linnell, Ph.D. is an associate professor of practice at Oregon State University. She is affiliated with the College of Health and Extension Service Family & Community Health. She has a Ph.D. in nutritional biology from the University of California, Davis. She has been involved in implementing and evaluating community health interventions in California and Oregon since 2009. At the University of California, Davis Center for Nutrition in Schools, she worked with schools and Cooperative Extension educators to develop and implement school polices and interventions to promote positive dietary behaviors among students and their families. She then joined the Extension Service at Oregon State University Extension Service, where she has worked with rural communities to implement and evaluate interventions to improve food security, vaccine access, and mental health. In 2021, she was the recipient of the Western Extension Director's Association award for Excellence in Extension Diversity, Equity, and Inclusion.

Lindsey Lunsford, Ph.D., is a respected educator and advocate, originally from Indiana and now ingrained in the vibrant heritage of Alabama. As a third-generation graduate and esteemed faculty member of Tuskegee University, Lunsford upholds and extends the impactful legacy of the institution. She is deeply passionate about seeking justice for Black communities, specifically through unraveling and sharing the diverse and vital stories surrounding food within these communities. A compelling storyteller, Lunsford in her work illuminates narratives that provoke thought, foster understanding, and cultivate societal connections. With a profound belief in revisiting the past to sculpt the future, her substantial contributions to Extension emphasize the critical roles of diversity, equity, and inclusion as cornerstones for community development and empowerment. Lunsford's relentless pursuit stands as a beacon, continually amplifying silenced voices and weaving threads of understanding, justice, and equity across communities.

Leslie Lytle received a B.S. in medical dietetics from Pennsylvania State University and a master's in education from Purdue University. Her doctoral degree in health behavior and health education is from the University of Michigan. She was a postdoctoral fellow in cardiovascular health behavior in the Division of Epidemiology at the University of Minnesota and a professor in the Division of Epidemiology at the University of Minnesota for more than twenty years. She served as professor and department chair for Health Behavior at the University of North Carolina at Chapel Hill, 2012–2017. She continues to work at both the University of Minnesota and the University of North Carolina as an adjunct faculty member. Lytle's research focuses on the health promotion of youth and young adults, particularly on preventing obesity and promoting healthful diet and physical activity through multilevel interventions involving families, schools, and communities.

Erin L. Martinez, Ph.D., serves as an associate professor and Extension Specialist in the Department of Applied Human Sciences at Kansas State University. Her primary areas of focus are promoting health and well-being across the life span to encourage optimal aging, and implementing policy, systems, and environmental changes that positively influence health equity and the social determinants of health. She holds a Ph.D. in family sciences and a graduate certificate in gerontology from the University of Kentucky.

Allison Myers, Ph.D., M.P.H., serves as associate dean for extension and engagement at the College of Health and is program leader for Extension Family and Community Health at Oregon State University. The College of Health and the Extension Service share a vision for lifelong health and well-being for every Oregonian, and work in tandem to build community–university partnerships. Earlier in her career, Myers served as a health policy fellow to U.S. Senator Sheldon Whitehouse (D-RI) and co-founded Counter Tools, a nonprofit technology startup dedicated to advancing place-based public health. She has also led research and strategy development for health organizations at Innovation Management, LLC. Myers earned her B.S. in environmental resource management from Pennsylvania State University, and her M.P.H. and Ph.D. in health behavior from the Gillings School of Global Public Health at the University of North Carolina at Chapel Hill. She was a Peace Corps volunteer in Gabon.

Kylie Pybus is the assistant director for the Expanded Food and Nutrition Education Program (EFNEP) at Washington State University. She supervises educators delivering EFNEP classes to youth and adults in their community. In addition, she facilitates policy, systems, and environmental change regarding food security and nutrition education in Washington. Kylie received her master of public health degree from the Colorado School of Public Health. Her interests include program evaluation, youth curriculum development, and health promotion and literacy.

Elizabeth H. Weybright, Ph.D., is an associate professor in the Department of Human Development and an adolescent Extension specialist in the Youth and Families Program Unit at Washington State University. She also codirects the Northwest Rural Opioid Technical Assistance Collaborative. With a background in adolescent development and prevention science, her research and programming spans basic research on topics such as leisure experience (e.g., boredom), youth behavior (e.g., rural youth firearm engagement), the dissemination, adaptation, and implementation of substance use prevention, and positive youth development programs and approaches to building capacity among professionals and systems for delivery of evidence-based approaches. This work has been funded by federal and state agencies and is conducted in collaboration with community-based partners. Ultimately, her work seeks to use the Extension network and related strengths to deliver community care more effectively in rural areas to address health inequities.